A VIEW FROM THE CHAIR

A Festival and a Theatre that Helped to Shape a City

A VIEW FROM THE CHAIR

A Festival and a Theatre that Helped to Shape a City

PETER WILLIAMS

William Peter Williams is Welsh, only son of William Edgar Williams and Gladys Mary Thomas. He left Cotham Grammar School in Bristol at 15 to take a job as office boy on the Bristol Evening Post. After 12 years in newspapers in the West Country and Fleet Street, he has had a distinguished career in television with ITV and the BBC, and as an independent film-maker. He was for 21 years chair of the Canterbury Festival and then of the New Marlowe Theatre Development Trust. He was awarded the MBE for services to the Arts and Television, and has written several books.

In Black and White, the story of a coalfield, its life and death
Winner Stakes All, a profile of Lynn Davies, Olympic Gold Medallist
McIndoe's Army, the badly-burned airmen, reconstructed by
Sir Archibald McIndoe (with Ted Harrison)
Unit 731, the Japanese Army's biological warfare experiments on
human beings (with David Wallace)
Being There: Titanic, Marlon Brando and the Luger Pistol

FEATURE-LENGTH DOCUMENTARY FILMS (a selection)

Everyone's Gone to the Moon, on the US space programme
Test Tube Explosion, in vitro fertilisation (IVF) and its implications
Ruth Ellis – The Last Woman to Hang
UNIT 731 – Did the Emperor Know?
D-Day – The Shortest Day
The Queen and her Ceremonial Horses
Hilary Lister – A Race Against Time
The Challenge (for Salon Pictures)
A Canterbury Tale – The Battle for Hill 112
A Century of Coal, the unique story of the Kent coalfield
Titanic – A Question of Murder
The Night Football Changed For Ever, the formation of the
Premier League
The Clone a Human Being
Hillary on Everest, Sir Edmund Hillary's conquest of Everest
(with Tom Scott Productions)

Book Dedication

Do all the good you can, by all the means you can, in all the places you can, at all the times you can, for as long as you can...

John Wesley

...but the truth, of course, is that you cannot ever achieve this on your own.

My thanks to my friend Sir Robert 'Bob' Worcester, who loves the Festival, and financially supported the birth of this book, and to my wife and best friend Jo, who has been with me every step of the way.

Some Festivals have a
French connection...

...and are launched on a Cross Channel Ferry in the rain.
Credit: Gareth Fuller / Alamy Stock Photo

Introduction

Historians are like anglers and fishmongers. They fish for facts and what they catch makes up their presentation, the fish on their slabs. Eminent historian, EH Carr, believed that recorded history depended both on the areas in which the historian "chooses to fish, and on the kind of fish (facts) he wants to catch." In other words, most of the history from which we should learn our lessons is subjective and open to debate. Elsewhere, Carr confirms "the facts of history never come to us 'pure' since they do not... exist in a pure form. They are always refracted through the mind of the recorder..."

This book then, does not pretend to be an official history of the Canterbury Festival. It has no plot, save for the fact that the passing of time is a plot. It is about the importance of theatre in the history and the shape of Canterbury. It is also an assembly of views and recollections gathered over the 50 years in which the Canterbury Festival was an important part of my life.

I have tried to put the voices of individuals centre stage. But, having spent a year surrounded by copious files, even the longest book could barely embrace the detailed memories of all those who have contributed so much to the cultural adventure that is the Canterbury Festival. They know who they are and, if they are not listed here, my gratitude to them is undiminished.

This story is largely chronological and it falls into four phases: First, the early Festivals with Canterbury Cathedral at its heart; second, the establishment of the modern Festival, a decade of brilliance, determination and turmoil; third, the years of growth and development under the guidance of Festival Directors Mark Deller and Rosie Turner, leading to the fourth phase which culminates in the creation of the magnificent 1200-seat Marlowe Theatre in the heart of Canterbury.

Many people who have played important roles in this chronology have been generous with their views and memories, for which, my sincere thanks. Seventy years in journalism have taught me the value of listening and, because there is, frequently, a close relationship between what people are and what they say and do, I have made occasional forays into private lives in order to provide a context for decisions made, hopes encouraged and ambitions fulfilled...

...Or, disappointingly, dashed.

Peter Williams
Boughton-under-Blean
2022

Preface

Culture can be an explosive word. Seldom is it neutral because a basic truth about 'culture' is that it stirs passions. It gives rise to battles for dominance between conflicting values; for instance, you are either for or against red meat or fox-hunting, Rangers or Celtic, Yorkshire or Lancashire, working from home or attending the office. Occasionally, culture fosters deep and important discussions in society, as with debates over gender and sexuality or religion or slavery and those associated with that diabolical trade. Sometimes, the cultural collision is more trivial. I remember discussing with an American friend, quite fiercely, the semantics of his determination to remove letters from the English language – such as in 'color' or 'flavor' – but his unwillingness more logically to add letters to the English spelling to match the way he spoke: why not 'cawfee' rather than 'coffee'? Anthropologist, Ernest Crawley, called this sort of discussion 'the narcissism of small differences' – the ability to become heated over trivial matters. 'Coffee' or 'cawfee' was an interesting diversion but not worth reviving the War of Independence.

The Germans – of course – have a word for this emotion, *Kulturkampf*, literally 'cultural struggle'. The description emerged in the 18th and 19th centuries in Prussia during a battle for supremacy between the Catholic church and the state. Between 1872 and 1878, the Kingdom of Prussia, led by Otto von Bismarck, confronted Pope Pius IX over the church's dominance, particularly in the field of education. Since 1870, Catholics had considered the Pope infallible, an infallibility that was now being taught to children as a literal truth. This was unacceptable to the Prussians, to von Bismarck and to many European liberals. There was a stand-off whence church and state agreed to differ and then went their separate ways.

Given the average adverse reaction to change, it is surprising that more blood is not shed in pursuit of deeply-held beliefs. The arts are by no means immune from *kulturkampf*. It occurs in almost every corner of the world of music, the visual arts, drama and dance. It is sparked by commitment and fuelled by ambition and, when they come together in a concentrated form, called a 'Festival', the scope for disagreement is doubled and redoubled.

Or so you would think…

In the pages that follow, I will suggest quite the opposite – that the coming together of different skills in the setting of a community is potentially a great healer of rifts, an example of a creation being superior to the sum of the contributing parts. The annual Edinburgh International Festival is a prime and admirable example; established in 1947, its founders' motivation in a war-weary world, was to rebuild relationships between nations which, for six years, had been intent on destroying each other. Festivals are peacemakers in these culture struggles although, inevitably, and as you will read, there are some skirmishes along the way…

A festival is an expression of a place's identity. It sets down how it sees itself and how, it hopes, other people will see it. The carnival of the Rio de Janeiro festival in Brazil; the jazz and colour of the Mardi Gras in New Orleans; the Diwali Festival of Light in India; the heaving, swaying icons of Semana Santa in the Roman Catholic world every Easter; Germany's Oktoberfest, all beer and Bavaria; the small hall, side-street surprises of the annual Edinburgh Festival Fringe and the explosive celebration of Wagner at Bayreuth every year… each community puts on its best bib and tucker to impress the visitor. The town is on its best behaviour.

Yet crises are an integral part of any festival. If one were to draw up a business plan for an initiative, one wouldn't start here, as the Irishman once famously observed. Festivals invariably begin with an idea and no money, develop into a living entity with no money, and they live or die, year on year, dependent on the ability of supporters to defy financial logic and meet the annual challenge of satisfying artistic ambition while recognising economic reality.

Is it worth it? Of course. Because festivals embrace and dispense a message of hope, delivered lightly through the international language of theatre, image and music. Festivals simply encourage us to rediscover enchantment.

IN THE BEGINNING

Hitch-hiking – or the art of waiting patiently, 1952.
The author (right) and Ray Hill

Ray Hill (right), the author (left) and his wife Jo Taylor Williams

The Festival of Britain, 1952 – King George VI and Queen Elizabeth and an explosion of national pride – the author's first festival. (Alamy)

The Dome of Discovery

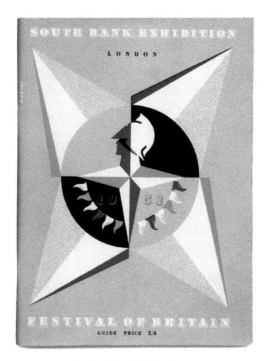

Festival Star. Credit: Alamy

The Skylon – a symbol sullied by controversy. Credit: Alamy

Chapter 1 – "Somewhere there's music…"

I can honestly say that becoming chairman of the Canterbury Arts Festival for 21 years was not part of my life plan. I came to Kent in my late twenties from Wales and the West Country where I had been working as a journalist for 12 years. I had a six-month freelance contract to open the new ITV studios for South East England – a hurriedly-adapted former bus garage in Russell Street, Dover. It was my first job in television.

While in Bristol working for the local newspaper, the *Evening Post*, my interest in the arts had been more social than thespian. The Bristol Old Vic was one of the most thriving and vigorous theatre companies outside London and the post-production parties at the Llandoger Trow[1] next door to the theatre on King Street, were equally vigorous. Peter O'Toole, who played Hamlet on the Bristol stage in 1957, set the pace and, if you had told an elfin Dorothy Tutin that she would one day become a Dame, she would have believed you were booking her for the next Christmas pantomime. Tom Stoppard was an exact contemporary of mine on the rival paper the *Western Daily Press*. He, too, had sidestepped university to earn a living with words. Bristol in the 1950s was a merry place to be young.

I liked actors and acting. Practically speaking, in the pursuit of a career in television and in the belief that learning to project my voice might improve my ability to talk to an inanimate camera, I

---

1. Llandoger Trow built in 1664, one of Britain's most ancient public houses, named after Llandogo in Wales where they built 'trows', flat-bottomed river boats

had joined the drama group at my local church, St Saviour's, in Redland, Bristol. There I had stumbled through a number of roles in plays by Emlyn Williams, Noel Coward and Arnold Ridley's *The Ghost Train*. Whether or not the experience improved my fluency, the experience on stage confirmed one important lesson: teamwork was crucial to success. It was in the church drama group that I vividly recall hearing for the first time, from a wise am-dram director, the assertion that *"there is no 'i' in the word 'team'"*.

The very first festival I ever attended was in 1951. I was 17, two years a journalist, and intent on using my two-week annual holiday to explore the horizon. In 1951, the world had emerged from the violence of World War Two, ready to give friendship and rehabilitation a priority, so much so, that teenagers, both boys and girls, hitchhiked all over Europe in comparative safety. That summer, my friend Ray Hill and I decided to take in the national Festival of Britain on our way to France and Holland. Outside Bristol, on the old A4, we bummed a lift on a lorry and were in London in four hours. It was a furniture truck and we travelled in comfort in the back on someone else's armchairs.

It was an optimistic time, reflected in the pop music in the charts. 'How High the Moon' was one of the 1951 favourites – a driving, timeless exercise in guitar skills by Les Paul and Mary Ford...

"Somewhere there's music, how faint the tune.
Somewhere there's heaven, how high the moon..."

Wonderful lyrics embracing young and old in joy and hope and confidence in the future. That was the tone of the Festival of Britain. It was a huge success. It had set out in 1947 to celebrate the centenary of Britain's Great Exhibition in 1851. It became more than that. Clement Attlee's Labour Government wished to encourage in the electorate a feeling of successful recovery from the devastation of war. They set out to stress the excitement of Britain's achievements in science, technology, design, architecture and the arts. It was a bold, well-funded project, led by deputy Prime Minister Herbert

Morrison. It cost around £10 million[2] and, nationwide, more than half of Britain's population of 49 million visited the exhibitions or took part in the celebration.[3] I was one of them. We headed straight for the South Bank, the Festival Pleasure Gardens and, later, to the exhibition area at Waterloo. Unlike its predecessor, the Great Exhibition a hundred years earlier, the Festival of Britain concentrated on Britain and the qualities of Britishness, ignoring matters international. It stressed Britain's ability to rise from the ashes of blitz and bomb site, with the quick fix of prefabricated housing and long-term plans for redesigned cities and rebuilt industry. It was, said the Festival publicity, *"a united act of national reassessment...and reaffirmation of faith in the nation's future...a tonic to the nation"*.[4] To a teenager, the breadth and optimism of the exercise was both apparent and impressive. This was the initiative of a Labour Government, remember, which had already delivered nationalisation, a co-ordinated council housing policy and given substance to the Liberal Lord Beveridge's image of a National Health Service – yet I don't recall an undue emphasis on any of these achievements. The images of the Festival that live in my memory are the structures – the Festival Hall on the South Bank where the arts have flourished ever since; the Dome of Discovery, where the exhibits concentrated on land, earth, sea and sky and, in an atomic age, the potential and perils in the word 'progress'. And then there was the Skylon, an ambitious cigar-shaped aluminium-clad steel tower. The Skylon had no practical use but, suspended as it was in mid-air, with barely apparent cables and a base 50 feet from the ground, it reflected the pervading mood that anything was possible.

The Festival's heart was in London, but the whole nation joined in. A Festival ship, the Campania, took an exhibition to all the four nations of the United Kingdom, from Cardiff to Glasgow, Southampton to Belfast. As for Canterbury, the city celebrated the

---

2. Around £250 million in 2022 money
3. Richard Weight: Patriots: National Identity in Britain 1940–2000, Pan Macmillan, 2013, pp 193–208
4. Gerald Barry, director of the Festival of Britain

Festival over several weeks in high summer. Bombs that had fallen from Dorniers and Heinkels ten years earlier had cleared the sites on which Canterbury now built an exhibition of Kent's heritage. It was in the shadow of the cathedral, which had been saved from greater damage by the bravery of volunteer fire watchers, who had stayed on the cathedral's roofs throughout the blitz, to hurl the incendiary bombs from roof to ground. Local film-maker, John C Clague, recorded on film the civic service at the cathedral, which opened Canterbury's Festival of Britain celebrations. The 'Red Dean', Hewlett Johnson, greeted the dignitaries – a chain gang of 20 mayors, each representing Kentish boroughs, the entire city council of Canterbury and the barons of the ancient Cinque Ports, which in centuries past had supplied vessels to create the foundation of King Henry VIII's Royal Navy. On August 2nd 1951, an elaborate and lengthy procession of floats, each depicting a historic moment in the history of the front-line county of Kent, wound its way through the City's streets – and, in a competitive world, Deal won the award for the best float. Canterbury sent out "*a message to the world*", said film-maker Mr Clague; it reflected the optimism of the time: "*We are showing what a small town can do when it has the will to do it*".

Tens of thousands of people flocked to London's South Bank in 1951 to wander around the Dome of Discovery and gaze at the Skylon. Historian, Kenneth O Morgan, wrote of the nation that "*a people curbed by years of total war and half-crushed by austerity and gloom, showed that it had not lost the capacity for enjoying itself... Above all, the Festival made a spectacular setting as a showpiece for the inventiveness and genius of British scientists and technologists*".

Regrettably, politics intervened in what was an exercise of national unity and positivity. The Skylon, 300 feet (90 metres) high, and floating heavenwards, became a symbol of dissent. Attlee's Labour Government, in power since the end of the war, was losing focus. In the General Election of 1950, its majority had been reduced to five. Governing Britain was hard work – Attlee was ageing, Stafford Cripps resigned through ill health and Ernest Bevin died in 1951. At the end of that summer, Attlee, buoyed by the success of the Festival of Britain, decided optimistically to go to the country again in 1952. But the Conservatives, led by Winston Churchill, won relatively easily[5] and formed a government with a majority of 28 seats.

Churchill saw the Skylon as an irritating symbol of the radical changes that the Labour Government had made to the British way of life. He ordered it to be removed. It was dismantled, toppled into the River Thames and most of it was sold for scrap. It was an ignominious and unnecessary end for a fine work of art, part of the legacy of the Festival of Britain. Still, looking back on an inspirational year, the Festival's guidebook summed up the Festival thus:

'It will leave behind not just a record of what we (as a nation) thought of ourselves in the year 1951 but, in a fair community founded where once there was a slum, in an avenue of trees, or in some work of art, it will be a reminder of what we have done to write this single, adventurous year into our national and local history.'

Nearly a century later, I see no reason to alter a single word of that assessment.

The story of festivals is a thread that runs through the tapestry of history. In all communities, men and women have told their stories to each other since the beginning of time, handing down their memories in gesture and speech, carving and outline, music and dance. The tidy-minded Greeks identified speech and drama in what they described as *'dithyrambs'*, hymns to Dionysus, the god of wine and fertility. *Dithyrambs* were led by a poet, who was chosen to deliver the spoken word. In the 6th century BC according to Aristotle, the Greek poet Thespis became the first person to portray a character in a play, instead of speaking as themselves. Thus, 'thespian' to describe the art of an actor. Initially, only one person spoke amid the music, using a variety of masks to illustrate the changes from comedy to tragedy, laughter to tears.

---

5.   Labour won the larger share of the national vote (49.4% to the Conservatives' 47.8) but gained only 293 seats compared to the Conservatives' 321.

Later, the entire ensemble were similarly masked, to portray the diversity of drama.

The world's oldest festival, according to Harvard University's Center for Middle Eastern Studies, is Nevruz,[6] established 4,000 years ago to celebrate the spring equinox in March. Nevruz was also the Persian New Year, celebrating food and music. Festivals continued to embrace a culture of plenty, giving thanks to the gods who provided it. In Britain, festivals were historically low-key and local, often created by cathedral-based religious orders. But in the 18th century, the centenary of the birth of Handel was flamboyantly marked by *"a grand, national event, the like of which had never been seen before. It was not for the greatest general, politician or king, but for a 'mere musician'".*[7] Curiously, and at roughly the same time, actor/manager David Garrick's attempt to celebrate nationally the bicentenary of William Shakespeare's birth in 1769, made little impact outside Shakespeare's birthplace, Stratford-upon-Avon, where *"thanks to torrential rain it was literally a wash-out even there".*[8] The secret of the success of the Handel celebration was that the King, George III, supported it; he loved Handel's music and had been a devotee since childhood. As part of his patronage, the King decreed that Westminster Abbey should be at the heart of the Handel centenary festival. The great nave of the Abbey was transformed into *'a royal musical chapel'*[9] with the addition of galleries and stands. Fashionable London queued for tickets. To create more space, ladies were instructed not to wear excessive hoops under their dresses, and so high was the demand for seats that two of the events had to be repeated. If properly organised, supported by royalty and touched by magic, festivals could be high-profile brilliant showcases. Historian, David Starkey, describes the scene in the Abbey thus:

---

6.   Pronounced 'No-rooz'
7.   Music and Monarchy, David Starkey & Katie Greening, BBC Books, 2013 pp2
8.   Ibid pp2
9.   Dr Charles Burney, author of the history of the event

'Before the festival proper began, the royal family, headed by the King, visited Handel's tomb nearby in the south transept to pay their respects; then, they processed to their box and listened, rapt, as Handel's Messiah *was performed. The towering stage facing them became a sort of altar; and Handel's music, written to the glory of God, became instead part of the composer's own cult.'[10]*

Starkey pursues this parallel with the religious experience by writing that *'music had once honoured kings; now the King led the nation in honouring – worshipping scarcely seems too strong a word – Handel and his music.'*

As in London, so, too, in Canterbury. It was in Canterbury Cathedral, the mother church of the worldwide Anglican Communion, that the Canterbury Festival would be born.

---

10.   Music and Monarchy, David Starkey & Katie Greening, BBC Books, 2013, p4

*Queen Elizabeth the First from a detail in a document
in Canterbury Cathedral archive.*

Becket's shrine, from a detail in a window at Canterbury Cathedral.

Illustrations in this chapter copyright Canterbury Museums and Galleries

Dean George Bell, fifth from left, front row.

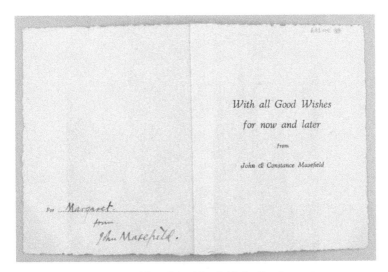

A greetings card from John Masefield, the Poet Laureate;
believed to be to Margaret Babington

Illustrations in this chapter copyright Canterbury Museums and Galleries

The Coming of Christ: actors in the Precints

Canterbury Cathedral from the Christ Church Gate

Illustrations in this chapter copyright Canterbury Museums and Galleries

Chapter 2 – Drama in the Cathedral...

The established church often turns to symbols to express its message. In the early church, the fish[11] was the badge that proclaimed membership of a small but fast-growing faith. The dove, the olive branch and the cross also expressed symbolic reminders of the breadth of Christian belief. Symbols were an introduction, readily used to promote among non-believers a further and deeper examination of an idea and of the Christian way of life. The church's rejection, then, of the imagery of theatre for more than a thousand years, seems puzzling. But, in medieval Britain, belief in an all-powerful God was central to everyday living. The major objection to acting as a vehicle to convey a Christian message was a fear that imagery could fast become idolatry, the worship of the object rather than the substance of the message and, though joy as much as penance lies at the heart of Christianity, there seemed – and sometimes still seems – too little room for laughter and applause in religious observance. This estrangement from the theatre with its ability to express chronologic and human behaviour in its every mood, grew from an entrenched attitude in English society that, in 1592, even led to a decree forbidding the sale of hot cross buns, which originated to alleviate the hunger of the poor, except at burials, on Good Friday or at Christmas. The sensitivities surrounding religious symbolism were stifling. But, thankfully, there were those, within the established church who recognised that fact, and I guess loved hot cross buns!

---

11.   Ichthys (fish) believed to be an acrostic of the Greek words for 'Jesus Christ, Son of God, Saviour'

The organisation known as The Friends of Canterbury Cathedral was launched through a letter to *The Times* newspaper on June 20th 1927. The letter is significant in the history of the Canterbury Festival for two reasons: firstly, because the Cathedral Friends organisation gave birth to the modern Festival and, secondly, because the signatory to the letter was George Bell. Bell was Dean of Canterbury in 1927. Throughout his career, Bell was both fearless and controversial and we will return later to him and to his dedication to the arts and to Canterbury.

The response to Bell's letter, which sought supporters to raise funds for the cathedral's needs, was immediate and enthusiastic. *The Times* later carried an article by Bell announcing the launch of 'a society of men and women to be known as 'The Friends of Canterbury Cathedral'…a body of supporters…prepared to take some share in caring for (the cathedral) and in preserving it for posterity…The Prince of Wales *(later the uncrowned King Edward VIII)* is today the first friend entered on the roll,' he announced.

The minimum subscription was five shillings.

Some 800 'friends' were recruited in the first six months. Sir Anton Bertram,[12] barrister, retired judge and former Chief Justice of Ceylon (now Sri Lanka), was appointed Honorary Steward and Treasurer of the new body. However, he left Canterbury for Cambridge after a year and was succeeded by Miss Margaret Babington, daughter of the vicar of nearby Tenterden. Miss Babington had moved with her father to the cathedral precincts on his retirement; she was a woman for whom the word 'vigour' was probably invented. She had, for years, run 36 societies or committees from her home in Tenterden and, in 1928, she brought that dedication to the formation of the Friends. Dean George Bell and Margaret Babington immediately identified the potential of the arts to invigorate both the profile of the newly-formed Friends and, potentially, its balance sheet. Part of Bell's vision, his credo, was that music and drama could, and should, play an important part in the life of the church. Miss Babington shared that vision

---

12.   Sir Anton made his home in Canterbury and died there in 1937 aged 68

and pursued it with charm, charisma and determination. Thus, in that first year, a 'Festival of Music and Drama' was born within the hallowed walls of Canterbury Cathedral. The birth was both splendid and controversial.

It is important to consider the context in which this first Canterbury Festival would take place in 1928. Bell knew that, for centuries, his church had deplored and outlawed any drama performed in a place of worship, overlooking the fact that the Christian faith sprang from one of the greatest dramas ever told. Thespian activities in the church had been confined, broadly speaking, to liturgical drama and biblical pageants, conspicuously and most successfully, in York and Chester. The construction of theatres – buildings that were set aside specifically for performance – would not reappear in England until the reign of Elizabeth the First (1558–1603).[13] The renaissance of theatre and the arts – the Golden Age – led by Queen Elizabeth and embracing the works of William Shakespeare, Christopher Marlowe and the creation of the Globe Theatre, was still more than half a century away as, in 1505, Canterbury considered a bold move of which Bell would have undoubtedly approved. The then city fathers debated a suggestion that they should hold a St Thomas Pageant. It was an initiative both exciting and practical.

During the 15th century, England had lived through a debilitating slump that had lasted three decades. Canterbury had suffered as much as any other city. In addition to the economic downturn, England had endured a number of outbreaks of the plague. Canterbury did not escape, and the impact was similar to that experienced during the COVID-19 pandemic in the 21st century but without the medical knowledge and scientific aids to combat it. People died in their hundreds. It is estimated that plagues killed up to 50% of the population of the British Isles. Among

---

13.   Her people called her 'Good Queen Bess' or 'Gloriana', but Queen Elizabeth was also champion of the performing arts. So rare were theatres in England that the first purpose-built theatre for a thousand years was constructed at the express wish of the Queen in 1576 in Shoreditch, London. Founded by actor James Burbage (1530–1597), it was named, simply, The Theatre

those who survived, the appetite for religious observance actually increased. People threatened by a quick and painful death sought prayer to strengthen their souls as they prepared for purgatory and the promised life thereafter.[14] Families living closely together were decimated. Three generations could be wiped out in a single week. To avoid the plague, some travelled to holy places, to Canterbury, to the Eastbridge Hospital, where in warmth and comfort that would prove deadly, they died on the straw-strewn floor, infected by lice, fleas and rats that had done for the previous occupants only days before. The mortality rate, particularly among the monks in their cloistered environment in Christ Church Priory, was high.

The wool trade, which provided work for a third of the city's residents and was a bedrock of Canterbury's prosperity, fell into decline. So stressed was the city's economy early in the 16th century, that the mayor and aldermen imposed an embargo on the sale of wool to spinners and weavers outside the city walls, in an attempt to protect the shrinking cloth-making trade. In addition, every civic officer was ordered to buy annually a length of locally produced cloth.[15] Yet, amid this crisis, Canterbury was one of the few cities whose population increased, from 4,500 souls in 1377 to 5,500 in 1524.[16] In addition, it had improved its standing in the country, moving up from 13th in England's national ranking to ninth during those 160 years. It was growing in importance and it was intent on proclaiming its resilience. Canterbury shrewdly recognised that the martyred Archbishop Thomas Becket had unique appeal both to pilgrims and to residents. After all, if a pageant could benefit York and Chester, why not Canterbury?

Religious attitudes were changing. Champions of a new, humanist movement were gathering strength in northern Europe. But the relationship between cathedral-dominated Canterbury and Thomas Becket, its 'hooly blissful martir', was profound and very saleable. It was now 300 years since the Translation of Becket,

---

14.   Lucy Worsley, the Black Death, BBC, May 2022
15.   Historical Manuscript Commission, 9th report and appendix, p174
16.   These are approximate figures drawn from national taxation records, Shelia Sweetinburgh, Archaeologia Cantiana, Vol 137, 2016

the day in July 1220 when Becket's relics had been moved from the crypt in Canterbury Cathedral to a magnificent shrine in a newly constructed apse[17] at the east end of the cathedral. To emerge from the slump, Canterbury needed inspiration, both spiritually and financially. On July 6th 1505, the mayor and the aldermen decided they would gamble on a 'St Thomas Pageant'.[18] They were nothing if not ambitious. They planned five sections in the pageant, which would be led by giant puppets, followed by gunners and pikemen. The first procession was the Annunciation; the second, St George; the third, the Nativity; the fourth, the city's mayor and aldermen preceded by archers and the city's great two-handed sword, and lastly, the fifth, St Thomas himself. The pageant was spectacular; it wound its way through Canterbury's narrow streets and market places, probably starting and finishing at the city's Guildhall in the heart of the walled community.

Unlike York, Canterbury's pageant probably contained little drama, with the conspicuous exception of the St Thomas section of the procession in which 'St Thomas, the murdered Becket, was probably portrayed by a puppet. Detailed financial records of the time indicate that money was spent on building and fitting out 'the pageant waggon', which included 114 feet of board for the floor of the cart', and '10 yards of new canvas', presumably for a backdrop or painted scenery. Props were also used to depict the murder of Archbishop Becket and the accounts indicate the purchase of a leather bag of 'blood' that must have been attached in some way to the puppet of St Thomas. Ledger entries for the regular repainting of St Thomas' head in subsequent years may imply that it became bloodstained during the enactment, a scenario that may also have included slicing off part of the puppet's head to dramatise the tragic event. It appears, too, that the knights were well-equipped as, in addition to wearing armour, the accounts show annual payments for tin, silver and gold foil, leather, points, needles and thread, as well as the swords that they carried. The pageant may subsequently

---

17.   Apse – a semi-circular recess
18.   Early Tudor Canterbury, Sheila Sweetinburgh, ibid, p164–173

have become even more elaborate; one piece of equipment that appears to have been introduced several years after its inception in 1505 was the 'vyce'. This device was worked by a man who was paid to operate a wire attached to an angel – also depicted by a puppet – which could be raised during the performance, presumably to indicate the elevation to heaven of the martyred archbishop's soul.[19]

All these findings point to a static performance of drama in order to portray the act of St Thomas' murder, which probably took place within the precincts of the cathedral. Sheila Sweetinburgh, in her assessment of the St Thomas Pageant, sums up the motivation of the city fathers who organised the event:

"By showing the archbishop's death at the hands of four assailants as he knelt, perhaps before an altar, the knights' swords and the pigs' blood adding to the horror of the moment, the leading citizens may have sought to emphasise Becket's sacrifice and suffering, especially if the crown of his 'head' was also sliced off. The subsequent carrying of the martyr's soul to heaven by the angel as it was wound up to the roof offered a spur to further pious thoughts of redemption and spiritual rewards, ideas that might have resonated at both personal and corporate levels."[20]

Given the context at the time, the St Thomas Pageant was bound to be controversial. However successful it might be artistically, spiritually and financially, the plans did not receive universal approval. There were those Christians who believed that praying to saints and honouring their images was a form of idolatry. The church's pomp and ceremony were anathema to them. They did not support the ceremonial practices that surrounded baptism and confession. They rejected the validity of papal pardons. They were described by the church establishment as 'Lollards', a derogatory nickname given to the poorly-educated who neither spoke nor read Latin and who vigorously supported the translation of

---

19.   Looking at the Past: The St Thomas Pageant in Early Tudor Canterbury, Archaeologia Cantiana, Vol 137, Sheila Sweetinburgh
20.   Ibid

the Bible from Latin into English to make it more accessible. Lollards followed the teachings of John Wyclif (or Wycliffe), an Oxford philosopher and priest, who argued that knowledge of the scriptures was the best guide to understanding God's intentions and that the church's money and effort should be devoted to helping the poor and needy rather than indulging in ceremony and artistic extravagance. Wycliffe encouraged priests to live in poverty; he also criticised many aspects of the monastic life, including what he saw as corruption within the holy orders. He had, as you would imagine, his enemies within the established church, but his teachings became part of the drive in England towards Protestantism.

Wycliffe had died in 1384, but support for his ideas had gathered strength. By the 14th century, the established church moved to describe 'lollardy' as 'heresy' and Wycliffe's teaching became a major issue, politically as well as spiritually. King Henry IV used the powers of church and state to combat its spread and, in a series of trials for heresy lollards were persecuted and executed. Wycliffe had himself been declared a heretic in 1415 and the fact that he had contributed to the translation of the Bible into English was taken as evidence of that heresy. He was posthumously excommunicated, his papers were destroyed and his remains were dug up, removed from consecrated ground and burned. His ashes were dumped into the River Swift, which flows through the market town of Lutterworth in Leicestershire.

It was amid this ongoing and seminal struggle for the soul of the church in England, that Canterbury's St Thomas Pageant took place. There is no doubt that 'lollardism' had legion supporters in Kent, nowhere more than in the Tenterden area. The Weald was a hotbed of religious dissent and Benenden and nearby villages were at the centre of a lollard network. Archbishop Warham,[21] pursuing his King's wishes, visited Tenterden and found that many parishioners *"use to sitt stille in the churche atte processione*

---

21.   William Warham, archbishop of Canterbury (1503 until his death in 1532)

tyme",[22] thus indicating their disapproval of the ornate religious ceremonial. A series of heresy trials were held between 1511 and 1512, at which long prison terms and the confiscation of estates were among the punishments meted out to those found guilty of heresy. Against this simmering background, Canterbury's elders continued to support its St Thomas Pageant until the shrine's destruction in 1538 and its subsequent revival and rehabilitation decades later during the reign of Queen Mary.

There is a parallel between the creation of the St Thomas Pageant and the rebirth of the Canterbury Festival. This persistence and resistance to criticism that surrounded the creation of the St Thomas Pageant in 1505, typified the attitude of both Margaret Babington and Dean George Bell 400 years later as they prepared to restore drama to the ecclesiastical calendar. In 1928, they set out to launch, in Canterbury Cathedral, their Friends' Festival of Music and Drama, with a production of Poet Laureate John Masefield's *The Coming of Christ*. Their targets were spiritual in the subject and content of the programme and practical in that the money raised would pay builders, plasterers and glaziers to restore the cathedral's water tower, which was severely dilapidated and would cost an estimated £1,000 to restore.

The performance of *The Coming of Christ* was remarkable, a game-changer. No drama of any kind had been seen in an English cathedral in 400 years as the Church of England had expressed its total opposition to drama in any form. Historian, Kenneth Pickering, writes thus of the importance of the Canterbury event in 1928, 'the first festival of its kind in Britain':

'*English cathedrals make unlikely playhouses: some would even think it blasphemous to think of them as such. Yet some of the more interesting developments in twentieth century drama took place within their walls.*'

---

22.   Robert Lutton, Lollardy and Orthodox Religion in Pre-Reformation England: Reconstructing Piety (Woodbridge, 2006) See also R. Lutton, 'Connections between Lollards, Townsfolk and Gentry in Tenterden in the Late Fifteenth and Early Sixteenth Centuries.

The Coming of Christ, written by Masefield, would become the foundation stone in this planned restoration of the bridge between church and drama. Bell was unequivocal in his championship of the initiative. He felt that drama must be enlisted to forward the cause of Christianity "*and I wish to see my church taking the lead*".[23] George Bell believed that his church was "*above all things a creative body*".[24] He recalled the genesis of Masefield's play in a sermon which he preached in the village of Wittersham's parish church, near Ashford in Kent, in December 1953:

"*John Masefield stayed at the Deanery in Canterbury, one summer's night in 1927. As Dean, I took him round the Cathedral after supper. He was thrilled with all he saw, and the light in which he saw it. The great nave and the long flight of steps with their separating platforms leading up to the choir...I told him of my dream of a nativity play in Canterbury Cathedral on that very place...*"

Bell invited Masefield to write the nativity play. Masefield responded by telegram: '*Will gladly do all I can to help.*' He was as good as his word. That summer, he wrote *The Coming of Christ* during a holiday in Cornwall.[25] That year, Bell's persistence and determination were rigorously tested. He knew that 26 years earlier, the Chapter of Canterbury had refused to allow the 15th century play, *Everyman*, to be staged in the cathedral. Kenneth Pickering summarises the challenge facing both Bell and the Cathedral's Chapter; the Chapter '*was now confronted with a more daring proposal* (than *Everyman* had been) *from its own Dean. Even the Archbishop* (Randall Davidson), *with his declared sympathy towards the stage, had advised Bell against the project; but Bell made his determination clear and, with some reluctance, the Chapter gave him the permission he requested. Bell at once asked Masefield to invite Gustav Holst to compose a score...not only was Holst enthusiastic about the Canterbury project, he also agreed to*

---

23   George Bell, Ronald CD Jasper, Oxford University Press, 1967, p41
24   Canterbury Cathedral Chronicle LIII (1955) E Martin Browne
25   Drama in the Cathedral, Kenneth Pickering, J Garnett Miller, 2001, p88

*provide a choir for the performance, as difficulties had arisen over
the use of the cathedral choir* (an incident which we will examine
later in Chapter 3). *Bell next contacted Laurence Irving, Sir Henry's
grandson, who lived at nearby Whitstable. This was an inspired
move as Irving was not only a theatre designer of repute, but was
steeped in almost every aspect of the theatre of his day.'*

Bell invited Charles Ricketts, who had worked with Oscar
Wilde, to produce and direct the play. At the first meeting between
Ricketts and Bell, Ricketts asked:

"What backing have you?"

"None," said Bell.

"What are you charging for seats?"

"Nothing," replied Bell.

Ricketts cast his eyes towards heaven.

"Truly, the spirit of St Francis is abroad."

He agreed to produce the play,[26] despite later confiding to Irving
that *"as a good atheist, I cannot approve."*

Two observations on this verbal exchange between Ricketts
and Bell: first, it is not surprising that Bell intended to charge
his audience nothing. In 1925, he had abolished any payment by
those who wished to visit Canterbury Cathedral. Secondly, Bell
was determined that this performance would be an exercise in
Christian outreach, an act of faith so strong that it would impress
and persuade others to support the initiative and to embrace the
Christian faith.

There were still sensitive production issues to be negotiated,
however. Masefield's description in his text of Jesus as *'the
brightest of the heavenly host'* was removed. In addition, careful
diplomacy was required to reach agreement on how Christ should
be portrayed. By an actor? As a veiled figure? Simply as a voice?
Bell eventually and laconically reported that *"all difficulties were
overcome".*

Part of his solution to the sensitivities was to insist that none of
the cast was named. Each actor remaining anonymous, particularly

---

26   George Bell, Ronald CD Jasper, Oxford University Press, 1967, p42

the actor playing the Anima Christi[27] character. In this striving for anonymity, he was remarkably successful. The only cast list surviving is an incomplete set of pencilled names on the back of a production photograph. A young, regular soldier named Bernard Storrs played the Anima Christi character, but according to *The Daily News*' review of the production, the part was attributed to the cathedral's precentor. Masefield's play may certainly have offended a small minority of the audience, but the enthusiastic reception it received generally suggested that Bell's confidence and approach were justified.[28]

On the Tuesday and Wednesday of Whitsun week in 1928, *The Coming of Christ* was performed five times in the nave of Canterbury Cathedral. More than 6,000 people came to watch it, free of charge. The event was 'of considerable importance in the history of drama and English theatre', said the drama critic of *The Daily News*, who went on:

'Since the murder of Thomas a Becket, Canterbury Cathedral has not been the scene of a more startling event than the performance of John Masefield's The Coming of Christ. *For the first time since the Middle Ages, an English cathedral had opened its doors to the religious stage. Canterbury's lead was significant; it set the seal of the Church's approval once more upon an art which the church had banished for 300 years.'* [29]

Bell looked back on the event 25 years later in his sermon to the villagers of Wittersham:

"On that day, history was made. In a moving and enchanting form, the Poet and the Artist together re-entered the Church. They had only to be asked, and with a ready response to a lead which was not afraid to offer sympathetic direction, they brought their gifts. I

---

27   Anima Christi, a prayer relating to the Eucharist, the body and blood of Christ

28   Drama in the Cathedral, Pickering, p93

29   The Daily News, May 29th 1928

think I may justly claim that it was the combination of a lead from the Church of Canterbury with the response from the Three Kings in their respective arts, Poetry, Music and Painting, which started a new chapter in the history of English drama."

Bell said that, as far as the ecclesiastical records could tell, it was the first performance of its kind ever to be staged within Canterbury Cathedral. *"It is certainly, as I believe, an incident of great significance in the history of the Cathedral. I look upon it as a religious event, an act of religious dedication and inspiration, very proper to the Whitsuntide Festival."* It was *"an offering of gifts – poetry, music, beauty of colour and design, singing and acting, arts and crafts, and a great religious truth."*

In addition, the play provided the financial opportunity to launch further similar ventures. The voluntary collections taken at the performances amounted to more than £800. The money was set aside for commissioning new plays.[30]

Bell, supported by The Friends of Canterbury Cathedral, and benefitting from the organisational enthusiasm of Margaret Babington, had *"faced much criticism"* in producing an event so successful that, thirty years later, *The Coming of Christ* would be described in the history of drama in Britain's schools and churches as *"the one (play) which will longest be remembered."*[31]

The first annual meeting of The Friends of Canterbury Cathedral in the precincts on May 19th 1928 was attended by more than 500 members. It rained, so the gathering moved from the Water Tower Gardens into the Chapter House. The enthusiasm that the Festival had engendered spilled over into the formal meeting. One Friend, according to the local newspaper, *'speaking in feeling tones, said he was sure there was a feeling of thankfulness pervading all who were present at the festival...the beauty they had experienced... was beyond words and it would sink deep into their hearts...'*[32]

30.   George Bell, Ronald CD Jasper, 1967, pp 42–43
31.   KM Lobb, Drama in School & Church (London), 1955
32.   Kentish Gazette & Canterbury Press, May 1928

There were messages of congratulation from the Prince of Wales, Prime Minister Stanley Baldwin and Archbishop Davidson. Dean Bell immediately set about building on this triumph. He looked forward to a new and expanded festival of music and the arts in Canterbury in 1929.

But the best laid plans...

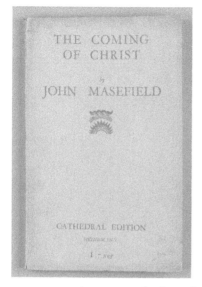
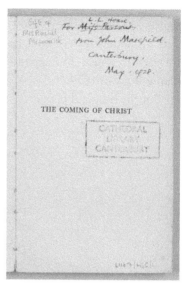

A programme for the performance of John Masefield's
The Coming of Christ, signed by Masefield.

Margaret Babington, at her desk, above the Christ Church Gate.

Illustrations in this chapter copyright Canterbury Museums and Galleries

Great Deans of Canterbury – George Bell (1924-1929) and Robert Willis (2001-2022).

Actors rehearse for Tennyson's Becket (1932) in Canterbury Cathedral.

Illustrations in this chapter copyright Canterbury Museums and Galleries

Dorothy Sayers, who wrote two plays for Canterbury,
The Zeal of Thy House (1937) and The Devil to Pay (1939).

Costumes for a Dorothy Sayers' play The Zeal of Thy House, performed in
Canterbury Cathedral in 1937 and 1949.

Canterbury Cathedral suffered considerable damage in the World War. Two bombing raids in June 1942

Illustrations in this chapter copyright Canterbury Museums and Galleries

Chapter 3 – Babington and Bell

The partnership between Dean George Bell and Miss Margaret Babington, forged during the formation of The Friends of Canterbury Cathedral, had flourished during the successful production of John Masefield's *The Coming of Christ*, performed in 1928. They made a formidable couple: Babington, the vicar's daughter from Tenterden; Bell, the innovator, who would, in the years ahead, shock and inspire with his thoughts on ecumenism and with his very public anti-war stance in World War Two. Together, they had brought drama back to the cathedral. Their skills were complementary; their enthusiasm was shared and focused.

But in February 1929, the Bishop of Chichester, Dr Winfrid Burrows, died, and his death would have an unexpected significance for the nascent Canterbury Festival. It wasn't immediate, however. Dean Bell and Miss Babington pressed ahead with plans for a second festival of music and drama in Canterbury Cathedral in August 1929. They would repeat *The Coming of Christ*, which had been so successful in 1928 that queues had wound their way through the precincts at each of its five performances. Bell would also embrace Mr Nugent Monck and his players from the Maddermarket Theatre, Norwich, to perform *Everyman*, a work previously banned by the cathedral. Local Kentish players who would come from Rochester, Maidstone, Herne Bay, Tunbridge Wells, Folkestone and Canterbury, would make up the cast. Gustav Holst agreed to conduct a performance of his rousing suite *The Planets* and, thanks to his acquaintance with the BBC's Director General, Sir John Reith, Bell reached agreement with Dr (later Sir) Adrian Boult and the BBC Orchestra to play in this second Festival. As the programme for 1929 developed, *The Times* published a letter from Bell, calling attention to the *'Festival in which the best music and the best drama are combined'*, emphasizing its local character and pointing out that *'the special and intimate association of the Festival with Canterbury Cathedral recalls the old inspiration which religion gave to art of all kinds and not least to drama and music.'* *The Times*, in a third leader headed 'The Church and the Arts', took up this theme. After referring to precedents in the Middle Ages, it commented that *'last year when* The Coming of Christ *was acted in the Cathedral, and this year when* Everyman *is played at the West Door, a stream, which had long been flowing underground, is seen coming to the surface; and it may be permissible to ask whether the staging of Dr Faustus in the Chapter House does not show that the stream has grown to be wider and deeper than of old.*

'At Canterbury, the Church is resuming her old and proud connection with the Arts.'

But Bell, the first chair of the Cathedral Friends and effectively, therefore, of the Festival, found that assembling performers for a Festival was not without its challenges; first, there were difficulties over one of the centrepieces of the 1929 programme, Masefield's returning nativity play *The Coming of Christ*. In December 1928, Bell had written to Masefield to say that *'we are very definitely counting on having* The Coming of Christ *on Whit Monday and Whit Tuesday (1929). I write now to clinch the matter…firmly and plainly as far as Canterbury, and my wife and I are concerned.'*[33] Yet, by March 1929, only three months later, Bell was writing to Masefield cancelling the play: *'To my great disappointment, circumstances have arisen which make an immediate repetition (of* The Coming of Christ) *impossible. Some of the causes are local, some due to the fact that leading helpers and players of 1928 are unable to take part; and there is, besides, the tumult of a General Election in the last part of May.'* In reply, Masefield begged him to reconsider. *'Don't give up on* The Coming of Christ…*people can be*

---

33. Lambeth Palace archives, extracts from Dean Bell correspondence

found to take the places of those who are gone...even if we have to get the blind from the hospitals and cripples from the workhouse...I do beg you to let Holst...and myself do two performances.' But Bell was adamant.

It is not wholly clear from the correspondence what the detail of the 'local circumstances' might have been. Presumably they would have included the fact that Dean George Bell had been invited to become Bishop of Chichester,[34] about which Bell could not speak publicly. Besides, he had not yet made up his mind.

Initially, Bell refused this promotion to bishop. One can imagine his dilemma. His investment in Canterbury was immense. Canterbury also provided him with a platform for everything that he held dear. Locally, in Kent, he was both active and vocal in his support for the underprivileged; he argued for full employment, better housing and improvements in standards of education. If he moved to Chichester, he would have to give all that up. His friend, Archbishop Davidson, had retired in 1928,[35] but Bell now sought him out and consulted him. Davidson urged him to accept the appointment as bishop. But on March 19th, Bell wrote a letter declining the nomination 'with great regret and only after the fullest deliberation'. He didn't post it immediately, however. In the afternoon, he went for a drive with his wife, feeling very uncomfortable about this refusal. Was it not his duty to accept? The next morning, at prayers, he decided he must say 'yes', and he wrote to the Minister accepting the bishopric. He noted in his diary that he had *'no doubt of the rightness of choice – but beastly'.*[36] It was during this period of indecision that he wrote to Masefield, cancelling his play.

Bell was consecrated as Bishop of Chichester at Canterbury Cathedral on June 11th 1929. He would now live and work more than a hundred miles away from the city and from the Festival which, in partnership with Margaret Babington, he had inspired.

---

34.   Lambeth Palace archives, Dean Bell correspondence
35.   To be succeeded by Archbishop Cosmo Gordon Lang
36.   George Bell, RCD Jasper, p54

With the knowledge that he was about to leave Canterbury, Bell nonetheless toiled on to create the programme for the 1929 Festival, and to do what he could to secure its future. He had met T.S Eliot two years before, and had recognised Eliot's talent and the potential in a friendship that could benefit the Festival. Using the profits from the 1928 production of *The Coming of Christ*, he offered Eliot £100 to write a play for the Cathedral, with a performance guaranteed. It came to nothing but, years later, the result would be *Murder in the Cathedral*.

Bell certainly included in his 'local circumstances' the cathedral's organist and choirmaster, Clement Charlton Palmer, who had held the position since 1908. There had been issues between them during the 1928 Festival. On May 14th 1929, the situation between the Dean and Dr Palmer became so strained that Bell wrote to composer, Gustav Holst, a detailed letter of explanation and apology:[37]

'*My dear Holst, I am sorry to say that Dr Palmer is very sore about the Festival. He complained bitterly that he was not consulted. What happened, as a matter of fact, is this. I was at Salzburg last August, and on my return, saw Sir John Reith,[38] and I said I should very much like a Festival at Canterbury; could he help? He at once arranged to let us have the BBC Orchestra, and all the BBC entered into the idea with enthusiasm. Simultaneously, I got hold of Nugent Monck and the Norwich Players to give a couple of plays at the same time. In the very early stages, I told Palmer about the Festival, and said that the BBC Orchestra were coming and that I hoped, but it is not settled, that Boult[39] would conduct. He raised no sort of objection on his own account, but said that August was not a good month as people were away from Canterbury; and he said that he himself intended to be away. Some time later I saw him again and told him that Boult definitely would conduct, and that I had been asked whether it would be possible to get a chorus together for two of the events: what did he*

37.   Ibid, Lambeth Palace, Bell correspondence, May 14th 1929
38   Director General, BBC
39   Adrian Boult, later Sir Adrian

think? He again raised no sort of objection, but said that in August local people were very busy and it would be very difficult to get any singers; but he was quite ready to ask his choral society, and would do it at once if I liked. I thanked him and said I would rather wait until I knew how large a chorus was required. I also talked to him about the possibility of the Lay Clerks helping with incidental music in the Plays, quartets etc. and he said that would be a good idea, and I said that the terms would of course be professional terms. He again said that he would be away.

'I took it that, in accordance with his regular habit, he disliked things out of the conventional order, and saw and magnified the difficulties. But that he raised no objection and, that while he would not help very much, (he) would acquiesce completely. I also took it that, as he was away, this was simply an indication that he did not want to be bothered with anything. I felt it was rather foolish of him to be out of it altogether, but that was his own wish.

'When, however, the announcement was made at the end of Easter week that the Festival was to happen, and he realised it was all going on apart from him, and that the choruses would be wanted and the whole thing was really taking very positive shape, he developed a great indignation, and when I was abroad I heard about it. When I came back, I saw him and he was very angry, though admitting that he ought to have objected in the very first instance, and he said that he would not help the Festival at all and, indeed, that we should find it very difficult to do some things without his help. I am sorry to say that his indignation is considerable and it persists; and he is particularly angry with me, and also apparently with Boult for asking for his co-operation!

'I worry you with all this silly business because it effects (sic) a particular point in The Planets. I understand you want some boys to sing. I have not asked Palmer, but I know from what he has told others, that nothing will induce him in his present frame of mind to let the choristers take any part at all, though they would be very sad.'

Holst replied understandingly and soothingly. Bell decided the Festival would go ahead without Dr Palmer. Bell then explained to Holst how best to go about getting a choir for the Festival:

'I hardly feel that it would be right for me, as Palmer has taken this line, to over-ride his authority with the choristers altogether and say that they must sing for, after all, he is 'the master of the Choristers'. If you feel that the choristers are necessary (as you may) you could of course approach Palmer yourself to ask him as a personal favour to let the boys come, for it can be managed, I know, in spite of choristers' holidays, with goodwill. The boys will be dreadfully disappointed if they are not in the Festival. Probably it would be better for you to wait before approaching him, till I am out of the way. I leave about June 12, and Palmer might oblige you when I am gone.'

I cannot trace whether Dr Palmer ever relented.

Throughout 1928 and 1929 Margaret Babington supported Bell in his every move. She bristled with activity. From the outset, she had suggested initiatives to enable the Friends to flourish – corporate membership for schools, links with the English-speaking Union, lantern lectures, circulation of those lectures 'as part of (the Friends') propaganda'.[40] In January 1929, she chided Dean Bell for underestimating the need to spread the word of the Friends beyond Britain; it might, she suggested, be 'desirable for you to write a letter deploring the fact that the Dean and Chapter get in touch with…so few…of those who visit England and Canterbury from overseas'. She shared with him her annoyance at criticism of the Friends' outreach that had been printed in an editorial in the local newspaper, the *Kentish Express*, written by its owner, Sir Charles Iggleden. Sir Charles had just returned from a visit to America with the Institute of Journalists,[41] of which he was president, and his words, wrote Babington, 'had rather cut me to the quick…I feel we must do something drastic before this

---

40   Margaret Babington correspondence, Canterbury Cathedral archive
41   A professional association of journalists

coming season'. That same month she urged Bell to write to the BBC's Sir John Reith asking that she (Miss Babington) could give 'one of the educational talks on the wireless' about the Cathedral and the Friends' initiatives. She added that perhaps Bell could think about this and other matters 'at your leisure'. Bell replied that Babington's suggestions were 'excellent'. He added that he was 'anxious to get the Friends interested and, if possible, associated with the Canterbury Festival of Music and Drama'.[42]

I can find no correspondence relating directly to the shock Margaret Babington must have felt at the news that George Bell was going to become Bishop of Chichester, a position he took up in June 1929. What *is* apparent, however, is that, from March onwards, she made communication with him in her letters as simple as possible, asking her questions and delivering her information in short and separate paragraphs and leaving a space beneath each paragraph so that Bell could scribble his reaction. Which he did. In May, she consulted him confidentially over the appointment of a new member of the Friends' council. There were two candidates – Mr Aylmer Vallance and a Dr Cotton. Mr Vallance was not a member of the Friends, but Dr Cotton was. However, in Margaret Babington's words, Dr Cotton 'is certainly not quick enough on the uptake and he so easily worries over things...I would rather not have him as a member of the Council, living at its doors!... Now there is so much going on, we rather want a Council who are quick of brain'. Whether or not she enlisted Bell's support, if Miss Babington ever changed her views on Dr Cotton's mental agility, it is not recorded.

Dr Cotton was elected to the Council.

The Friends' first Steward Treasurer, Sir Anton Bertram, returned to Canterbury in May 1929. He hastened to write to the Dean: '*I hope you will make it quite clear to Miss Babington and to all concerned that my return...must not be considered as in any way affecting her position.*'

It didn't.

---

42   Margaret Babington correspondence. Canterbury Cathedral archives

George Bell left in June to take up his new responsibilities in Chichester. There is no hint in the correspondence between them that this was either the end of their friendship or of George Bell's interest in the Festival. Just before he left, George Bell wrote to Margaret Babington. He enclosed a cheque for five guineas from a new member of the Friends, a Mr Crow. Because Mr Crow was a member of the Old Stagers,[43] he urged Margaret Babington to try to recruit the dramatic society as corporate members; and he concluded with a compliment to Miss Babington, noting with pleasure that *The Times* newspaper in an article and leader, had given 'special praise to the Steward and Treasurer' (Miss Babington) for the initiatives of The Friends at Canterbury Cathedral.'

In Chichester, Bell faced not only settling into his duties as Bishop, but he also had to write the biography of Archbishop Randall Davidson, a promise he had made to Davidson when he had accepted the appointment as Dean of Canterbury. His correspondence indicates that he sustained his interest in the Canterbury Festival and, between the years 1928 and 1948, a number of unusual plays by Laurence Binyon, T.S. Eliot, Christopher Fry, Christopher Hassall, Laurie Lee, Dorothy L Sayers and Charles Williams had their first performance in the nave or the Chapter House of Canterbury Cathedral. Among these plays was an acknowledged masterpiece, T.S Eliot's *Murder in the Cathedral*, which was premiered at Canterbury in 1935.[44]

Murder in the Cathedral was first performed in the Cathedral's Chapter House and was a milestone in the growth of the Canterbury Festival. By 1935, the Festival's reputation as an important entry in the nation's arts calendar was becoming recognised by established voices in the English theatre. Dame Sybil Thorndike had chosen to make a strategic speech at the 1934 Festival, in which she maintained that the church should not have *"turned its back on theatre, for so many years"* and she declared that *"the beginning of*

---

43. Old Stagers, claimed to be the oldest dramatic society in Britain, with close links to Kent County Cricket Club and its Canterbury Week of matches
44. Drama in the Cathedral, Kenneth Pickering, J Garner Miller, 2001, Introduction, p3

the downfall or perversion of the theatre was when the Church let it go...The theatre had become an excrescence instead of an integral part of religion and life...and a gulf between actor and spectator had stopped theatre from becoming 'the common art' for the people".

Building on his friendship with T.S. Eliot, George Bell was wholly responsible for recruiting him to create *Murder in the Cathedral* for the Canterbury Festival. It is not clear how they met, the cleric and the American poet, but it may have been in Margate where, following a nervous breakdown, Eliot spent many months resting and recovering. He and his wife, Vivien, stayed at the Albemarle Hotel in Cliftonville, the up-market end of town. Its address, No 47 The Esplanade, was grand enough as a letterhead but the establishment was, in truth, a superior guest house, 'marvellously comfortable and inexpensive', as his wife wrote to a friend.[45] While he was in Kent, though recovering from illness, Eliot continued writing, much of the time in a seaside shelter overlooking Margate Sands. He reached this haven by catching the tram outside the Albemarle in select Cliftonville and alighting at the stop that, conveniently, was right beside the seated seaside shelter. At the end of each day he would take the same route home, manuscript in hand.[46] *Murder in the Cathedral* confirmed Eliot's place at the forefront of English theatre. Had Eliot written no other play, his reputation as a dramatist would have been established, and had the Canterbury Festival produced no further commissions after 1935, it would still be entitled to claim its part in a revolution of the English theatre. Like the first productions of *Waiting for Godot* or *Look Back in Anger,* a single theatrical event created a watershed for the modern stage.[47]

Murder in the Cathedral was the first play to be written especially for the new, open stage that Laurence Irving had designed in Canterbury Cathedral's Chapter House. Irving wrote later:

45. All the Devils are Here, David Seabrook, Granta Books, 2002
46. Ibid
47. Drama in the Cathedral, Kenneth Pickering, J Garner Miller, 2001, p171

'...Bell asked Eliot down to Chichester, liked him very much, then wrote to me...to negotiate with Eliot. Eliot was very diffident – awfully quiet, friendly chap...and then he came down to stay with us. I spent the next morning taking him all over the Cathedral and showed him the stage. Then we went and had lunch somewhere and I remember my dismay when I said to him: 'Has this given you any ideas for a play?' And he said, 'Oh yes, I shall write a play about Thomas à Becket!' We thought we'd had enough of Thomas à Becket – but of course he was quite right (what he wrote) was entirely new.'

The 1936 Festival in Canterbury was particularly star-studded. Poet Laureate John Masefield gave a talk and Alfred Noyes gave a lecture on Charles Dickens. There was a new work by Arthur Bliss and a new play by Charles Williams titled *The Masque of Thomas Cranmer of Canterbury*. It was 'a worthy successor to Mr Eliot's play', declared the *Canterbury Cathedral Chronicle* that year, and *The Times* felt that the Canterbury Festival had 'created a new school of drama'.

Meanwhile, Babington in Canterbury and Bell in Chichester remained regular correspondents. In 1932, she had found time to support Bell's call for '100,000 churchmen and churchwomen to form a Society of Sussex Church Builders', describing it as 'an irresistible appeal...' which she 'liked enormously'. She reported that, in a successful example of the importance of international outreach, 'Mr Johnson, vicar of St John's Parramatta, in New Zealand, is devoting the offertory to The Friends of Canterbury Cathedral'. She invited Bishop Bell and his wife to the 1935 Festival, which had Youth as its theme – though 'there is literally not one seat left for the performance at 2.30pm...but I will, of course, make places for you'.

In 1936, Dorothy L Sayers, playwright and author of the Lord Peter Wimsey detective novels, was commissioned to write a play for the Festival. As Kenneth Pickering notes in *Drama in the Cathedral*:[48]

---

48.   Ibid, p106

'Few playwrights have projected themselves so completely into the production of one of their plays as did Dorothy Sayers. From March 19th 1937, when she gave the first reading of The Zeal of Thy House, *until June 19th when the cast gathered after the final performance, she took up residence in Canterbury. She helped in the sewing of costumes, discussed theology long into the night with Ben Travers, the writer of farce who was staying with Laurence Irving, and attended rehearsals. The Chapter House was filled with the beautifully modulated voice of Harcourt Williams, who had once played Paolo to Dorothea Baird's Francesca in Stephen Phillips's play and, in* William of Sens, *the architect who rebuilt the Quire of the Cathedral shortly after the murder of Becket, Williams created a memorable role.'*

Dorothy Sayers' enthusiasm even extended to giving signed and inscribed photographs of herself to the cast and stage management[49] and she became so attached to Harcourt Williams and Frank Napier, the joint producers, that in 1938 she bequeathed them in her will the rights of the play. Part of this gratitude was due to the fact that Williams and Napier arranged for the play to be produced at the Westminster Theatre after the Canterbury Festival, and thence at the Duke of York's, the Garrick and, finally, with virtually the same cast, at the New Theatre Oxford, in May 1939. A second Sayers play, based on the story of Faust, and titled *The Devil to Pay*, was written for, and presented at, the 1939 Festival.

This relationship with Canterbury resulted in a close friendship between Dorothy L Sayers and Margaret Babington. World War II suspended the annual Canterbury Festival, but Sayers and Babington continued to correspond. In 1942, Miss Babington told Sayers 'how touching it was to receive so great a number of letters from friends telling me how much they miss the Festival'. Never one to miss a trick, she also asked Sayers: 'Are you thinking of a new play for when peace returns and a Festival is once again possible?'

---

49.   Sayers gave to electrician, Mr Fairbrass, a photograph inscribed *'To Sparks, with all gratitude and kind remembrance'*.

Canterbury was heavily bombed in 1942. Forty-three people lost their lives and 100 were wounded. Around 800 buildings were destroyed but the Cathedral escaped virtually unscathed – only the deanery and the library were damaged. Miss Babington's home in the precincts was hit. Bishop George Bell wrote to Margaret Babington[50] on June 17th:

'*My dear Miss Babington,*

'*What a relief it was to me when I heard that, though your house had fallen in ruins about you, you yourself had got clear with your bicycle. I heard that you were seen busily touring the streets of Canterbury almost immediately after. I am afraid you must have lost some treasures and many things which you valued for various reasons. I hope some things that you cared for have been saved.*

'*I saw Alec Sargent yesterday, and my wife had already seen Mrs Temple* (wife of Archbishop Temple) *last week, so I have gathered the general course of the terrible damage which was done to Canterbury. What a mercy that the Cathedral did not suffer more seriously. How strange Canterbury will look with the middle gone. I wonder whether the County Hotel was spared.*'

Miss Babington replied:

'*My dear Bishop,*

'*I am ashamed not to have sent your receipt[51] before now. A letter was written to you the day before our first raid and did not get posted. Now I send it with much gratitude and write to give you a little of the information for which you ask.*

'*The County Hotel is quite uninjured. The whole of the damage was from Timothy White's* (a chemist shop) *just beyond Mercery Lane to the Cattle Market. In that part on both sides of the road nothing exists for on the night of the first raid it was just a burning*

---

50. Bell correspondence, Canterbury Cathedral archives
51. A receipt for the Bishop's annual subscription to The Friends of Canterbury Cathedral

fiery furnace so that none of us could hope to save a thing and all my books and all my family things are gone.

'*It is fortunate that so few people were sleeping in this business part of the city; otherwise I think the casualties would have been far less light than they were.*'

Barely had the sirens sounded for the last time when the irrepressible Margaret Babington was planning the first post-war Canterbury Festival. By October 1945 she was negotiating with the BBC for Sir Adrian Boult to bring the Symphony Orchestra to a Festival planned for August 1946 – and, in a letter to her friend Dorothy Sayers, she asked: '*Is there any chance that you could give us the promised play? It would be marvellous if you could?*'[52]

She pursued with energy and determination her mission to spread the word of Canterbury, its Festival and the Cathedral's achievements, and in 1949, 1950, 1954, 1956 and 1957, she visited North America, presenting a demanding series of talks with Canterbury at their heart. It was too punishing a schedule. Early in the morning of August 21st 1958, the cleaners found her dead in her office in the upper reaches of the Cathedral's Christ Church Gate. She was still sitting at her desk.

The tireless and remarkable life of Miss Margaret Babington is recorded in the Precincts in two memorials – one in the cloisters and the other close to the main West Door – the only person so honoured in the 2,000-year history of the mother church of the Anglican Communion.

Bishop George Bell died on October 3rd 1958, aged 75. During World War II he had been an outspoken critic of the blanket bombing of German cities by the Allied air forces. He had also championed Protestant ecumenism and a united Europe with an Anglo-German alliance as its cornerstone. Thirty-seven years after his death, a complaint was made that he had sexually abused a girl in the 1940s and 1950s, and a second and similar complaint against him was made as recently as 2013. The Diocese of Chichester

---

52.   Ibid, Canterbury Cathedral archive

paid compensation to the first complainant and, in 2018, Sussex Police declared that the matter was now closed. As I write, a debate continues over whether a statue in memory of George Bell should be created to stand in the precincts of Canterbury Cathedral.

George Bell served as Dean of Canterbury for only five years, but in that time "he transformed the Cathedral from Victorian mode to modern mode". The words are those of another great Dean of Canterbury, Robert Willis; they were part of a speech he gave to mark the 75th anniversary of the foundation of The Friends of Canterbury Cathedral. Dean Robert explored the faith that had driven George Bell. When Bell had been elected to a dining club called Nobody's Friends, he had written an autobiographical poem which looked back humorously on his life and ministry, including his Canterbury years. He wrote:

> 'From Lambeth I, with full courage,
> Made a decanal pilgrimage;
> Succeeding to the dead Dean Wace,
> I sat where now is the 'Red Dean's' place,
> And helped all NOBODIES to see
> The whole Cathedral without fee.
> We were young, we were wise, and very,
> very merry
> And founded the Friends of Canterbury.'

Dean Robert Willis[53] quoted from the poem and recalled that Bell had been quite young, only 41, when he was installed and, as his poem suggests, he had come from Lambeth where he had been Archbishop Randall Davidson's chaplain for 10 years. Dean Robert recalled that his experience as Chaplain to the Archbishop had often brought Bell to the Old Palace in Canterbury; his first night spent as the Archbishop's chaplain included a performance of Spohr's 'Last Judgement' in Canterbury Cathedral. He said:

---

53.   Robert Willis, Dean of Canterbury from 2001 until 2022

'Perhaps one of the most significant clues to the faith and character of George Bell who would become the friend of Dietrich Bonhoeffer and would jeopardise his own chances of the highest preferment with his courageous speech in the House of Lords following the bombing of Dresden, lies in a simple letter about his faith which he sent to his friend Dick Rawsthorne a year before he became Chaplain.' He quoted Bell's words:

'Why am I a Christian? First of all I was born one. I was taught certain things about God and Jesus Christ and the Holy Spirit, and learning and receiving them on the only authority real to me, my parents, I tried in my small way to live by them.

'The fact that so many great and holy men had believed, and by their faith had done all the things which Hebrews XI says men do by faith, seemed a guarantee that faith worked; and I could not see how such faith could be, in all these cases, a mere illusion. This experience then led me to test Christianity on my own...I have been led rather than taken by storm: guided by quiet thinking and doing rather than driven by tumult and violence. And so I go on, continually reassured by my own experience and the experience of those among whom I work.'

Dean Robert went on:

'Many of the things that we take for granted, can be found in Bell's ministry. He realised that Canterbury Cathedral was ministering to people who came for a multitude of reasons, as pilgrims and as sightseers from right across the world and with these people he was determined to share the faith of Christ. Our whole ministry of welcome to visitors, which again we now take for granted, finds its origin in this vision and determination. Bell also saw that the cathedral was a great place for music and drama and he believed that the Gospel could be effectively proclaimed by both. He was therefore at the forefront of the movement in Cathedrals to commission works *of art and to have them performed both in Chapter House and later in the Cathedral itself…*

'*The years he was here, from 1924 to 1929, seem all too short in the Cathedral's long history. But Bell filled them with significance and we owe him a deep debt of gratitude for he filled them with an affection for and pleasure in the community of Canterbury.*'

Which is an appropriate epitaph for a rich life, remembered in this city with admiration and affection…

Prime Minister Margaret Thatcher with Lord Boston at the opening of the TVS studios in Maidstone.

TVS excutives: Lord Boston of Faversham, Chairman; James Gatwood, Managing Director; Michael Blakstad, Director of Programmes

Martin Jackson, Controller Public Affairs; Bob Southgate, Controller News and Current Affairs

Nicolas Stacey – administrator, athlete,
priest and member of the TVS Trust.

Terence Boston, Baron Boston of
Faversham, chair of TVS Television

The TVS Factual Programme team. Standing: Philip Dampier, Olivia Russell,
Roy Francis, Steve Bergson, Adrian Edwards, Graham Hurley, Lisa Davies, Rose
Ashfield, Ted Harrison, Jamie Barrett, Paul Slater, David Pick
Sitting: Pat Daniels, Anita Rimmer, David Sawday, Stuart Nimmo
Pearl Livingstone, Jan Jones, Andrew Barr, Peter Williams, Peter Urie

Chapter 4 – The Influence of Television

In the latter part of the 20th century, there took place in the world of television an event that was a combination of the Grand National and a coronation. It was known as The Franchise Round and it was run by the Independent Television Authority (ITA), later renamed the Independent Broadcasting Authority, or the IBA. Independent Television (ITV) was launched into a BBC-dominated Britain in 1954. Its aims were to be regional and to make money for its shareholders, and the richest franchise, London, would later be divided between two companies, a weekday and a weekend broadcaster. It would be, as its name implied, a wholly independent national network run by completely separate companies but regulated nationally by the ITA.

The southern franchise was won by Southern Television, which went on air from its studios in Southampton in August 1958. They did a good job. They were not one of the biggest companies – Granada, ATV and Associated-Rediffusion dominated daily national programming. But Southern professionally produced local programming and news coverage and a number of series for the network. In 1960 it expanded its coverage to include Kent and Sussex. At that time, I was a newspaper reporter and sub-editor on the *Bristol Evening Post*. Television was the new growth industry and, having watched Alan Whicker on the BBC telling the stories we journalists had only written about in the past, I fancied trying something similar. Southern Television advertised for keen, young, ambitious journalists. I applied.

In 1960, I arrived from Bristol outside Southern Television's studio in Dover in my blue Austin A40 motor car, slightly dented as during the journey I had had a brush with a very much larger vehicle on the A2 near Sittingbourne. The 'studio' was a single-storey former bus garage in Russell Street, Dover, and I was late. Within an hour, it seemed, I was introducing the local news programme, *Day by Day*, in a two-camera studio, with only one very busy cameraman called Hughie who moved repeatedly from one camera to the other.

I came to Kent on a six-month contract. I stayed here for the rest of my life.

Southern Television was run by a former BBC senior executive named Berkeley Smith and, as their programme controller, he brought BBC standards with him. It was a good place to learn a trade and I stayed in Dover for three years, an apprentice embracing this new grammar of television. I lived near Canterbury and, over the years, I never moved far from this remarkable city. Even though I subsequently worked in London at Thames Television and the BBC, Kent was the place to bring up a family.

In 1979, the IBA decided it wanted to strengthen the regional nature of ITV. Among their concerns was the poor coverage of events in South East England. There were plans for a new, multimillion-pound studio to be built in Kent, in addition to the existing studio in Southampton. A major studio on my doorstep had an obvious appeal.

The Franchise Round equated to the insertion of a fox into a henhouse. Pretty well everyone in the industry considered his or her position and pondered the opportunities. I was, at that time, working as an executive producer in BBC Science and Features at Kensington House in London.[54] The three major priorities for any group seeking to compete for an ITV franchise were to convince the IBA that their programming was innovative and comprehensive; to pack the group with talent, both national and, particularly,

---

54.   I was executive producer of two series of *Open Secret* and contributed on-screen both to *Horizon* and *Panorama*

local, that could deliver the promised programmes and to assemble enough committed investors to sustain the business plan presented to the IBA, including the multimillion-pound annual 'rental'. I became part of a consortium called Television South and South East. It was a strong group. The money would come from Charterhouse Bank, through Bruce Fireman; Bill Hodgson from ITN was our chief executive; David Elstein, from Thames, would be Head of Current Affairs and Factual programmes; Paul Bonner from Channel Four and the BBC was our programme controller and Peter Graham Scott our Head of Drama. I was to be in charge of Regional Programmes.

Two years previously, Paul Bonner had headhunted me from Thames Television where I had worked for 14 years as a reporter/ producer for the ITV current affairs flagship, *This Week*. We now worked in the same building at BBC Kensington House and we found secret opportunities to plot and to assess.[55] One morning, another of my colleagues, Michael Blakstad, who ran the much admired *Tomorrow's World* scientific series, called in for a chat. He carefully closed the office door. Was I interested in joining a group that was being assembled to go for an ITV franchise in the South and South East? I stopped him in full flow. I was, I said, disqualified from doing so. I said no more than that – but he knew damn well that I was already committed. We looked at each other in some amusement. I'm not sure exactly when Michael found out that there were in fact three of us, including Paul Bonner, on the same corridor in Kensington House, vying for the same franchise.[56]

In the weeks leading up to the franchise awards, the atmosphere was both fevered and conspiratorial. The IBA held meetings across the regions "to test the water…to assess local feelings". I was never convinced they did either. Meaningful progress in any business is achieved through individual inspiration and/or concentrated hard graft by a small group. The public franchise meetings became exchanges of pre-written position papers, an exercise in point

---

55. BBC staff were explicitly forbidden to be part of the ITV Franchise Round.
56. Michael Blakstad subsequently confirmed that he was not aware of Paul's involvement in my consortium

scoring delivered at high volume and debated in a very public shop window.

Columnist, Patricia Williams, reflected in the magazine *Broadcast* on one such meeting, at the Gulbenkian Theatre in Canterbury in September 1980. It was chaired by the wonderful Mary Warnock *"whose DIY haircut contrasted sharply with the blue-rinse ladies in the auditorium."* Representatives of the incumbent Southern Television said their piece and so too did we, the suitors anxious to replace Southern, careful not to make our promises too wild because, in the audience, IBA stalkers were busily taking notes. Patricia Williams wrote of the meeting:

'It was a strictly middle-class, middle-aged, middle-of-the-road affair. Amid the swathes of grey suits, Women's Institute bouffant hairdos and neat Marks and Sparks shift dresses; there was not a black face to be seen. And the only brown ones were, one suspected, carefully cultivated on the beaches of Corfu. The only young woman to speak happened to work in the bar of the Gulbenkian Theatre where the meeting was being held. The only young man who ventured a word or two turned out to be the ACTT[57] area shop steward.

'Half of the gathering turned out to be directly involved in applying for the franchise. At least half of those left were from umpteen warring local councils determined to secure the site of the new South-East studio for their particular patch.

'The nice poshly-spoken man made a pitch for Canterbury, which of course is the intellectual, cultural centre of the county. Everyone by now knew what he was leading up to. We just waited expectantly for the punch line. "It just so happens I have in my briefcase", the posh man went on, "plans for..." The rest of his speech was lost in gales of laughter.

'Of those 300 people at the meeting, only a handful were bona fide, disinterested genuine 22-carat viewers, claiming no interest whatsoever other than the one issue which the IBA had come down to listen to: the quality of programme output.

---

57. The Association of Cinematograph, Television and Allied Technicians, a television industry trade union

'One local organisation after another got up to bemoan and berate Southern's lack of coverage of this, that and the other. The Women's Institute, South East Arts people, watchdog committees, all claimed too little interest by the incumbent in what they were doing. An ex-employee of Southern said the company had a lot to answer for in its lack of commitment to news coverage of Kent. Teachers complained about the nature of schools broadcasting and a conductor felt the BBC was alone in its support of music, despite Southern's coverage of Glyndebourne opera. 'Why can't these music programmes go out earlier in the evening?' wondered one of the many gentlemen from South East Arts. No-one on the IBA panel ventured an explanation of the art of scheduling. However, Mrs Warnock reassured him that the IBA would closely question each applicant at the interview on this subject and whoever won it would be closely watched to ensure they kept their promises.

'But the plaudits should go to the IBA panel who, like the good civil servants they are, behaved immaculately. Rarely did they show boredom or imply they'd heard it all before, which they have. Nor did they betray the slightest glimmer of emotion sitting stony-faced and still in listening mode. It was 10 o'clock and the tinkle of bottles announced the bar was open. The audience made a dive for welcomed refreshment.'

I report this at some length; firstly, to stress the importance of 'local' in our democratic process; secondly, to illuminate the difficulty in persuading the man and woman in the street to become involved in decisions that will affect their everyday lives and, thirdly, to stress that, of the few questions posed at that, and other similar meetings, 'information' and 'community' issues were indeed at the heart of most concerns expressed. I recall a feeling of relief that night that, when a single question was raised on religious broadcasting, we were able to remind the meeting that the then Dean of Canterbury, the Most Reverend Victor de Waal, was one of our Board members. Sport? We had the Kent and England cricket captain, Mike Denness. Local politics? The then Leader of Kent County Council, Sir John Grugeon, was also among our supporters. We thought we had covered all the bases. I quote a paragraph from a paper on regionalism I wrote at the time:

'...*a television company must be involved in the life of the region it serves. Involved for two reasons; first to understand the significance of events within the region and the potential impact of national trends and decisions; second, to use its influence and its money to support and encourage that which is good, and which will benefit the region.*'

In the months leading up to Christmas 1980, we beavered away amid the uncertainty and isolation shared by all the competing groups. A week before the announcement of the results, *The Observer* newspaper claimed in a front-page banner headline scoop from a leaked IBA document, that Southern Television would be replaced. Television South and South East would win the franchise. That was our group. We were about to win. It was there in black and white. We quietly celebrated. On December 28th 1980, our chairman, Lord Nathan, went to the IBA headquarters at no 10 Brompton Road, London. He was given a letter. It began: 'Dear Lord Nathan, I write before we make a public announcement to give you news which I know will be very disappointing to you...' It was signed by the IBA chair, Lady Plowden.

We had lost and, ironically, that was to have a considerable – and financially favourable – impact on the future of the Canterbury Festival.

The team that won the franchise to broadcast television in the South and South East of England was titled Television South, or TVS. Its Director of Programmes was Michael Blakstad who, as we know, worked in the next office to mine at BBC Kensington House. I rang to congratulate him; he thanked me and asked me to join his victorious team as Head of Documentaries. This was an unexpected offer and, on reflection, a pleasant surprise. I knew many of the team with whom I would be working if I accepted the role. I accepted. It was a post that the Blakstad team, I learned later, had deliberately left vacant in their bid. I think TVS were mildly surprised that they had won; the late Martin Jackson, their head of Public Affairs, pop pundit and Kent County Councillor, confided as much, years later. From a purely programming viewpoint, the incumbent Southern Television had done little wrong. Their output was tight and professional under Berkeley Smith, their Programme Controller. They had, however, turned up at the IBA with plenty of financial muscle for the interview which every applicant had to undergo, but without Berkeley Smith as part of their interview team. Berkeley was the lynchpin of their output. The IBA parked the Southern Television team in the waiting room until they could find Berkeley; this they did, and rushed him to Brompton Road before the interview would begin. That had been a silly omission and a fatal error.

I had little time to settle into this new TVS team. It was led by James Gatward, and they were all thoroughly steeped in the detail of their application. My attraction, Gatward once said to me, was twofold – that I had an established track record with both the BBC and ITV in making documentaries but that I was also embedded in the community of Kent and the South East. In 1980 I was chairman of Canterbury's Conservation Advisory Committee and of the Oaten Hill Society, both of which I had helped create in order to try to curb the worst excesses of the city planners at the time. I was a member of the Canterbury Society and a trustee and member of the Canterbury Theatre and Festival Trust. In this regard, I was delighted to discover in the TVS bid, a pledge to set up a 'TVS Trust' into which a percentage of the company's revenue would flow, then to be utilised for community initiatives. This was a unique idea much praised by the IBA as evidence of the new company's commitment to the community it was now going to serve. This Trust would, with generous donations, play a vital role in the survival of both the Canterbury Festival and Chichester Festival.

TVS fulfilled the promises made in their winning application. The converted bus garage in Dover was phased out and a new, state-of-the-art studio was built at Vinters Park, Maidstone. Network and local programming for the new, enlarged South and

South East region rolled out and, because TVS now had two major centres of production, an aeroplane was leased to fly executives and production personnel from Maidstone to Southampton and vice-versa. Every day a Britten-Norman Islander light aircraft shuttled between a specially-laid grass runway beside the Maidstone studios to the airport at Eastleigh in Hampshire. The service was accepted gleefully and with some amusement. Sadly, it didn't take long for winter to grip the schedule, necessitating diversions to Bournemouth and Rochester airports and involving much stress in the minds of those who were buffeted about amid the storm clouds on their way to the already much-delayed budget meetings. Communication in this twin-centred company was always challenging. Some controllers and heads of department lived near Maidstone, others near Southampton. The M25/M3 became familiar strips of motorway for the company's executives. On one occasion, the Controller of Current Affairs (Clive Jones)[58] headed to meet the Controller of Factual Programmes (me). There was confusion over the meeting place; one dashed from Maidstone to Southampton, the other from Southampton to Maidstone. We must have flashed past each other somewhere near Bagshot. Each of us picked up a speeding ticket. The meeting eventually took place by telephone.

TVS took seriously its promise to involve itself in the community. Its chairman was Lord Boston of Faversham in Kent, and the TVS Trust met in the boardroom of the Maidstone studios. Terry Boston knew Kent. He had been Member of Parliament for Faversham from 1964 until 1970 and seated in the House of Lords since 1976. For a Labour peer, his style and formal manner of speech wouldn't have been out of place in the Bullingdon Club. He was lighthouse tall, patrician, immaculately dressed and married to a down-to-earth Australian, Margaret (née Head), who had been a market research consultant. They were at home in rural Kent and when Boston spoke he usually had something worthwhile to say.

---

58   Now Sir Clive Jones

The TVS Trust embraced the community in its choice of board members tasked with distributing the thousands of pounds set aside annually from the profits of the parent broadcaster. One of them was the Reverend Nicolas Stacey, Nic Stacey, Olympic runner, friend and contemporary of Christopher Chataway and of Roger Bannister who, on May 6th 1954, had fallen into Nic's arms as he finished running the first four-minute mile. For a year or two, sprinter Nic Stacey was also the fastest white man on earth. He was wickedly funny and a pioneer in the treatment of mental health when he became Director of Social Services for Kent. As with any good priest, he had a questioning faith and a love of his community. He was an active member of the TVS Trust and the Trust would prove important to the future of the Canterbury Festival. So important that in five years, the Trust would intervene with grants that, though not guaranteeing the survival of the Festival, would allow it to continue its mission to 'reach out into the community to produce an annual arts festival of international branding throughout the years to provide creative opportunities and to commission and produce performance and events.'[59]

---

59.   Quote from Canterbury Theatre and Festival Trust Strategic Plan

GROWING PAINS

"THREE WISE MEN"

Reg Brown

Peter Williams with Festival administrator Clarrie Middleton

Robin Carver and his wife June.

Henry and Mary Villiers, Henry on the Kent Opera board,
Mary a driving force in the Arts-Collection Fund

Lord (Melvyn) Bragg

"Do we have a seconder for the amendment '... that an ambulance and the police be sent for'?"

"Do we have a seconder for this amendment
'... that an ambulance and the police be sent for'?"
A reflection on the Canterbury Festival board meetings in the late
1980s; sent by board member Caroline Collingwood to the chair.
(Private Eye, April 1986)

Ken Reedie, curator of the Royal
Museum, (The Beaney) in Canterbury.

Arthur Porter, leader Canterbury City Council, determined the old Marlowe Theatre should be demolished.

Marlowe Theatre, which stood in what is now the Marlowe Arcade.

Norman Platt, Kent Opera

Keith Lucas, Chair, Canterbury New Theatre Ltd

Brian Arnold, "Mr Music" for many years, who encouraged the Canterbury Choral Society to become a major player in the Festival.

Chapter 5 – 'The Liveliest Show in Town'

'It is now recognised that those who reside in, or visit, a large part of Kent generally to the east of the River Medway, are almost completely deprived of the opportunity to enjoy performances of plays, opera, dance, and light entertainment in a modern theatre similar to those available…in other parts of the United Kingdom.

'It is also recognised that the area in general, and Canterbury in particular, suffers in its appeal as a centre for national and international tourism by virtue of the lack of entertainment and allied attractions for the overnight visitor.'

This was the depressing summary set before Canterbury's city fathers at the end of the 1970s by[60] consultants they hired to assess the magnitude of the problem they faced as they debated how they would develop the centre of the cathedral city – a process that threatened the demolition of Canterbury's Marlowe Theatre. They will have taken comfort, however, in the final pages of the consultants' report, which concluded, presciently, that *'we consider the future development of Canterbury is very closely tied to the future of the arts in the city, and that rather larger issues are at stake. We think that the city has everything in its favour to make a much greater impact in a number of respects than appears to be happening at present, and are certain that theatre and music have important roles to play in realising this potential. We appreciate the difficulties*

---

60.   Reports by Martin Carr, Carr & Angier, March 1980 and May 1981

facing the council, but it is an opportunity for the future that must be grasped with courage and determination, and now!'

If this was a call to arms – which it undeniably was – let us examine the players who would try to answer it. First, there was the city council who had commissioned the report. They were led by an autocratic but farsighted councillor, Arthur Porter, who was very much in the Tammany Hall mould of council leaders. The council ran the city's theatre, the Marlowe, through a trust led by councillors Maurice Steptoe and Cyril Windsor, both solid and dependable champions of the arts.

The city's small, 400-seat Marlowe Theatre run by Peter Carpenter and, later, Bill Preston, limped along year by year with a six-figure annual subsidy from the council. It provided a mixed programme that included plays from a small repertory company,[61] some pop groups, contributions from touring companies and leading local amateur societies, both musical and dramatic. My impression was that a committee made up of Trust members plus the theatre director, created the theatre's programme each year.

Then there was Kent Opera, England's first regional opera company founded in 1969 by Norman Platt. Kent Opera was a brave and innovative venture that sought to produce first-class opera outside the main traditional centres in the nation's big cities. It played in Dartford and Royal Tunbridge Wells as well as "squeezing into"[62] the Marlowe Theatre in Canterbury.

And there was a new kid on the block, Canterbury New Theatre Limited (CNTL), set up by a group of enthusiasts who feared the disappearance of theatre altogether in the city, and which had strong links both with Kent Opera and with South East Arts. The city council were also considering "very seriously" a massive proposal from developer Lew Cartier, who wished to build a sports, hotel and theatre complex in the Northgate area of the city. The early minutes of the CNTL indicated a determination to liaise with Mr Cartier 'but no-one knew how to contact him.'[63] Ultimately, Mr

61. Joanna Lumley was a member of the repertory company
62. Phrase used by Norman Platt in conversation with author
63. Canterbury New Theatre Limited minutes (CNTL) April 9th 1980

Cartier's development plans expanded to four sites in Canterbury and did not find favour with the city council.

The 1970s were a decade of intense local protest in Canterbury; decisions and suggestions made by the city council, most of them concerning planning, stirred opposition from residents and ratepayers all over the city. At one time, there were 14 separate amenity societies or protest groups within the city boundaries. The city council was predominantly conservative; the Chief Planning Officer was Percy Jackson who had 'form' in a similar role in Chester. The amenity societies banded together, dismayed at the lack of a coherent voice to oppose the worst excesses being suggested by the city council. They consulted the University of Kent's Law Clinic, which was led at the time by Larry and Linda Grant, who would go on to become leading lawyers in the civil rights movement. They suggested we should form a Canterbury Conservation Advisory Committee (CCAC), which would have the statutory right to call councillors and officers to explain and defend the decisions they intended to make. The CCAC[64] was for many years the most effective forum for discussion on planning in the city – and I salute the architects who might frequently be bidding for work from the local authority, for their courage and social conscience in openly supporting the views of those who were opposing the council's view. Among them were Frank Lee Evans, Anthony Swain, Andrew Clague and Anthony de Moubray.

One of the amenity societies set up at that time came into being because Percy Jackson was suggesting the construction of three tower blocks of flats just outside the city walls on St George's Place, close to the current site of Waitrose. It was called the Oaten Hill Society and, during a series of brisk exchanges in the local press, a senior council member referred to the society's members as 'urban terrorists'. For a brief moment, a member of the Oaten Hill Society, Miss Tibbles, held centre stage. She was in her eighties, tiny, stylish and with a penchant for cloche hats. She said she had never seen herself as an 'urban terrorist' and objected to the description. She

---

64.   I chaired the CCAC for five years

said that she simply could not see any justification for a historic city such as Canterbury even to consider the construction of tower blocks of flats in a cluster so close to the city walls. Miss Tibbles' view prevailed. The tower blocks were never built.

The Oaten Hill Society, which I chaired, also argued anxiously and vigorously about the future of theatre in the city. Early in 1977, the council applied to demolish the Marlowe Theatre in the city centre. The application was accompanied by the words: '...*it is not the intention of the city council to demolish the Marlowe Theatre until a replacement theatre has been built on another site...*' This was an important pledge and, in 1977, the Oaten Hill Society wrote to Percy Jackson, the city's Architect and Planning Officer, to emphasise its importance and to question the strength of the council's commitment for 'intentions' may change.

'The view of this society, expressed at two public meetings, it that the Marlowe Theatre should not close until a new theatre is open or – at the very least – under construction. For Canterbury to lose its theatre for whatever reason – lack of available cash, or lack of motivation from a future council – would be a major indictment of those of us living in the city today when the decisions are being taken.

'Our concern is over the legal validity of the guarantee which accompanies the application. The City Council say: We wish to apply to knock the theatre down – but don't worry, we won't do it till another site is guaranteed. We are worried that, with the best will in the world, such a promise from the City Council may not be legally binding. Certainly, it will not have the legal status of an approved order permitting the demolition of the theatre.'

This view was widely supported. Edred Wright, Director of Music at The King's School and a member of the CNTL, told the city council that they had no moral authority nor power to decide whether or not Canterbury had a theatre. '*We must*', Edred wrote '*affirm our positive intention that Canterbury will have a theatre and we call upon the council to tell us in detail what their proposals are.*'

In April 1977, Percy Jackson responded that the favoured alternative site for a theatre was on the Watling Street car park – a proposal which, incidentally, was never progressed – but his final paragraph contained as firm a commitment as we in the Trust and in the Oaten Hill Society, felt we were going to get:

'You will appreciate, of course, this does not commit the Council in any way to a date or cost for building a new theatre, but the Council, by several formal resolutions, have made it clear that they do not intend to demolish the Marlowe Theatre until a replacement theatre is ready. I trust this explanation will move any misapprehension within your society regarding the City Council's intentions. Yours sincerely, Percy Jackson. City Architect and Planner.'

The growth of CNTL became increasingly important in the debate over an issue that was now widely considered vital to Canterbury's future. The members of the group included a number of names who would make significant contributions to the revival of the modern Canterbury Festival. They were:

- Brian Arnold – farmer, stalwart of the Canterbury Choral Society, chairman of the National Federation of Music Societies (now Making Music) and of the trust of the Menuhin Competition;
- Norman Platt – vastly experienced founder and director of Kent Opera as a baritone, a director, administrator and a translator;
- Mark Deller – countertenor, director of the Stour Music Festival and member of the Deller Consort, famed for its concerts throughout Europe, the USA and South America;
- Robin Carver – City Councillor and a former mayor of the city;
- Reg Brown – director of the University of Kent's Gulbenkian Theatre; and
- Keith Lucas – artist and director of the British Film Institute, who chaired the CNTL.

I was a founder member of the group and I remember the meetings held at the Platt family home at Pembles Cross near Ashford. The major issues at that time were that, if we could save theatre in Canterbury, where would a new theatre be sited? And how big would it be? The year was 1980. Thirty years later, those two questions would still be exercising those who cared about the city!

It was apparent from the outset that the majority of the city council wished to retain a theatre and to face the challenge set them by their consultants; but, year by year, as they considered the size of the subsidy necessary to keep the existing Marlowe Theatre open, the competing demands of refuse collections, social services, uneven pavements and housing needs pressed in on local politicians. Among councillors elected to ensure value for the ratepayers' money, there was evidently increasing unease at continuing to allow a Trust to run a theatre and to be subsidised by the city council to do so.

The annual report on the 1978–79 season in the Marlowe Theatre reveals the reasons for the city council's misgivings about leaving the future of Canterbury theatre in the hands of the then Trust. It was an optimistic, even glowing, report. Nine productions had been staged, attended by 66,690 people. They included *Joseph and the Amazing Technicolor Dreamcoat* and the pantomime *Dick Whittington* but, on examination, those two shows had attracted nearly 40,000 (or two thirds) of the theatre's total annual audience. Kent Opera had appeared twice, performing *Ulysses* and *Il Seraglio* (total audience 3,196); 14 concerts, from 'pop' to Gilbert and Sullivan, which had sold 7,007 tickets. The local Canterbury Amateur Operatic Society presented *Die Fledermaus* to 4,810 during its week's run and 2,897 people came to see the Woodman School of Dancing pantomime, mostly mums and dads of the cast of local schoolchildren. As a local theatre, then, it was providing a varied programme and encouraging local, amateur talent. The problem lay in the Trust's accounts. The theatre took £95,870 at the box office and income from hiring out the building produced a further £12,000. But the grants to enable it to run were enormous – £57,000 from the Arts Council and a total of £64,164 from the city council who also covered the theatre's operating deficit of £12,164. It was an annual haemorrhage of cash that even the most dedicated theatre-goers among the councillors found hard to justify.

The city council's logic was clear. They had ambitious plans for the commercial heart of the city that would involve the development of the site currently occupied by the Marlowe Theatre; therefore, their view was that the theatre would have to be demolished. This was certainly the opinion of the council's leader, Arthur Porter. Christopher Gay, the city's Town Clerk and later, Chief Executive, recalls:

"Arthur was determined that the theatre should be demolished. The city centre had to be developed and the theatre, and its local supporters, were standing in the way. Arthur would produce, time and again, back-of-the-envelope financial calculations which he would discuss with me, showing what the theatre was costing the city. Arthur's priority was always to transform the city centre. He thought Kent Opera's demands were elitist and he was impatient with them. I was lobbied, privately, by Kent Opera but, whatever I felt personally, I had to remain even-handed."

Chris Gay[65] was always sympathetic to the arts. He had been a cathedral chorister at Southwell in the Midlands, his father was Welsh and a singer and he was a member of choirs all his life. He supported the Marlowe Theatre and remembers meeting Cleo Laine when she briefly joined the repertory company: *"I was a fan of Cleo and Johnny Dankworth's jazz, for as long as I can remember..."*

The pressure on the city council to reach a decision became intense. The matter was resolved when the full council confirmed again that they would not demolish the theatre until a site for a replacement theatre was agreed and, to prove it, the council moved decisively and bought the site of the Odeon cinema near the West

---

65.   Chris was a nephew of Constance Chapman, a leading actress in the 1980s whom I had met and admired in the repertory company at the Little Theatre in Bristol. Connie's maiden name was Coulsting, a name she shared with Christopher Coulsting Gay. On his retirement in 1996, Chris joined the Festival board

Gate, which was one of the sites already being considered for a new theatre. With this reassurance, in January 1980, Canterbury New Theatre Limited changed its name to the Canterbury Theatre *and Festival* Trust (CTFT), with charitable status.[66] Theatre and festival were now indelibly linked. The Trust's aims were twofold: to support and help to build a new Marlowe Theatre in the city and to create a modern Canterbury Festival. The Trust pledged to raise £20,000 towards the interior decoration of the new theatre.[67] The first, new Canterbury Festival was planned for 1984.

The city council's decision to buy the Odeon cinema and convert it was both shrewd and timely. The Odeon was a relatively young building and it had one characteristic that made it both suitable and swift to convert into a theatre. The Canterbury Odeon was one of the very few buildings in the Odeon chain of cinemas that had a relatively large stage, intended by the owners to accommodate stage presentations in addition to a major feature film at a single performance. The move to buy the Odeon site, which we welcomed, was not without controversy, however. *'Who needs a larger theatre?'* trumpeted correspondents in the local *Gazette*. Composer, Alan Ridout, questioned whether the reputation of the old Marlowe Theatre was as high as was claimed – *'certainly not with the distinguished directors and actors who have worked there in the past; nor with the audiences which, in droves, keep clear'*. The £15 million that it would cost to convert the Odeon cinema would be better spent on raising the money paid to actors and playrights, Alan went on to suggest, and he concluded that *'£15 million of concrete and plastic will not produce living theatre'*. In addition, there were misgivings about the height of the fly tower that would be necessary to accommodate the sets required for the onstage productions. Would that not detract from the magnificence of the cathedral nearby? And what about road access to this newer, bigger building? A recipe for more traffic snarl-ups? Nonetheless,

66. CTFT minutes, February 25th 1983
67. To help transform the cinema into a theatre, Roger Butlin was commissioned to paint a cloud effect on the auditorium walls

Canterbury generally welcomed the initiative, not least because – as the local *Gazette* declared in its leader column in February 1984 – *'Canterbury is at last going to have a regular Festival, with many events being staged at a new Marlowe Theatre'*.

The Duke of Kent formally opened the new, adapted Marlowe Theatre in 1984 in time for a Festival later that year. He unveiled a commemorative plaque in the foyer, which also marked the contribution of £20,000 from the Canterbury Theatre and Festival Trust. In the background, as the Duke spoke, Kent Opera could be heard vigorously rehearsing *King Priam* for that night's performance. Norman Platt commented that the *"new freedom of the extra space on stage was liberating"*.

The new Trust was a strong pressure group. It embraced representatives of the National Art Collections Fund (now Art Fund), South-East Arts, the chair of Kent Opera, Lady Northbourne, and a number of benefactors. Its target was to revive the Festival in 1984 and we had already taken preparatory steps – but a programme of events had to be created from a blank canvas and whoever took on the job faced a huge task. Mark Deller stepped forward as he records in his fascinating autobiography:[68]

'With my experience as director of Stour Music for the previous eight years, and before that running the Salisbury Festival of the Arts in 1967, I approached Norman Platt (who was essentially the power behind the throne) and suggested to him that I might be the person to take on the task (of Festival Artistic Director), *for a small fee, and he agreed. So in November 1983 I began work, initially from home, on putting together all the elements for a festival the following September.*

'I had the task of finding a Festival Office in the city, and producing a three-week mixed arts festival for about £50,000. I think I was paid £4,000 as my fee for doing so. We had some support from South-East Arts and KCC, but no direct financial support from the City Council although they did allow us free use of the theatre for the three weeks

---

68.   Mark, My Words, 2021, p145

which, considering the Trust's involvement with the creation of a new Marlowe Theatre, was probably the least they could do. I managed to find office space, with the help of Michael Waterfield, in the shop room at the front of his new restaurant in Best Lane, and begged, borrowed or stole furniture and equipment to establish a Festival Office. I employed Valerie Paterson as a part-time, two days a week secretary, and Di Kaufmann, Kent Opera's publicity officer used to come in for one day a week to oversee the marketing and publicity.'

Within a matter of weeks, he had produced an outline programme, a budget that forecast a deficit of £15,800 on events, but a festival attractive enough to draw good audiences and therefore healthy sponsorship. This first Festival in 1984 would include a week of the National Theatre at the Marlowe, another week with the Ballet Rambert and a third week with Kent Opera performing Mozart's *Il Seraglio* plus a much-praised production of Michael Tippett's *King Priam*, attended by the composer. Sir Charles Groves would conduct the Philharmonia Orchestra in a concert that would include Walton's Symphony No 1 and a young Nigel Kennedy playing Elgar's Violin Concerto. There were exhibitions, walks, talks and events in the University's Gulbenkian Theatre and, of course in the cathedral, and a separately-organised Festival Fringe. Mark Deller prepared us for an overall deficit of around £5,000.

He was determined to embrace the visual arts and, in this he was helped by the intervention of the National Art-Collections Fund. The fund, no longer in existence, provided support for an exhibition titled Treasures from Kent Houses. It would become a highlight of the first Festival, largely due to a small group of influential women led by Mary Villiers, who, persuaded Kent's great families to allow their treasures to be gathered together at the Beaney museum in Canterbury. Working with the Beaney's curator, Ken Reedie, their success was truly staggering. Portraits by Van Dyck, Mytens, Janssens, Batoni, Gainsborough, Angelica Kauffmann, Ramsay and Beechey; works by Sailmaker, Van Goyen and Stubbs; a grand opening by the Arts Minister Lord Gowrie, sponsored by Christies. Mary Villiers was 'quite pleased'[69] with the NACF teams efforts. So were we. Mary was well-connected and worked with a group including art historian Niamh Lloyd-Thomas and Ginette Cobb. Ginette became a spiky, hard-working member of the Trust's Board. Altogether the Fund introduced a fresh dimension to the Festival, bringing seldom-seen treasure into public view.

Money was a constant concern in the monthly meetings of the Trust – funds to create the new Festival but also to support the city's ambitions to build the new theatre. The Trust's £20,000 contribution to the new theatre was not going to be easy to find, but the pledge was important as a declaration of the Trust's support for the local council. In August 1983, chair Keith Lucas, expressed his concern that concentrating on raising money for a 1984 Festival might *"jeopardise the front-of-house fundraising"*, so the Trust decided to separate the two efforts. Kent Opera's Robin Jessel reported that the Trust had *"£155 in the bank"*, and suggested an approach to prospective "emergency funders", including John Swire, whose wife Moira (now Lady Swire) would later become a board member of the Trust and one of its most vivid and important supporters. But money remained a problem.

As the months of debate wore on, it became apparent that there were two factions within the Trust: On one side, the Kent Opera team, which had laid the Trust's foundations by employing their own administrative structure, and on the other, some trustees who shared the objectives of building a large theatre but whose interests spread more widely to embrace the arts other than opera. The structure of the governance of the Festival was a recurring item on the Trust's agenda. In January 1984, looking ahead to 1985, the Trust had considered three models of management structure and opted for "a Festival Director, with an assistant, plus three or four advisors in various fields of the arts, to whom he or she could turn

---

69. One of the most unusual objets in the exhibition loaned by Lord Harris of Belmont was a hat worn by Tippu Sahib Sultan of Mysore, who fought the British, leading to the treaty of Seringapatam in 1792. It was shaped rather like a bonnet. Its provenance was subsequently questioned.

for advice". Mark Deller, then organising the 1984 Festival, had commented that this would enable the Trust's board to meet less frequently.

Kent Opera's Carole Patey was then appointed the Festival's Artistic Director for 1985. At the Trust's June meeting in 1984, she presented a 'comprehensive report...on the general structure of the 1985 Festival' which, in the Trustees' opinion, 'seemed to be a sensible path to development'. It was certainly a helping hand offered by Kent Opera to a cash-strapped Trust. A dispassionate observer might also have commented, however, that this was either a confirmation of the primacy of the Kent Opera lobby or another step towards an inevitable and potentially damaging disagreement over the future shape of the governance of the Festival.

It was probably both.

The press launch of the 1984 Canterbury Festival took place in London. TVS had helped produce a video for the occasion and actress, Dora Bryan, famed and much loved for her scatty personality, gave TV interviews. Carole Patey then produced her thoughts on the 1985 Festival. It would have an Italian theme, she said. All this while, simultaneously, Mark Deller continued to direct and assemble the 1984 Festival. It was an odd arrangement that had the potential to disturb those of a sensitive nature.

With their eyes on a European audience, Mark Deller with Lady Northbourne, Jack Bornoff and Robin Carver, cultivated the links with France and with Reims, the French town with which Canterbury was twinned. Importantly, Michael Waterfield and Sandra Drew for the Festival Fringe, reached an agreement[70] with Canterbury's Urban Studies Centre, based in St Alphege's Church, to use the centre during the Festival as a Festival Club between the hours of 6pm and 11pm. Both these partnerships would prove valuable for future festivals. Mark's 1984 Festival with its European theme had been meticulously prepared, both artistically and financially.[71] I still recall the excitement of that

70.   CTFT minutes, April 27th 1984
71.   One of Mark Deller's strengths, as was the case later with Rosie Turner, was his accuracy in financial projections

weekend, September 25th 1984, and the three weeks that followed – the opening Festival service in the cathedral[72] and the children's opera *Doctor Syn* at the Gulbenkian; the jazz concerts with the late, great George Melly; the Philharmonia Orchestra at the Marlowe; Ballet Rambert and Robert Tear; the films of Peter Watkins and the shock of watching his forecast of nuclear disaster in *War Games*, and the explosive climax at the St Lawrence Cricket Ground when the Retreat was impressively beaten and fireworks filled the night sky over Canterbury. Keith Lucas, the Trust's chairman, wrote in this first Festival programme:

'For those of us fortunate enough to be close to Canterbury, the establishment of a major Arts Festival, should provide a focus for the growing cultural vitality of the City and its significance as the historic centre of the region. The aim of the Festival is of course to provide entertainment and enrichment but a festival must have a theme and a context. The theme of the Canterbury Festival derives from the historical and geographical situation of the City itself, set as it is on the main route to Europe, an ancient centre of pilgrimage, commerce and, more recently, tourism. We have merely to look around our own streets to see in the buildings the influences of Flanders and France, and enter our churches to listen to the influence of Italy and Germany on our own great musical inheritance. Our Festival seeks to relate the strands of this continuing process of cultural interchange.*

'We wish to thank all those who have given their support in so many ways and with a generosity which confirms a shared conviction. The Cathedral, the City Council (for their enterprise in providing the new Marlowe Theatre), the County Council, the University, colleges, schools, arts organisations and societies and in particular Kent Opera and the National Art-Collections Fund...*

'Together we have planned what we believe will become a corner-stone of the cultural life of the country and an important event in the European calendar.'

---

72. This festival evensong in the cathedral became an annual tradition at the start of every festival

Composer, Alan Ridout, in his critique of the Festival at the final curtain, regretted the absence of drama written by Canterbury's own Christopher Marlowe in this celebration (as, after all, the city's theatre bore his name) and wished for a less conservative choice of music performance. Nevertheless, he commented that *'those Jeremiahs who thought, and said that it* (a festival) *couldn't possibly work have been confounded'*. He praised *'the sheer size and enthusiasm of the audiences'* in *'an astonishing three weeks'*. More phlegmatically, *Classical Music Weekly* declared *'This could become a very important festival in the future…this first festival is subtitled 'Britain in Europe', and administrator Mark Deller seems to have assembled a pretty wide-ranging assortment of entertainment to illustrate this not-too-restrictive theme'.*

Meanwhile, Stuart Deas in his review of the Festival said:

'The city of Canterbury has such obvious attractions for the millions of tourists who visit each year that it seems strange it has not jumped on the festival bandwagon before now. Perhaps it was thought, quite reasonably, that there was no need to trumpet its wares, although surely in the past there must have been events other than purely ecclesiastical to justify a fanfare or two. But the Canterbury Festival made an auspicious beginning on September 23rd, naturally with a Cathedral service led by its Archbishop, but more importantly from a musical point of view, with an orchestral concert in its new theatre known simply as 'The Marlowe'.

'This building takes the place of the much smaller (and by some, much lamented) Marlowe, but, although it is a converted cinema, the conversion has been done in such a thorough manner that a newcomer might never guess its previous existence. The acoustics, it is true, tend to have that rather harsh brilliance which seems to bedevil all modern halls and theatres, but other comforts have not been forgotten, and the size – some 2,000 (sic) seats – ensures that major productions can benefit from its wide stage and sunk orchestra pit.'

In fact, the new Marlowe Theatre could seat only just over 950, and through judicious use of huge chandeliers, the capacity could be reduced to 500 to create a more intimate atmosphere for drama productions. The mechanics of this process were complex and the adaptation was seldom used, but 30 years later, the theatre's capacity for only 950 seats would have an important bearing on the ongoing debate over theatre in Canterbury.

Four weeks after the event on Friday November 2nd, the Trust met at the Gulbenkian Theatre to debrief and reflect. The meeting was understandably upbeat. The city's Chief Executive, Chris Gay, complimented the Trust on the accuracy of its financial forecasting. South East Arts' chief Chris Cooper, lauded the Trust on the quality and variety of the Festival. Chairman, Keith Lucas, praised Kent Opera's treasurer, Robin Jessel, for his *"comprehensive grasp of the financial challenges and his hard work on the accounts"*. He thanked the cathedral's Dean and Chapter and Lord Boston, chairman of TVS, who had supported the Festival financially, including vice-chair, Brian Arnold, and the entire staff for their *"devotion"*. Keith also formally introduced Carole Patey to the Trust as Artistic Director for the 1985 Festival. Mark Deller, having delivered the 1984 Festival, agreed to remain as Festival Administrator.

The Trust was, by now, a strong body with many talents and the right networking connections. The minutes of the meetings during 1985 list among members and contributors: Keith Lucas (chair), Brian Arnold (vice-chair), Lady Northbourne, Lady Swire, Bill Dorrell (*Kent Messenger*), Mrs Ginette Cobb, Reg Brown, Robin Carver, Mrs Caroline Collingwood, Col Ken Gross, Dr David Ingram, Robin Jessel, Michael Marriott, Norman Platt, Peter Rolt, Mrs Margaret Scott-Knight, Mrs Mary Villiers, Doug Abbott (secretary) and myself. Kent County Council gave the Festival a grant of £5,000, plus an interest-free loan of £10,000 and, having adopted an Italian theme for 1985, it was 'hoped that donations from Italian sources would amount to £25,000...'[73] Total expenditure on the 1985 Festival £100,000.

---

73   CTFT minutes, April 26th 1985

But, with the advantage of hindsight, it was becoming obvious that the flaw in the structure of the group between two competing priorities – the ambitions of Kent Opera and the rebirth of the Canterbury Festival was fundamental and dangerous. Mark Deller, working closely with Reg Brown and others, had produced a highly successful first 'modern' Canterbury Festival. The programme had embraced Kent Opera, but in Mark Deller's words, *"it became apparent that Norman Platt's overriding concern was success for Kent Opera, whereas the objective for many of us was a wider, community-based celebration of the arts"*.

On July 22nd 1985, Mark Deller resigned from his role of Festival Administrator. Kent Opera members now occupied two key positions in the Trust. The Artistic Director was Carole Patey of Kent Opera and Di Kaufman was in charge of marketing and publicity. Deller resigned for a number of reasons. He had devoted nearly two years to the CTFT and he wished to concentrate more on his career as a solo countertenor with the Deller Consort and with Stour Music. His resignation letter contained these paragraphs:

'During the past two years many changes have occurred and I now find myself at odds with the general artistic policy of the festival and no longer in a position where I can bring any influence to bear.

'I have for long been aware that there was a danger of the festival becoming another platform for Kent Opera and its protégés; indeed I have voiced this concern on several occasions in the past. Not only has this element exceeded my fears, but it has been carried out with little regard for financial considerations.

'Everything has been made subservient to 'artist integrity', which virtue, it seems, has been bestowed on one person only. To try and work with someone who is apparently omniscient and infallible is both tiresome and fruitless.

'The Kent Opera participation in the festival is, I believe, wholly desirable and indeed demonstrates precisely that degree of excellence which we all agree should be the hallmark of the Canterbury Festival. However, during the past year as Administrator, I have found that on too many occasions I have been the last person to hear about

important developments within the festival. Much of this, I'm sure, was unintentional, but altogether, it puts the administrator in an intolerable situation.'

Mark Deller's resignation, as one member of the Trust observed, '*put the cat among the pigeons!*' Every member of the Trust, it seemed, had a view. Mary Villier's husband, Henry, served on the Board of Kent Opera. Mary remembers that he *always* (her emphasis) came home irritable after a Kent Opera meeting; "*that man, Norman Platt, is impossible. Talented he may be but he will jeopardise the whole initiative.*" The chair, Keith Lucas, wrote a paper before the 1985 Festival advising Trust members, '*I hope that we all recognise that everyone involved is striving for the highest (standards)... however, this objective must be balanced and measured against the likely financial viability of events and the resources available.*' He proposed that a co-ordinating committee be duly formed for the Festival that would '*monitor the policy brief of the Artistic Director (Carole Patey) and, on the advice of the Financial and General Purpose Committee, (should) set up the budgetary limits and targets within which the Festival should operate.*'

The 1985 Festival went ahead amid simmering unease. It ran for three weeks. It opened with a torchlight procession and masquerade beside the River Stour at the Westgate gardens. The genuine Italian gondola carrying the mayor, Councillor Hazel McCabe, became entangled in reeds, separating the stranded mayor from the opening ceremony. We hoped it wasn't an omen. The Italian theme embraced music from St Mark's, Venice, in the cathedral, a talk on Leonardo da Vinci, an Italian film festival and the history of pizza- and pasta-making. To the general public, the Festival was both varied and successful, but a paper presented at the meeting of the Festival Co-ordinating Committee, immediately after the Festival on October 28th 1985, set out reasons for urgent concern.

Preliminary results of the 1985 Festival forecast a loss of £92,000, which was £23,000 higher than had been anticipated in June. Particularly in the light of Deller's resignation letter, the message to Carole Patey was clear. Firstly, communicate better and, secondly, artistic ambition had to be tempered with financial reality. The schism between the two camps widened. Four weeks later on Friday November 15th, vice-chair, Brian Arnold, appealed for '*an attempt to strike a balance between the opposing points of view expressed on the 1985 Festival…and* (a recognition of) *the financial constraints the Festival was experiencing*'. That rapprochement did not take place.

On December 4th, chairman Keith Lucas wrote to Carole Patey. The first section of his letter indicates how serious the rift had become:

'*This letter is a formal warning that your continuing failure to consult and communicate with me as chairman of the Trust and of the Festival Co-ordinating Committee, even at the most basic level, constitutes a gross breach of professional behaviour and is completely unacceptable. As you will recall from an earlier letter warning you that you needed to change your attitude, I instructed you to keep closely in touch and to meet normally at least once a week. This you have singularly failed to do, and you are now putting the efficient running of the Trust and management of the Festival at risk by your failure to inform me of what you are doing, planning or failing to achieve.*

'*You must recognise that your behaviour puts your continuing employment at immediate risk.*'

Carole Patey responded immediately. She resigned. The first paragraph of her response read:

'*I have recently been subjected to severe criticism, insults, shouting, swearing, lies and abuse by the chairman of the Festival Committee. This is an intolerable situation which must be immediately resolved.*'

Whether or not all this was true, she went on to accuse the chairman and the Festival of a lack of vision:

'I believe that every Festival must have a unique identity. You do not create this by simply employing established 'international stars' at random, but through a unique vision informed by knowledge and awareness, which also includes the discovery of new talents...one of the great strengths of the Canterbury Festival is that it embraces all the arts. Why not have the most exciting and enterprising company in our area (Kent Opera) as the focal point of the music of the Festival? We should probably have more Kent Opera, not less. The Deller Consort falls into the same category, though on a smaller scale, and it is wholly right that we should base our festival in this way...'

Carole's Kent Opera colleague, Di Kaufman, also resigned. Despite the efforts of Lady Northbourne, Kent Opera's chair and Robin Carver of Canterbury City Council who negotiated with them, the two sides seemed irreconcilable. Norman Platt, Kent Opera's founder, then resigned, and in February 1986, the Trust accepted all these sudden resignations. The final paragraph of Norman Platt's resignation letter read:

'There is no way in which I or Kent Opera can be associated with a regime that treats its (sic) employees in this way, nor with a Festival which has no central artistic direction; I therefore offer my resignation...There are around this table some honourable people dedicated to the idea of a Festival of quality in Canterbury who could have prevented this situation. It need not have happened.'

Chairman, Keith Lucas, then considered his own position and offered his resignation at a meeting on February 12th at Rutherford College at the University of Kent. The Trust responded to this welter of resignations by setting up an official Working Group. It comprised Councillor Robin Carver, the Gulbenkian director, Reg Brown, and myself. We became known as 'the Three Wise Men' and, proposed by vice-chair, Brian Arnold, and seconded by Caroline Collingwood, the Trust passed a vote of confidence in our ability to sort out the mess. I guess they had, at that moment, little choice. The minutes that day recorded that the Trust's liabilities exceeded its assets by £6,000, plus debts of £10,000 to Kent County Council and £8,000 to two charitable trusts, a total of £24,000. I recalled a phrase in Norman Platt's resignation statement: *'The damage to the Festival* (of all this) *is incalculable'.*

The two friends who joined me in making up the Three Wise Men, Reg Brown and Robin Carver, brought contrasting skills to the task. I recall the first words we shared over a cup of tea in a restaurant in St Margaret's Street; they were: *"Well, where do we go from here?"* I guess we shared two important characteristics – a determination that the Festival should survive and an instinctive optimism.

Reg Brown was a man of the theatre. Born in London's East End, he knew Kent because the Brown family spent their annual summer holidays picking hops in and around Canterbury. He left school at 14; his first job was in the family's greengrocer's shop, boiling beetroot. After National Service in the RAF, he obtained an honours degree in English and American Literature at the University of Kent. He then became director/administrator of the University's Gulbenkian Theatre, a position he held for 22 years. He programmed every season, contracted the visiting companies, produced and directed in-house productions, frequently acted and sang in them, designed and built the sets, created posters and programmes and usually found costumes for the performers from the thousands of garments and gewgaws he collected from around the country. He kept the Gulbenkian Theatre solvent and usually full. As if this weren't enough, as well as balancing the accounts and managing the staff, he would sometimes be found selling tickets before the show or an ice cream at the interval. If we needed someone who understood theatre, Reg Brown was the man.[74]

Robin Carver was very different. His background was in banking and science. He had worked in the Middle East for the Ottoman Bank before joining Shell and becoming head of public relations at their Research Centre in Kent in 1970. Robin was indomitable. He was born with spina bifida and had had to have a

---

74.   Reg Brown died in 2016

leg amputated at the age of 21. You would never have guessed it. He had played in a Baghdad cricket team as wicketkeeper – he loved the game and spent much of his rare spare time watching cricket at the St Lawrence Ground in Canterbury. Robin lived at Fordwich with his wife, June, and won the city council seat of Sturry South in 1973 – a position he would hold until his retirement in 1991. He was elected mayor in 1979. In our deliberations, he spoke for the city council. How he found time to devote to our concerns, I don't know. He worked tirelessly for the disabled. To my knowledge, he supported the local Harry Barker Handicapped Club, the Disabled Drivers' Association and had travelled to Mongolia and Kyrgyzstan to speak for the disabled and to help improve their lives. He was erudite and funny. He was loved and respected. He was just the man for a crisis.[75]

I was asked to chair this Working Group. We took a number of steps. Though he did not wish to continue as chair, we did not accept Keith Lucas' resignation from the Board. Instead, we created a new role of President of the Trust and invited him to take that office. He accepted. The future of the Festival was in the balance and we asked for three weeks to examine the feasibility of holding a Festival in 1986. Robin Carver, for Canterbury City Council, and Lady Northbourne, for Kent Opera, now proposed and seconded that we should also seek an Artistic Director immediately. We negotiated for a continuation of our office space in Ivy Lane, Canterbury, as part of a *Kent Messenger* sponsorship. We agreed to write to Carole Patey and Di Kaufman thanking them for their services, and seeking to terminate a growing correspondence between us.

In March, the Trust decided to go ahead with a 1986 Festival. We invited members of the Trust to report on certain aspects of a possible programme: Mary Villiers, visual arts; Mark Deller; music, dance and mime; Robin Carver, links with Reims; Reg Brown, drama; Professor Gibson, talks and Jack Bornoff, to help organise a concert from the Orchestre National de Lille.

---

75.   Robin Carver, Mayor of Canterbury in 1979, died in 2005

The first report we received that day was to inform us that Kent Opera had officially withdrawn from the Festival. We regretted it but were not surprised.

We were anxious to invite Mark Deller back into a position of authority and we asked him to return *pro tem* as Festival Administrator. We were also aware that the perception of the Festival's future was now, at best, 'shaky'. The Festival's reputation with some of the city's leading businessmen was not the highest. Tim Brett[76] recalls a meeting held early on in 1983, in Ricemans restaurant (now Fenwick department store) when most of Canterbury's commercial world had been invited to hear a presentation by the Canterbury New Theatre company. *"We attended with an open mind...But it was soon apparent that the speaker was interested only in money, and in stressing that it was our duty to help this cultural initiative. I think he was asking us each to find £10,000. Well, that was probably worth £100–150 thousand today. We weren't multi-national companies. We just couldn't consider that sort of money. He didn't win many friends that day."*

However secure one's lines of communication, Canterbury is – or was then – a village. Secrets were jealously guarded but easily overheard. Negative chatter needed to be silenced. Through my friend and colleague, Greg Dyke, I slightly knew Melvyn Bragg.[77] Melvyn ran and hosted *The South Bank Show* on ITV, the nation's most watched programme on the arts. Mark Deller and I sought an appointment with him and visited his office at London Weekend Television on the South Bank. Would he be our Artistic Consultant? He would – provided he had to do nothing other than believe we were doing a good job. We reassured him. Melvyn stuck completely to his word. We never saw him in Canterbury; in fact, I don't think we even contacted him except to send him an outline of the Festival's events, but the name 'Melvyn Bragg' appeared on the programme of every event in that 1986 Festival. It inspired confidence. I do not believe Melvyn even claimed the

76.   Tim Brett, chairman of Robert Brett & Sons for more than 40 years
77.   Now Baron Bragg

£500 we offered him in our letter that confirmed his engagement.[78] His intervention was crucial to the future of the Festival.

Finance was, as usual, a problem as the Trust prepared for the 1986 Festival. The final deficit from 1985 was £48,700. The TVS Trust answered our plea for help with a grant for £20,000, confirmed, it is said, by a casting vote from Nic Stacey, canon of this parish and founder member of the television company's trust. Peter Rolt produced a deficit budget indicating that the 1986 Festival would need to find £54,700 to break even. This would have to be found through a combination of box office receipts, sponsorship, grants and the generosity of benefactors. It would not reduce the debt the Festival had accumulated. Lady Moira Swire and Lady (Marie Sygne) Northbourne immediately pledged their long-term support. Keith Lucas pledged £4,000.[79] We reflected that it was in critical times such as these that you found out who your friends were.

This was a troubling time in the history of the revival of the Festival. One trustee commented that the Festival meetings were so scarred by disagreement and aggression that the meetings themselves were, for a period, *"the liveliest show in town"*. I have tried to record in detail how the schism developed for two reasons; firstly, because it threatened the future of the Canterbury Festival and secondly, because, in the eyes of those bodies who might contribute to the growth and success of Kent Opera, the bitter arguments that had raged raised questions about the governance of this brilliant initiative in regional opera. As it was to prove, the latter consideration was to have the more profound effect.[80]

The Festival would survive. Kent Opera would not.

---

78. CTFT minutes, March 21st 1986: 7(a) Mr Melvyn Bragg is confirmed as the 1986 Festival artistic consultant with fees not to exceed £500
79. CTFT minutes, April 26th 1986
80. Mark Deller wrote a note on file in this crisis (see Appendix 2)

The Deller Consort, Alfred is on the far right; Mark is sitting next to him.

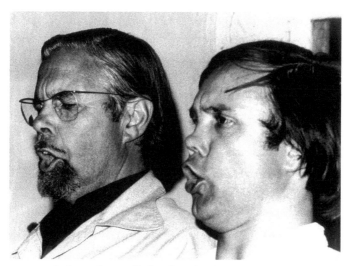

Father and son; Alfred and Mark Deller, counter-tenors

The Dller Consort play to a packed Palais du Music, Barcelona

John Round, as treasurer, kept the finances on a tight rein.

Mark Deller, Festival Director

The Orient Express – A journey for a Festival with a French theme.

Improvisation – not to be repeated!

The Theatre Royal, Margate

Chapter 6 – Turmoil and Tantrum

At first, I thought the high, clear notes faintly heard might be birdsong. Then, as I followed the garden path through the roses to the back of the timbered Tudor cottage, I realised it was a human voice. I was a month or so into my job with Southern Television and the assignment that day was to make a short film on Alfred Deller.

Alfred George Deller, CBE, was a countertenor almost wholly responsible for the revival of the countertenor voice in Renaissance and Baroque music in the 20th century. The script I wrote that day explained for a lay television audience that a countertenor was a man who sang in a high register, that Alfred Deller had been born in Margate in 1912, that he had sung in his local St John's Church choir and that, when his voice had broken, he had continued to sing in this high, flute-like manner. I remember thinking, when confronted by the commanding figure of Alfred Deller that day, how odd it was that so huge a figure could produce so delicate a sound.

My report included an observation that, even in the 19th century, countertenors in Italy were castrati[81] – males castrated in boyhood in order to retain their soprano or alto voice. This prompted the story from Alfred that day (not broadcast!) that once when singing in France he had been approached by a French woman who exclaimed, "*Monsieur, vous êtes eunuque*",[82] to which Alfred promptly replied: "*I think you mean 'unique'*, madame."

This encounter with Alfred at his home on the outskirts of Ashford was my introduction to the Deller family and the beginning of a lifelong friendship with Alfred's son, Mark, with

---

81.　Castrati – the practice was made illegal in 1903
82.　Literally, 'you are a eunuch'!

whom I have worked and planned and laughed over the last 50 years. Mark Deller followed the musical road already trodden by his father. Alfred had been a lay clerk in the Canterbury Cathedral choir during World War II[83] and Mark, his mother, Peggy, and his brother, Simon, moved to live in the Cathedral precincts. Mark then became a cathedral chorister and, in 1948, took part in his first 'Canterbury Festival'. As we have seen, the Friends of Canterbury Cathedral had, since 1928 and throughout the 1930s, held their festival in Canterbury based on the cathedral itself, and young Mark was cast as one of the singing monks in the 1948 festival play *Thor, With Angels*, written and produced by Christopher Fry. He never appeared in the play because the monks sang offstage; he was heard but not seen. The following year, however, he "*trod the boards of the festival properly, for the first time*" (as he put it) in the role of Henry Purcell in Sydney Nicholson's opera *The Children of the Chapel*.

Mark's links with Canterbury Cathedral are lifelong and precious. Services in the cathedral during the war took place in the Eastern Crypt and as a schoolboy he used to attend evensong quite often. The boarder choristers had been evacuated to Cornwall to avoid the bombing anticipated on the East of England; they went along with the organist, Gerald Knight, and the services in Canterbury Cathedral were sung by those who remained, the day boys together with the adult lay clerks. Mark became a chorister in 1946. The choir was directed by the precentor, Joseph Poole, with Bill Harvey, the assistant organist. Bill was also the resident organist at the local Regal Cinema, which had a Wurlitzer organ that rose from the depths to entertain the cinemagoers. Bill had a catchy signature tune when he played at the Regal, which he would repeat on the piano for the choristers at the end of their daily practice in the cathedral's Song Room. That piano, a 1910 Broadwood, now sits cosily in Mark's living room in his cottage home in Wye. It is an instrument of sentiment and memories. Not only was it the piano used in the cathedral's Song Room throughout his time as

---

83. Alfred Deller was a pacifist and worked on the land during the war

a chorister and until the 1990s, but it was also accompanied on this piano, that composer Michael Tippett first heard his father, Alfred, sing in 1943. When not so long ago cathedral organist and choirmaster, David Flood, told Mark he was replacing the ancient piano with a new Yamaha, Mark asked David what was going to happen to the Broadwood. *"He said: 'Make me an offer'. So I did, and I bought it for £300".*[84]

In his final year in the Choir School, Mark became head chorister and I remember once asking him how he would assess his time at the cathedral. He was *"not sure that the academic education at the Choir School was as good as it might have been",* but when he left, *"I was a pretty competent musician. We all were. We were expected to do everything to such a high professional standard. Leaving the Cathedral, when I was almost 14, was undoubtedly a wrench, and when I was first at King's School, I used to creep back into the North Transept occasionally to listen to Evensong. But I knew then that all I ever really wanted to do in life was to gravitate to the back row of the choir stalls and become a Lay Clerk, which of course is what I did in due course".*[85] At King's School, under legendary headmaster Canon 'Fred' Shirley, he became music monitor and was taught by the Head of Choirs at the school, Edred Wright, who was *"brilliant"* and became *"an important influence on the rest of my musical career".*[86] Wright, said Mark, *"could get even the most unlikely people to sing, and derive real pleasure from it. Simon Carrington described him as 'a maverick choral director, who lived and breathed music, but in a refreshingly irreverent and almost anti-establishment manner'. It was probably something of that rebel nature, and the sense that he was one of us, that rubbed off on us boys and made him such an attractive and inspirational personality. Certainly, I have him to thank for most of what I know about the technique of choral conducting, and any ability I have had to inspire others to sing".*[87]

---

84.   Mark, My Words, 2020, p23
85.   Ibid, p35
86.   Ibid, p38
87.   Ibid, p173

Mark also believed that what he learned from Edred Wright was influential in his winning a choral scholarship to Cambridge University. Professionally, Mark had, as a chorister, sung with his father in the newly formed Deller Consort. He now applied to fill a vacancy for an alto at Salisbury Cathedral. He made the 4½-hour journey to his audition at Salisbury on his tiny Lambretta motor scooter and got the job. It was the start of nine happy years, during which he successfully organised series of winter concerts in the city's market square by the Guildhall and, from 1961, taught English, history and French at the Cathedral School in Salisbury's Bishop's Palace. He also met Sheelagh, whom he married in 1965. Two years later, he was asked by the town clerk to inaugurate a Salisbury Festival of the Arts (now Salisbury International Arts Festival), which *"with the arrogance of youth and a touch of bravado, I was sure that it was something I could do"*.[88] Jenny Lee, wife of Health and Housing Minister, Aneurin Bevan, was Minister for the Arts at the time and, for a few brief years, anything seemed possible in the world of the arts. Mark (salary £1,500) went to the Arts Council for a financial grant and came away with a cheque for £3,000 *"without filling in a single form"*.[89] With the cheque in his pocket, he budgeted for an overall loss of £3,000. He was tellingly accurate. The Festival was a success, but the city council decided not to repeat the investment and it would be many years before the Salisbury Festival was revived. It was naturally a disappointment for Deller, but from that moment festivals have run like a golden thread through his life – from Salisbury to Canterbury, to Stour Music, to Canterbury again, to France for his summer Deller Academy and back to Canterbury.[90] Looking back on his years in Salisbury, Mark says: *"It was a significant experience and one which was to stand me in good stead when I took over running Stour Music, and, some years later, the Canterbury Festival. Were it not for the fact that the Town Clerk, George Richardson had enough faith*

---

88.   Ibid, p68
89.   Ibid, p69
90.   The Deller Academy 'early music' summer school at the Abbaye de Senanque and later at Lacoste, which ran from 1971 till 1996

in me to run the Festival, much of my future career might have been very different."[91]

Mark's varied duties at Salisbury also enabled him to sing, record and tour with the Deller Consort in Europe, the USA and Canada. By 1969, he was a vicar choral at St Paul's Cathedral in London, a post that had an established 'deputy' system, which allowed him to take other professional engagements. He toured all over the world – Australia, New Zealand, North and South America and most of Europe. It was in Argentina and Brazil that the Dellers realised how far and wide the appreciation of their music had spread; they played to audiences of 2,000 in Rio de Janeiro, São Paulo and Buenos Aires. By public demand, the Dellers returned every year for most of the 1970s. In 1979, Alfred died suddenly. A series of concerts had been planned in Buenos Aires. Amid his grief, Mark stepped in to conduct the concerts.

To survive the crisis that was gripping the fledgling Canterbury Festival in the spring of 1986, it needed someone with vigour, foresight, experience and flair. In the minds of the Three Wise Men charged with producing a survival plan, it was blindingly obvious that we should turn to Mark. The resignations from the Trust of the three members of Kent Opera early in 1986 left an unfinished programme of events for the 1986 Festival and barely six months to complete the task. Busy as he was as the director of the Stour Festival, Mark agreed to, as he put it, "fill in the gaps". In fact, although Carole Patey had previously produced an outline of the Festival and Melvyn Bragg was billed as its Artistic Consultant, that Festival would not have happened had we not been able to rely on Mark Deller.

The programme for the 1986 Festival had a strong French influence. This was due, in no small way, to the energy and contacts of Jack Bornoff and Marie Sygne Northbourne. Lady Northbourne had been chair of Kent Opera since its inception and was also involved from the outset in the campaign to create a festival and build a new theatre in Canterbury. She had remained

---

91.   Ibid, p70

above the atmosphere of tantrums and turmoil and, admirably, had managed to remain both loyal to Kent Opera and determined that the Festival should survive. She was also very clear about the ability of Kent Opera's Norman Platt to negotiate. He didn't.[92]

Marie Sygne's father had been a diplomat and the family had spent her wartime years from three to 11 in Washington, USA, away from her home in a divided and defeated France. As an aside, during her childhood, Antoine de Saint-Exupéry, author of *The Little Prince*, had been a family friend and she still has the drawings and watercolours that Saint-Exupéry had created for her amusement in the 1940s – and which, of course, are included in the millions of volumes of the hugely popular book.[93] Jack Bornoff was a quiet, gentle and entirely civilised man. He had been a staff officer in Germany in the Intelligence Corps during World War II and was a broadcaster and a UNESCO executive. Since 1963, he had been a founder board member of the International Institute for Comparative Music Studies in Berlin. He was about to retire and was setting up an organisation to liaise between the arts in South East England and Northern France.

The Festival proclaimed its links with France by hiring the *Venice-Simplon Orient Express*. For a single day, folk could catch the Orient Express at London's Victoria station and be delivered at Canterbury, having lunched on board. Luncheon was courgette and mint soup; Scotch salmon with prawns and tarragon mayonnaise; new potatoes with chives and spring onions; frilly bitter salad with a special dressing; hazelnut roulade with Melba sauce, and coffee from Colombia. The menu bore a replica of a drawing originally used on the Orient Express in 1884. The journey was two-way for some as they had already left Canterbury early that morning on a local train to arrive in Victoria in time to catch the Orient Express back to Canterbury! The journey was fun and incident-

---

92. Conversation with author, 2022
93. Lady Northbourne asked Saint-Exupéry to draw a fox for her; the fox's role in *The Little Prince* is central, as the Very Rev Robert Willis says: "The fox makes it evident that you only see things clearly through your heart rather than your eyes."

free; one Board member commenting that it was *"escapism…to get away for a moment from the problems crowding in on the festival."* Our outreach to France was of the highest quality. I still have the outline which Mark set out for the 1986 Festival. It reads:

'Principal Events
- Orchestre National de Lille
- École du théâtre du mouvement
- English Chamber Orchestra
- Molière's 'L'Avare' – drama week
- Ballet Rambert
- Exhibition: Bayeux Tapestry
- Exhibition: Stained glass
- Exhibition: Paintings by Pissarro
- Floodlit tattoo & fireworks
- Cabaret – 'Le Tango Stupéfiant' (Hélèn Delavault)

Recitals
- Esther Lamandier   (troubadour songs)
- L'École d'Orphée   (17th & 18th century music)
- Pasquier Trio   (19th century music)
- Jean Guillou   (organ)
- Jill Gomez   (French song)
- Trevor Pinnock   (harpsichord)
- London Oboe Band (Court of Louis XIV)
- Deller Consort   (*air de cour*)
- Ronald Smith   (piano)
- Hilliard Ensemble   (lute & Baroque guitar)

Plus
- Talks, city walks, excursions, exhibitions, jazz, French fashion…'

It all looked pretty good to us on the Board. Beside each event was its cost and the amount of sponsorship we would be expected to raise. I was elected chairman of the Trust in April 1986. I accepted on the understanding that I would serve only two years.[94] I remained chair for 21 years.

It had long been apparent that the governance of the Trust was top-heavy and, therefore, unwieldy. When the executive, the sub-committee members and all the staff met, there were often 30 people in the room. My solution was to select a strong but smaller board and offer those who had contributed so much to the journey so far, a seat on a new body, which we would call the Festival Council. This Council would be formed by 'members and supporters' of the Festival and would meet perhaps four times a year. The main financial board would hold executive power and take the decisions and then report back to the other members in the Festival Council. This was accomplished with very little upset, emphasizing the dedication of those who had helped create the Festival over the years.

The first matter however to be resolved was: Would there be a Festival at all in 1986? Having considered the cost of cancellations and the high hopes that would be dashed by a withdrawal, I proposed that the 1986 Festival should proceed. Robin Carver seconded the motion. It was passed with one abstention. The working paper I presented on behalf of the 'Three Wise Men' at that tense meeting contained the following opening paragraph:

'We were asked, without issuing contracts, to continue arranging a programme for the 1986 Festival; to advertise for an Artistic Director for a 1987 Festival; and to assess the financial situation and sponsorship possibilities. We have fulfilled those tasks...'

And the final paragraph:

'The Festival's gratitude to my two colleagues, Reg Brown and Robin Carver, should be recorded. The work has been done because we believe in the Festival. We have done, and are doing, our utmost to see that it survives and prospers – I am confident that it will do so...'

---

94.   CTFT minutes, April 25th 1986, Gulbenkian Theatre

That meeting also approved our suggestion that John Round and Desmond Connelly should become members of the Trust's executive. They were significant additions to the group. John came from Blue Circle Industries, the international cement company. He lived at Chilham and he became the Trust's treasurer, a position he graced for many years. Des was an excellent journalist, working for the Kent Messenger Group (now KM Media Group). He was based in Canterbury at the local *Gazette* and his relationship with the Festival in press and publishing terms would last throughout his life.

With so many issues facing the Trust, the core team of the CTFT had spent long days and evenings outside the committee meetings, in living rooms and quiet corners, discussing alternative strategies as well as the Festival's image. The public perception of the Festival was important: it should be innovative and not 'stuffy'. Should the Festival run for three weeks or two? The design of a logo[95] was given much thought and the shape chosen changed little over the years. The question of event programmes had recurringly exercised the team. Should there be a souvenir programme[96] containing all the Festival events? If so, how much would people pay for it? Outside the smoke-filled rooms where the decisions were being made – yes, in the 1980s they were still smoke-filled – there was a pressing need to present the Festival message to the people. The Festival team paraded through the city centre, from the West Gate to Ricemans department store, selling souvenir programmes as they went; among them, Keith Lucas and Rona, John Round and Pauline, Michael Irwin and Stella, Brian Arnold and Mary, Mary Villiers, Caroline Collingwood, Reg Brown, Robin Carver and June, myself and Jo and the team from the Festival office. We found the reaction to this public show of intent largely favourable. In 1986, that was important to us because there were those who declared that they *"didn't know there was a Canterbury Festival"*. But 50 years later, there are still folk in Canterbury who

---

95.　The Canterbury Festival logo is on page 7
96.　A souvenir programme priced at £1 and, later, £2, was produced for a number of festivals but constantly made a loss and, more recently, was superceded by single event programming

say that's the case – perhaps the same people who declare they were unaware that, for a century, Kent was home to a thriving and vibrant coalfield.

We revived the tradition of a chairman's message in the Festival programme and, looking back, the contrast between my first two 'messages' to the Festivalgoers is distinct. In 1986, in a Festival programme that ran to only seven pages, I assumed nothing. There is no reference to the future. I would describe its tone as 'tentatively informative'. The reader is addressed as a newcomer and was told that he or she 'would not be disappointed' with a Festival of 'variety, quality and fun'. We were 'a unique Festival' and 'if it is your first visit to us, we welcome you'. I added, rather as a tour guide, 'the charm and strength of Canterbury is not limited to the Cathedral. Pause, too, if you will, to visit other corners where the Festival is in evidence – the Poor Priests' Hospital, Blackfriars, the Old Synagogue and, at the Festival's end, the St Lawrence Cricket Ground, where the climax will be a spectacular fireworks display'. I concluded: 'A Festival is a time when a city is on show. It is a party to which we are all invited. But good parties that happen apparently spontaneously, are in fact the result of a great deal of planning and effort. Canterbury has worked hard to stage this, its third Festival'.

This last sentence was a heartfelt vote of thanks to those who had, and were, supporting the Festival at this critical time.

For the 1987 Festival, the chairman's message in a 92-page programme – which was 85 pages longer than the previous publication – would reveal an honesty that was built on growing confidence. It began:

'They say when you have problems, you discover your real friends. This is the fourth Canterbury Festival. It is true to say that over the past two years, there have been doubts over whether the third, let alone fourth Festival, would ever take place. The reasons, now irrelevant, are part of the growing pains of a lively idea...'

Twelve months separate those two messages; in those 12 months, Mark Deller and Administrator, Clarrie Middleton, had delivered a successful Festival. But, we needed to look ahead and, with Mark unlikely to take on a full-time role as Artistic Director, we followed the Board's instruction to find another professional to lead the Canterbury Festival. We advertised. We received 35 applications. It was an impressive list, by which I mean that the quality and track record of most of the applicants agreeably surprised us. They included established and immediately recognisable names in the world of music and drama. Among them was Robert Ponsonby.

Robert Ponsonby and Reg Brown

Robert Ponsonby, Artistic Director, Canterbury Festival 1987-1988

Michael Willis-Fleming

Chairman and Artistic Director, side by side

TVS excutives: (left to right) Author, Clive Jones, Jan Beal, John Kaye Cooper, Anna Home, Greg Dyke, Mick Pilsworth, Jane Tatnall, Pippa Cross and John Jones

Eurotunnel sponsorship supports the Festival and Alastair Morton, its chief executive delivers

Reg Brown (left) on stage, at the Gulbenkian.

Andrew Barr who recognised the energy and importance of British gospel music.

People Get Ready – shown nationally on television, ITV and Channel 4 featuring the best of Britain's gospel choirs, led by John Francis and produced by Roy Francis who says: "People Get Ready signalled the coming of the age of British gospel music."

Soloist: David Copeland and Beverley Wint

Chapter 7 – Crisis

All progress depends on the unreasonable person –
George Bernard Shaw

The capture of Robert Ponsonby to become Artistic Director of the Canterbury Festival in 1987 was something of a coup.

Robert was already a pillar of the British arts establishment in Edinburgh, Glasgow and London. He had been director of the Edinburgh Festival, general administrator of the Royal Scottish National Orchestra and, after 13 years directing The Proms, had recently retired as the BBC's London-based Controller of Music. He was a patrician product of Eton, Trinity College, Oxford and the Brigade of Guards and I know he had sounded out one of our newer Board members, fellow Etonian Michael Willis-Fleming, before accepting the job. He was born in Oxford and came with a glowing reputation, tempered by a reported personality that could be 'suavely managerial, charming or prickly in equal measure'.[97] His family history could be traced back to the battle of Waterloo and his reputation at Edinburgh, where he had embraced Alan Bennett, Peter Cook and Dudley Moore in *Beyond the Fringe*, was described as 'abrasive'.[98] Michael Willis-Fleming once confided about his friend that *'while steering the Swedish National Orchestra through a European tour in the 1960s, Robert paraded the players in front of the row of buses each morning and, on one occasion, inquired 'Who last night left their boots on the bed?'*

---

97.   Glasgow Herald, November 13th 2019
98.   Ibid

It was Mary Villiers, I recall, who suggested Robert might be approached. She knew his brother. *"He had a national, even international, reputation. I thought he might be interested."* He was clearly a man of pedigree and we – that is the interview panel of Brian Arnold, Reg Brown, Robin Carver, Michael Marriott, Chris Cooper from South East Arts and myself – welcomed him. He arrived with clear and exciting ideas about the shape of the 1987 Festival. The minutes of the board meeting of July 24th 1986 spell out the agreed working relationship between the Festival Trust and its new Artistic Director. He would be a freelance, that is, not full-time, 'working to a holding brief and being offered a fee rather than a salary'. He would 'deliver...the Festival programme...devised over 12 months which, in its final stages, would be submitted to selected members of the Executive Committee (Board) for final verification'. At that same meeting, the Trust (Board) welcomed Moira Swire[99] and financier, John Shipton, as new members. The strengthening of the Festival Board was continuing apace. It endorsed the interview panel's selection of Robert Ponsonby 'for the 1987 Festival with the option...of a further year's appointment'. Our new Artistic Director arrived on October 29th 1986.

The 1987 Festival, as Robert foresaw it, would be both exciting and innovative. The Board considered it, amid a continuing tide of appreciation and congratulation on the success of the 1986 Festival, from universities, South East Arts, major commercial supporters such as Ricemans and the city's museum and art gallery, through its visionary director, Ken Reedie. It culminated in a dinner party given by the Mayor and Mayoress of Canterbury, Councillor and Mrs Peter Baker, for the officers of the Trust and its administration. This civic gesture triggered a plea to the city council for increased financial support, which Robert, our Administrator Clarrie Middleton and I, vigorously pursued with the city's Chief Executive, Christopher Gay. We asked for a grant of £20,000 a year, arguing that, with regard to the city's profile, the Festival was

---

99. Later, Lady Swire, when her husband, Sir John Swire, was knighted in 1990

'generally seen to be a venture in need of greater support'.[100] In the same breath, we approached Kent County Council for a grant of £50,000. In January 1987, I told the Board that we would 'need at least £100,000 in grants or sponsorship if the Festival were to progress'.[101]

It is always important to agree on a strategy and then, as a team, to act on it. This was particularly so in the current perilous situation but, as chair, I was finding some difficulty in liaising, consulting and informing Robert. I am sure the fact that I was also busy running the Factual Department in a network television company contributed to this difficulty, but Robert worked in London and was seldom in Canterbury. This was in no way a complaint but this frustration reached a stage as early as January 1987 when I requested it be minuted that there was *'no information on the development of a marketing strategy because a meeting involving Robert and Clarrie Middleton had not yet taken place as planned.'* At the same time, the breakdown in relationships between the Festival and Kent Opera still bubbled away and the Board expressed disappointment at the difficulty of combining our two-week Festival with the commitments already made to others by Kent Opera.[102] Robert Ponsonby was also irritated by this lack of liaison. He reported that the offer of a concert by Kent Opera's orchestra had been withdrawn and that there was 'a possibility that Kent Opera would not take part even in the 1988 Festival'. In April, Robert produced his draft programme for the 1987 Festival. It was a cracker and I reproduce it in full:

---

100. CTFT minutes, December 1986
101. Ibid
102. CTFT minutes, January 9th 1987

CANTERBURY FESTIVAL 1987

DRAFT PROGRAMME (AS AT 3.4.87)

WEEK ONE

Saturday 26 September
- Eve of Festival event

Sunday 27 September
- am   Festival Fun Run
- 3.15pm   Cathedral Quire: Festival Evensong readings by
                Alec McCowen

Monday 28 September
- 2–5pm   Gulbenkian Theatre: Master classes: John Ogdon,
                Chopin, Liszt, Rachmaninoff
- 7.30pm   Cathedral Nave
                Tallis: 40-part motet: *Spem in alium*
                Vaughan Williams: *Fantasia on a Theme by
                Thomas Tallis*
                Tippett: The Vision of St Augustine (in the
                presence of the composer)
                David Wilson-Johnson (baritone), BBC Singers
                BBC Symphony Orchestra: conductor –
                Richard Armstrong
- 7.30pm   Marlowe Theatre: Vanessa Ford Productions.
                Shakespeare – *Twelfth Night*
                Anouilh – *Becket*

Tuesday 29 September
- 2–5pm   Gulbenkian Theatre: Master classes: John Ogdon, Chopin, Liszt, Rachmaninoff
- 5.30pm   Old Synagogue: *Can You Hear Me, Mother?* Hugh Wood, composer-in-residence during the first week of the Festival, talks about composing today
- 7.30pm   Shirley Hall: Purcell, Schubert, Wood, Britten, Gershwin; Lorna Anderson (soprano), Malcolm Martineau (piano)

Wednesday 30 September
- 7.30pm   Marlowe Theatre: Vanessa Ford Productions
- 7.30pm   Gulbenkian Theatre: Debussy, Ravel, de Falla, Gerhard, Wood; Lontano; Odaline de la Martinez Canterbury College of Art – Symposium

Thursday 1 October
- 2pm–7.30pm Marlowe Theatre: Vanessa Ford Productions Canterbury College of Art – Symposium
- 8pm   Shirley Hall, King's School: John Ogdon, Rachmaninoff – Preludes Liszt: Sonata; Brahms: Variations on a Theme of Paganini, Books 1 and 2

Friday 2 October
- 5.30pm   Old Synagogue (or Methodist Church): Talk – Robert Burchfield 'Skirmishes with English Grammar'
- 7.30pm   Gulbenkian Theatre: Beethoven. Hugh Wood, Elgar; John Ogdon/Britten String Quartet
- 8pm   Marlowe Theatre: Vanessa Ford Productions

<u>Saturday 3 October</u>
- 5pm   Marlowe Theatre Bar: Festival Question Time
              Festival personalities answer questions from the
              public about Festival policy and programmes
- 7.30pm   Gulbenkian Theatre: Tony Coe, jazz quartet
- 3pm–8pm   Marlowe Theatre: Vanessa Ford Productions

WEEK TWO

<u>Sunday 4 October</u>
- 3pm   Gulbenkian Theatre: 'Corno di bassetto'
              – Timothy West reads Bernard Shaw's
              music criticism
- 5pm   Cathedral Quire: Mendelssohn, Hugh Wood,
              Bach, Reger
              Allan Wicks (organ)
- 7.30pm   Cathedral Eastern Crypt: A Troubadour's World
              Martin Best sings troubadour songs, lute songs
              by Rossiter, guitar songs by Schubert and
              Shakespeare settings from: *The Tempest*

<u>Monday 5 October</u>
- 5.30pm   Old Synagogue: George Benjamin talk – 'My
              music – and some others: A View of the 80s'
- 7.30pm   Shirley Hall: Mostly Mozart; Elgar: Serenade
              for Strings
              Mozart: Piano Concerto 24 in C minor, K. 491;
              Benjamin: A Mind of Winter
              Mozart: Symphony 41 in C major, K. 551
              (*Jupiter*), with Eiddwen Harrhy (soprano) and
              Imogen Cooper (piano)
              London Mozart Players: Conductor –
              Jane Glover

Tuesday 6 October

- 5.30pm   Old Synagogue: Cormac Rigby says "Don't blame it on the wireless!"
- 7.30pm   Gulbenkian Theatre: B is Beautiful…and Nash is Nice: An Encounter With New Music – George Benjamin, John Buller, Denys Bouliane, Peter Paul Nash and the Nash Ensemble of London with Linda Hurst (soprano); music by Boulez, Bouliane, Buller, Nash and David Collins
- 8pm   Marlowe Theatre: Fascinating Aïda

Wednesday 7 October

- 5.30pm   Methodist Church: Alan Bennett talk (alternative dates: 28 Sept, 8, 13, 15 Oct)
- 7.30pm   Gulbenkian Theatre: Purcell, Britten, Schubert, Britten String Quartet

Thursday 8 October

- 7.30pm   Shirley Hall: Handel, Stanley, Geminiani, London Handel Orchestra Conductor: Denys Darlow

Friday 9 October

- 5.30pm   Methodist Church: Talk by Robert McCrum
- 7.30pm   Playhouse, Whitstable: John Amis, A Star of My Music
- 7.30pm   Cathedral Nave: BBC Singers, conductor: John Poole, Vaughan Williams – Mendelssohn

Saturday 10 October
- 5.30pm   Methodist Church: English Language debate
- 7.30pm   Cathedral Nave: George Benjamin: Jubilation;
            Holst: *Egdon Heath*, Vaughan Williams:
            Symphony No 5 in D major; Kent County
            Schools Choir and Symphony Orchestra,
            conductors: George Benjamin / Alan Vincent
- 8pm   Marlowe Theatre
            Richard Stilgoe entertains

WEEK THREE

Sunday 11 October
- 3pm   Gulbenkian Theatre: Literary readings about
            Canterbury OR Ted Hughes
- 7.30pm   Cathedral Chapter House: Deller Consort;
            Tudor and Stuart songs from Henry VIII to
            Henry Purcell

Monday 12 October
- 2–5pm   Gulbenkian Theatre: Master classes: Imogen
            Cooper, Mozart, Schubert
- 5.30pm   Methodist Church: Hugh Casson talk –
            'Ruskin in Venice'

Tuesday 13 October
- 2–5pm   Gulbenkian Theatre: Master classes: Imogen
            Cooper; Mozart, Schubert
- 7.15pm   Marlowe Theatre: Kent Opera – Mozart: *The
            Magic Flute*
- 7.30pm   The King's Hall, Herne Bay: Viennese Evening
            – Orchestra of National Centre for Orchestral
            Studies; conductor: Grant Llewellyn (soprano),
            Marilyn Hill Smith; Music by Mozart, Schubert
            and Johann Strauss II

Wednesday 14 October
- 5.30pm   Old Synagogue: Judith Weir – Talk 'The Night Before *A Night at the Chinese Opera*'
- 7.15pm   Marlowe Theatre: Kent Opera: Beethoven – *Fidelio* (first performance of a new production)

Thursday 15 October
- 7.15pm   Marlowe Theatre: Kent Opera – *A Night at the Chinese Opera*, Judith Weir
- 7.30pm   Gulbenkian Theatre: Medieval Players – An evening of Medieval farce

Friday 16 October
- 5.30pm   Old Synagogue: Carl Heap on 'Country love and village lust', with Dick McCaw (guitar)
- 7.15pm   Marlowe Theatre: Kent Opera – Mozart, *The Magic Flute*
- 7.30pm   Gulbenkian Theatre: Medieval Players
- 8pm   Shirley Hall: Bach – *French Suites* in G; Schubert – Sonata in A minor, D. 784; Schumann: *Davidsbündlertänze* – Imogen Cooper

Saturday 17 October
- 7.30pm   Gulbenkian Theatre: Medieval Players
- 7.15pm   Marlowe Theatre: Kent Opera – Beethoven's *Fidelio*
- 8pm   Shirley Hall: Loose Tubes – modern jazz

EXHIBITIONS (working titles)
- Joseph Conrad – Poor Priests' Hospital
- John Ward – Beaney Institute
- From Chaucer to Ted Hughes – Illuminated manuscripts from the British Library, the Cathedral Library and the King's School Cathedral Library

- Laurence Irving – Cleary Gallery
- 'Land: Sea: Air' – Twelve contemporary painters – Herbert Read Gallery
- Canterbury College of Art
- *Northanger Abbey* (or *David Copperfield*) – An exhibition of BBCTV costumes – Eastbridge Hospital
- Writing and Illumination – An exhibition by Kent children – Christ Church College (now Canterbury Christ Church University)

Kent Opera had been fully embraced and it was a fine programme. But it was also expensive. Treasurer, John Round, reckoned the cost would be £172,000, which would result in an estimated shortfall of £51,000. This was bad news. We felt Robert Ponsonby had overspent and so, before this was presented to the Board, John and I approached our bankers, National Westminster Bank, to ask if they would extend our overdraft to £45,000. The matter was referred to the bank's head office. They refused; it was, they said, *'an unbankable proposition'*.[103]

The Board considered the situation in April 1987. They had difficult decisions to make. I strongly felt that if the 1987 Festival were cancelled so early on its road to recovery, then 'a) the festival may not survive, b) the Board would be liable for all the debts that this cancellation would incur and c) the resultant deficit would be at least £40,000'.[104] I also 'apologised to Robert Ponsonby for the fact that the £75,000 that had been cited as being the sum he had to spend in the programme budget when…appointed, no longer appeared a reality.[105] The Board decided that £20,000 should be cut from the programme budget.'[106]

Robert's reaction was understandable but disappointing. If a £20,000 cut were deemed necessary, he would have to consider his position. He nonetheless took part in discussions on how savings

---

103. CTFT minutes, April 3rd 1987
104. Ibid
105. Ibid
106. Ibid

might be made while the Board pledged to redouble efforts to raise more funds – which they did, spectacularly.

From the outset, CTFT had sought closer artistic links with Europe. In 1987, Britain had plans for a physical link with Europe, through a tunnel between Kent and the Pas-de-Calais. The company that was about to start building this, the most expensive construction project ever proposed in the history of the UK,[107] was called Groupe Eurotunnel (now Getlink). Its chairman was a bluff South African, Alistair Morton.[108] I can't recall who made the introduction or whether it was simply a cold call, but he agreed to see us. He needed friends in Kent for this politically controversial venture. We needed money. We discovered that he had a strong interest in the arts; he would later become chair of the National Youth Orchestra of Great Britain. He gave us £50,000. We could restore some of the cuts dictated by the need to economise and he had rescued the Festival.

This sponsorship had an immediate impact on the quality of the programme for 1987. A rejuvenated Robert reported that the wonderful pianists, John Ogdon and Imogen Cooper, would now be able to give their series of master classes; Alan Bennett would lead a programme of talks and Judith Weir and George Benjamin would 'illustrate their own music'. Ponsonby wrote in his programme notes:

'The Canterbury Festival (in its present format) is very young – just four years old – and so are many of this year's participants. The Kent School's Symphony Orchestra and Canterbury School's Choir, Loose Tubes, the Extemporary Dance Theatre, the Medieval Players – all have boundless, youthful vitality. And a good deal of laughter will echo round Canterbury during the Festival – laughter with Shakespeare and Goldsmith, with Timothy West reading Shaw, with Kent Opera in Mozart and Judith Weir, with Richard Stilgoe and Fascinating Aïda.' He went on:

---

107. The Channel Tunnel, initially priced at £5 billion, eventually cost **£9 billion**
108. Sir Alistair Morton (1938–2004), later chair of Britain's Strategic Rail Authority

'Canterbury will be a good place to be this autumn. To misuse Shakespeare's Henry V – "and gentlemen in England then abed will think themselves accurst they were not here". To all who are up and about, welcome. Enjoy yourselves.'

But both Robert and I in our programme notes preparatory to the Festival emphasized the difficulties under which we were attempting to launch and consolidate the Canterbury Festival. I wrote:

'The policy of this Government has been to cut public spending. This applies to the Arts as much as to any other area. It could be said – it has been said – that strict adherence to such a policy threatens the quality of our traditions and our cultural life. As a former Secretary General of the Arts Council has said: "The wolf is not at the door. It is in the kitchen". The Arts Minister, Mr Richard Luce, has attacked "the Welfare State attitude" by arts organisations to funding – the feeling that "the arts are owed a living by right, and that if they do not get the money from central government, then the government are a lot of Philistines…"

'As you would expect, I can't support his view. At home, it undervalues a basic strand in the fabric of our society. Abroad, it overlooks the fact that our theatre, our opera, our music, our dance and our sense of fun in achievements in these areas, have a basic appeal to hundreds of thousands of tourists, every year. Without continuity and opportunities in our artistic life, how much poorer would we as a nation be? But when considering the government attitude – agree with it or not – of one thing there can be no argument: it offers us a challenge! With government subsidy at risk, we have looked to commerce, to local government, to the private individual for support.'

Robert also berated the government's policy:

'The Arts are at serious risk from the Philistines and from an indifferent Government, which does not even understand their *social value, let alone the pleasure and refreshment they give to mind and spirit.*

'Against this background, the fourth Canterbury Festival is something of a miracle (not that it yet qualifies for Arts Council support!) There came a point when, after all the fine tuning and pruning – not of quality, but of scale – had been done, the Trust had to commit itself, or cancel the Festival. It had the courage to go ahead, and was rewarded by Eurotunnel's handsome sponsorship...'

Board and Artistic Director spoke with a single voice, but the 'handsome sponsorship' was not a silver bullet. Some of the money went on giving Eurotunnel a proper return in publicity terms for their generosity. Thankfully, however, the Board confirmed that the proposed financial cuts in the Festival programme should be restored.

Nevertheless, in July even before the 1987 Festival began, it was apparent that the situation was still critical. Despite the injection of Eurotunnel's money, the predicted deficit now stood at £42,800. Such a loss would seriously jeopardise the Festival which, I reminded Ponsonby, had literally no reserves to cushion the deficit.[109] Given the bank's refusal to increase our overdraft facilities, members of the Board were asked if they would consider becoming personal guarantors if loans could be negotiated with Kent County Council and Canterbury City Council. Quite reasonably, Robert Ponsonby asked the Board that a decision be made that day (July 3rd) on whether the Festival would go ahead. To ease the crisis, Bill Preston, who was in charge of the city council's entertainment and manager of the Marlowe Theatre, offered to take over and therefore accept any financial liability for all the events to be held at the Marlowe. It was a generous offer which we accepted. Robert Ponsonby was not pleased, however. The Board decided again to press ahead with the Festival and, in October, the 1987 Festival was held. It was a success, but it did not solve our financial

---

109   It wasn't until 2004, when the Festival made a healthy £90,000 profit on a programme with a Hungarian theme, that it began to build a protective reserve.

problems. Audiences were smaller than forecast. In addition, as he looked forward to the 1988 Festival, Robert Ponsonby was voicing a growing dissatisfaction with the recurring financial constraints resulting from our difficult financial position. He also disagreed with some of the decisions that had been made by the Board and said so, observations with which we had some sympathy. In the immediate aftermath of the Festival, positions polarised and Board meetings became increasingly heated. Board secretary, Mark Rake, remembers them as *"traumatic. The elitism that Ponsonby pursued and presented was the polar opposite of what we as a group were attempting to do – to reach out into the community with the variety of riches that the arts have to offer and to emphasize that our Festival must be enjoyable. Our objectives did not mean a loss of quality"*. Mark's view had considerable support within the Board.

Privately, I tried to represent these views to the Artistic Director. He did not take kindly to them; he had his standards, he said, and he wondered whether the Board understood and were prepared to accept those standards. I sympathised but gave the simple message that spending had to be governed by the funds available. Ponsonby then took to communicating directly with the president, Keith Lucas. In November 1987, Keith and vice-chair, Brian Arnold; Robin Carver; treasurer, John Round and Professor Michael Irwin, wrote a letter to the Artistic Director, signed by Keith:

'The Board has delegated us to write to you to convey its concern about the rift between yourself and the Chairman arising out of your challenge to his office.

'There seems little point in prolonging discussion about the dispute itself and the arguments on either side and the Board has made clear what it thinks about the dispute...in its vote of confidence in the chairman...It really is essential that you agree to work within the appointed budgetary limitations (the unavoidable narrowness of which we all regret) and that you refrain from criticising the Chairman for his adherence to the financial policy which the Board has laid down and which it is his duty to enforce.

'It is also fair to say that because of the financial position, we

*must address the problems arising from the 55% attendance figures
achieved in the year's festival...It was very much apparent in
discussion that the Chairman and the Board are deeply apprehensive
about the possible consequences of a dispute of this kind and would
be most unhappy to lose your services as Artistic Director.'*

It was a difficult situation and Robert took exception to Keith Lucas'
criticism of the attendance figures at the Festival, which were lower
than Robert had anticipated. But the Board left the option open
for Robert to continue in post, which he did. His dissatisfaction
with the Board, and therefore its chairman as I pursued the Board
decisions, was apparent, however. He criticised the commitment
and ability of the Board and the way it had "allowed the Festival
to slide into a very difficult financial situation", ignoring the fact
that his spending had contributed to that situation. The Board,
throughout 1988, had continued to consider seeking a loan to
alleviate the financial pressure on the Festival. Having been
rejected by our bankers, Nat West, it was decided to approach the
City Council. Exploratory conversations indicated that personal
guarantees would be desirable. The figure needed was £40,000,
within two weeks, 11 Board members and supporters had stepped
forward to guarantee that figure; in alphabetical order:
Brian Arnold £5,000, Ginette Cobb £3,000, Caroline
Collingwood £1,000, Ken Gross £2,000, Peter Harris £5,000, Keith
Lucas £5,000, David Macey £2,000, Michael Marriott £2,000, Mark
Rake £5,000, John Round £5,000 and myself £5,000. The names of
the guarantors were forwarded to the council and the application
for a £40,000 loan, repayable over five years, succeeded. It would
be free of interest. The first annual payment of £8,000 would be
made in December 1989, said the then leader of the council, Jim
Nock. Jim, embedded in the Festival's struggle to survive,[110] was
well aware of the tensions between Robert Ponsonby and the
Board. He had helped to broker the loan, if only because, having

---

110. Councillor James Nock joined the CTFT Board in December 1988, at the
same time as businessmen James Bird and Peter Harris.

seen the names of the guarantors, he felt able to say that there were *"people we know and trust"*.

With the advantage of 50 years' hindsight, I regret that Robert and I found it difficult to work together. He did not endear himself when asking whether "we were bound to include Reg Brown and his very odd contributions (from the University of Kent) in every Festival we hold". I reminded him that Reg, and the University, were major reasons why the Festival had survived at all. This engendered a long-running discussion between us on standards, his standards. In fairness, Robert fought for the preservation of the arts as hard as any of us – harder, probably. I was at an age when, if given choices, I was seeking absolutes; it was black or white, survival or liquidation, co-operation and calm or conflict and chaos. My overriding concern was to maintain our standards and to balance the books because that is the only way to stay in business. I was fortunate during those months that my employers, TVS, were generous in the time they allowed me for Festival matters.

Over the years, TVS had forged a positive relationship with the Canterbury Festival. They had made a grant of £20,000 to the festival at a particularly difficult time and supported many events. By 1985, I was the company's Controller of Factual Programmes. That included its religious output.

As the Festival's chairman, I had a very clear idea of the responsibilities of a charity such as the Canterbury Theatre and Festival Trust. It was to see that its objectives and its method of governance were transparent, including being financially stable. It did not include interfering with the detail of the programming of artists and events. During 1987 and 1988 that was, as always, the prerogative of the Festival Director – in this case, Robert Ponsonby.

However, early in 1988, TVS originated and broadcast a programme, which I felt, would broaden the Festival's appeal and also earn money. I offered it to Robert. At TVS, my Head of Religion was Andrew Barr, a brilliant head of department who I had recruited from BBC Scotland and who had met Ponsonby in Edinburgh. Andrew had launched a gospel music series called *People Get Ready*. It was years ahead of its time; it was a reflection of the rapid growth of British gospel choirs. Its format was simple but its production was a challenge. The idea was to work with Britain's first contemporary touring gospel choir and band that fused gospel with pop, soul and jazz with rhythm and blues. John Francis was its inspiration, working with Sister J and Lavine Hudson. Andrew had trialled the programme at a cinema in Gillingham, which TVS had transformed into a studio. The pilot programme embraced the preparation and consumption of Caribbean food as well as the celebration of gospel music. The pilot recording overran by more than an hour. Everyone had a very good time. Andrew Barr described the experience as "joyfully chaotic – an inspiration". TVS's senior executives watched a carefully edited version of the programme and judged it "brilliant". Andrew commented privately that "it was a great success, especially when assessed by those who weren't actually there at the recording".

The quality, bounce and energy of the largely black choirs won the series a slot on nationwide television, Channel Four. The series ran for months. The shows were always recorded in the TVS studios, but there seemed no reason why we shouldn't take the programme on the road, as an outside broadcast, to a live audience. From a television point of view, the decision to commit to an outside broadcast was mine; from the Festival point of view, the decision to include the show in the Canterbury Festival was Robert Ponsonby's.

Robert was not keen on the idea. 'We have our standards', I remember him insisting, and he asked whether this was truly the sort of music that we wanted in the Canterbury Festival. I thought it was. He went away to London to reflect on the matter. He sent me a note a few days later, which indicated he had hardened his position. He had seen a performance of *People Get Ready* as I had sent him a recording of an early programme. He felt that this type of "freewheeling music…an ambiguity between a religious ritual and theatrical entertainment…isn't really for the Festival". He used the phrase "amateurish rather than amateur".[111] I argued that *People*

---

111. Correspondence between the Trust and the Artistic Director

Get Ready was a reflection of an emerging trend in ethnic music in Britain, and that a Festival should be bold enough to embrace initiatives such as this. I said that I would like it in the Festival programme, if he didn't mind too much. Robert *did* mind – but he reluctantly accepted with the remark: "This would never have happened at the BBC", where he had, of course, been in charge of music. He suggested modifications to the format to include stories or parables, but the format was already set and approved by the national broadcaster.

Andrew Barr, who originated *People Get Ready*, had also spent his life at the BBC as Deputy Head of Religious Broadcasting. *People Get Ready* duly graced the stage of the Marlowe Theatre, Canterbury, on October 10th 1988. For a television director, it was always going to be a challenge because the shows were unpredictable. Every week during the series, rehearsals were carefully plotted for each of the numbers, but the performances during the actual recordings were always different. Released from the confines of a studio, singing to a live audience of nearly a thousand, the London Community Gospel Choir let rip. Ten minutes into the recording, Dave Heather, a brilliant director who had brought Glyndebourne to the ITV network, threw his meticulous camera plots into the air above his control desk and busked the entire show. At that moment, I noted that Robert Ponsonby had been quite correct in describing the music as "freewheeling".

Before the performance, Andrew Barr, his wife, Liz, and my wife, Jo, had discussed how Canterbury might react to exposure to this new experience. Would the spirit and enthusiasm of these new wave artists move the residents of our cathedral city? Within half an hour we had an answer. Canterbury stood and clapped and stamped so hard that the floor shook beneath the weight of a thousand feet. It was a triumph for the choirs and we were proud of Canterbury. From the Festival's point of view, it was also a financial success.

Robert Ponsonby was in the foyer of the theatre as Andrew and I left. He needed to get back to London. He commented as he was leaving: "I was right. This should never have been part of the

Canterbury Festival." *The Guardian* newspaper, however, described the choir as 'controversial, professional, energetic, inspiring and spirit-filled.' I couldn't have put it better myself.

Unsurprisingly, the local press sensed this tension in the Trust. The *Kentish Gazette* ran a leader column that October that read:

'*Our Festival. Whatever you may think of this year's Canterbury Festival – which ends tomorrow (Saturday) – there can be no denying it has brought a range of reactions. This has been widespread indifference to parts of the highbrow programme, while some of the more controversial ideas have stirred the vitriol of armchair critics who normally don't know their art from their elbow.*

'*It is ironic the festival should have started with a fun run for, whenever the organisers have tried to bring the proceedings out of their cultural shell, there has been a chorus of criticism.*

'*Complaints ranged from the fireworks being too loud, the opening procession too small, the Westgate Towers' drapes too much and the John Dane washing machines too near the Mayor's home.*

'*Such criticisms have stolen the headlines but it should not be forgotten the festival has brought much pleasure, ranging from the laughter at Alan Bennett's lecture, through to the superbly performed concerts and fascinating exhibitions and excursions.*

'*Such a festival can never please all of the people all of the time. What it seems to be doing is not to please most of the people any of the time. Year after year the organisers have to fight rising costs, apathy and rely on the taste of a minority audience.*

'*Perhaps it is time for the festival to reappraise itself and widen its horizons and appeal. Then it can call the bluff of those who bleat: "There is nothing there for me".*'

In November with these comments ringing in our ears, the Trust's team moved on to the challenge of the 1988 Festival.

Robert produced an excellent programme. It began with a reception hosted and paid for by TVS and climaxed with a fireworks display at the university; it included the London Classical Players, The Fairer Sax, Fauré's Requiem with the Canterbury Choral

Society, opera master classes with Sena Jurinac, The King's Singers, *Aquarius* conducted by Nicholas Cleobury and an organ recital by Allan Wicks. But any hope of rapprochement between Festival and Kent Opera receded amid further harsh words between Robert and Norman Platt over Kent Opera's use of the Marlowe Theatre. Norman's final letter to the Festival Trust ended thus:

'I believe this incident makes any idea of future negotiations almost impossible (between us) *because we shall not know whether or not we can rely on invitations to take part in events in Festivals in the future. I would have much preferred to have carried on discussions with you on a professional basis in a friendly and civilised manner.'*

With this nagging dispute rumbling on just as the 1988 Festival was about to take place, I received a letter from Board member, Michael Willis-Fleming. Michael wrote that he was in no way in dispute with me but that he did not believe the Festival *'would achieve the budgets we need for the Festival we want, and repay our debts, without…help from the private sector…it is being said to me quite repeatedly that such help would be forthcoming if I were the chairman and I think that is probably true…although I am not looking for the job.'* I called Michael at his home in Betteshanger, both for clarification and to say that I would put his letter before the Board to discuss.

The letter did not come as a complete surprise to me. I had called him sometime before, wishing to ask if he was interested in co-ordinating sponsorship for the Festival. He had said he might be – but that he would be seeking to replace me as chairman. I had made a note to file following this telephone call and it reads:

'He (Michael) felt *"the style of the Festival was wrong"* and, when I asked in what way, he said *"Well – your chairmanship. A number of businessmen feel this."* I asked the identity of these people and he said that he had *"had a meal with 'A', who said he would support me* (Willis-Fleming), *financially, if I became chairman."* He said this was also 'J''s view. He further said that he and Robert Ponsonby had discussed the matter on a number of occasions and the Artistic

Director would "*support him*" as chairman and work with him. He asked me to step down and he felt sure there were other things I could do for the Festival "*for which I was well-suited*".

He had no personal animosity towards me. I asked Michael to put his thoughts in writing.

Ten minutes later, I telephoned Michael again and pointed out that the last thing a successful Festival wanted was a public upheaval. I also remembered that both Michael and Robert had been schooled at Eton and that some other members of the Trust had strong connections with Eton. A sizable and obviously dissatisfied lobby then, could exist within the Trust. I counselled Michael to be careful before writing the letter. He said he "*would think about it*".

Having thought about it, he wrote the letter I presented to the Board on September 16th 1988, with the Festival less than a month away. Michael was present and, according to the minutes, "*elaborated on his theme*". As chair, I then asked for a proposal and seconder for Mr Willis-Fleming to become chair. None was forthcoming. Those minutes record that those present were:

Peter Williams (Chairman)
Mr B Arnold, Mr R Brown, Cllr R Carver, Mrs G Cobb, Mrs B Collingwood, Mr D Connolly, Mr M Deller, Cllr M Dixey, Professor M Irwin, Mr K Lucas, Rear Admiral D Macey, Mr M Marriott, Dr M Rake, Mrs R Simpson, Mrs M Villiers, Mr Willis-Fleming.

In attendance:
Mr C Cooper, Ms C Mills, Mr A McLewin, Ms C McQuaid, Mr J Round, Miss C Hawes (Minutes Secretary).

Apologies for Absence:
Cllr P Baker, Mr J Bornoff, Ms S Drew, Mr R Ponsonby and Mr B Preston.

Before the meeting, I had briefed the Trust's officers and our treasurer, John Round, and had taken soundings on the accuracy of Michael Willis-Fleming's reading of the situation. John volunteered that he had spoken to Robert Ponsonby a number of times. The minutes recorded the substance of those conversations:

'Mr Ponsonby was not happy with the Marlowe arrangements that the City Council would be responsible financially for programming the events in the theatre, in consultation with the Festival, because he considered they would not work. He had expressed his uncompromising view that he could not accept the arrangement. He considered the City's grant puny; he had no confidence in the Board and was not prepared to work with it. He would not attend the present meeting and would not have any more to do with the Festival.

'It was pointed out that Mr Ponsonby's contract had one more year to run and that until a resignation in writing was received from him they (the Board) should honour the contract.'

Nonetheless, Board members took this as a clear intention to resign. They praised Robert Ponsonby's work for the Festival and regretted his "*uncompromising view*". The treasurer then announced that he had good financial news to report. The Policy Committee of the city council would recommend an interest-free loan of £40,000 to the Festival. And so a tense meeting at least ended with a smile…

The Festival announced Robert Ponsonby's resignation on November 29th 1988. The statement read:

'The Canterbury Festival announces with regret that it had released Mr Robert Ponsonby, the Festival's Artistic Director, from the final year of his three-year contract.

'The 1989 Festival will be co-ordinated by Mr Mark Deller, who acted as Festival Administrator from 1983 to 1985.

'Mr Ponsonby said today that new artistic and financial restrictions on the Festival programme were unacceptable to him. He added, "I am sorry to be leaving – particularly after the success of the 1988 Festival, which proved beyond doubt that there is a big public appetite for a serious arts festival of high quality in Canterbury".

Mary Villiers commented: "We had such high hopes of Robert, but, truthfully, it was a disaster. We were dreadfully disappointed. His ambitions and manner were too high-flown. I don't think that he ever recognised that he no longer had unlimited BBC money to spend and that every penny had to be earned and worked for."

The Stage, having spoken to Robert, and under the headline **Director Quits Over Council Veto**, wrote:

'Robert Ponsonby, has stepped down after refusing to allow the city council an effective veto over part of his programme or to make massive cuts to his artistic budget.

'Festival chiefs made the changes after the city stepped in with a limited cash guarantee when their own sponsorship drive failed to reach its expected target. After the 1988 festival the event was reckoned to be as much as £50,000 short of the amount needed to meet its total budget of £200,000.

'Organisers told Ponsonby that he must agree to let the council have a hand in some of the programme and would have to reduce his spending on artists from £80,000 this year to £30,000 in 1989. That would introduce a whole new ballgame and "it is something which anyone with any artistic integrity would not be willing to do," said Ponsonby.'

The Board did not recognise some of the figures contained in this statement, but for the Festival, this was a road crash. And, as with every such incident, witnesses seldom agree, even on its cause. But to me, the situation was quite simple – the festival had to survive – if there were causalities along the way, so be it. It is to Michael Willis-Fleming's credit that, although he resigned from the Board, he and his wife, Elizabeth, continued to support the Festival.

*Norman Platt and his wife Joanna at their home at Pembles Cross,
the headquarters of Kent Opera.*

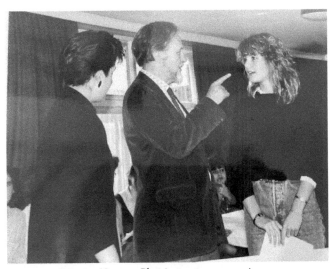

Director Norman Platt instructs younger singers.

Illustrations in this chapter copyright Kent Archive and Local History Service

Kent Opera's production of Fidelio, in Valencia, Spain.

Judith Weir's A Night at the Chinese Opera, opens on the London's South Bank

Illustrations in this chapter copyright Kent Archive and Local History Service

Lady Northbourne (chair) and the Duke of Kent battled for Kent Opera's future.

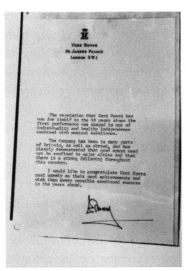

The Duke's letter to the Arts Council.

The Theatre Royal, Margate

Illustrations in this chapter copyright Kent Archive and Local History Service

Chapter 8 – Kent Opera – An Assassination

Even during the disagreements with Kent Opera over the governance of the Canterbury Festival, we had been aware that, among those who now controlled the funding of the arts in Britain, Kent Opera were not the most popular of clients. Chris Cooper, the director of South East Arts, told me as much. The relationship was, at best, tetchy. Writing from within the Arts Council, Robert Ponsonby, in the first paragraph of his message in the 1987 Canterbury Festival programme, was moved to criticise the Council for 'threatening' Kent Opera. He wrote that the Arts Council was *'regrettably, now aligned not with its clients but with the State...the arts are now at serious risk from the Philistines and from an indifferent government which does not even understand their social value, let alone the pleasure and refreshment they give to mind and spirit'*.

As I have indicated, in 1987–1988, the Canterbury Festival was determined to foster its relationship with Kent Opera despite the resignation from the Festival of its director, Norman Platt, along with two other representatives from the opera company.

In 1989, the Arts Council destroyed Kent Opera; it was unfair and was carried out in an underhand manner. Consider the facts... Financially, Kent Opera's performances required less public subsidy than the performances of any other opera company in the country. Artistically, its record of encouraging new work and sustaining production quality and innovation, was unchallenged, but it was *'common knowledge in the music profession for years that the (Arts) Council found Kent Opera and its artistic independence, fiercely*

guarded by...Norman Platt, to be an anomaly in the structure of regional opera, of which it would rather be rid'.[112]
The Arts Council had negotiated weakly with the government and was short of funds. Their solution would be to axe one of the regional opera companies. The crisis for Kent Opera came to a head in December 1986. The Arts Council called an emergency meeting of all seven British opera companies – Covent Garden, English National Opera, Welsh National Opera, Scottish Opera, Glyndebourne Touring Opera, Opera North and Kent Opera. Norman Platt, who was at the time directing *Il Seraglio* in Metz, prepared to fly back to London for the meeting but freezing fog cancelled flights from Luxembourg. At short notice, Kent Opera's treasurer, Robin Jessel, represented the company at a meeting, which informed the seven companies that 'there was simply not enough money to go round'.

Any unity among the seven companies was immediately threatened. They were now competing with each other for financial support. Old rivalries resurfaced. The crisis became personal. It was all becoming a soap opera in itself. Norman Platt found himself at the heart of the storm. He recorded in his autobiography:[113]

'One evening early in 1987 I had an unexpected evening visit from Kent Opera's Chairwoman[114] and another member of our Trust Council, who told me on the authority of 'an Arts Council officer' (later identified by them as Jack Phipps) that unless I resigned immediately the Arts Council subsidy to Kent Opera would be cut off. I questioned the legality and morality of such a threat, and asked what sort of company they would be preserving in such circumstances.

'The Secretary General of the Arts Council, Luke Rittner, in his reply to my letter raising these points said: 'I cannot imagine that action of the kind you suggest was taken by any member of the Arts Council staff'. He also expressed his warm admiration for the company's work and thought that the Arts Council's future behaviour*

---

112. Graeme Kay, Classical Music, January 1990
113. Making Music, Norman Platt, Pembles Publications, 2001, p100–101
114. Lady Northbourne

to Kent Opera 'will convince you that you have been misinformed in this matter'.

He did not mention that, at that very moment, the touring committee 'working party' was within days of giving birth to the report that would recommend the extinction of Kent Opera. Perhaps he forgot.

Norman Platt went on: *'A few weeks later we were informed by the Arts Council that a report had been written recommending the solution to their opera problems, i.e. that Kent Opera should have its grant withdrawn from 1st April 1988.'*

Kent Opera immediately resisted the announcement. They raised, through donations, £60,000 as a fighting fund. They were touring at that time and letters of support, indicating horror at the decision, arrived at the Arts Council in their hundreds. There was no love lost between Platt and Jack Phipps who had been the Arts Council's Head of Touring and who was the author of the report recommending that Kent Opera's grant be cut. Norman Platt's record of the whole affair[115] confirms this tension. But so fierce was Kent Opera's resistance, so staunch the views of its supporters expressed to the Arts Council and in the national press, that the recommendation in the Phipps Report was overturned. In June 1987, the report was quashed and Phipps apologised to the Kent Opera chair, Lady Northbourne, 'for issuing misleading information'.

The reprieve coincided with a purple patch in Kent Opera's fortunes. With funds provided by the BBC, the premiere of Judith Weir's *A Night at the Chinese Opera* took place in October at the Marlowe Theatre as part of the 1987 Canterbury Festival. It was 'the debut of a very memorable composer' (*The Times*) and Kent Opera 'could not have found a more compelling reason for survival' (*The Guardian*). In the next 18 months, Kent Opera undertook two tours of England, performed *Don Giovanni* for three nights in Singapore and took *Don Giovanni* and *Fidelio* to Valencia in Spain.

---

115. Making Music, Norman Platt, ibid pp102–109

'All in all, the Arts Council has reason to be pleased with Kent Opera', wrote *The Sunday Times*.

Norman Platt was looking to the future and planning his succession. With Iván Fischer, the Hungarian conductor and composer who had been the company's music director since 1983, he had agreed a Three Year Plan that included a production in 1990 of Michael Tippett's *King Priam* at Covent Garden, directed by Nicholas Hytner and conducted by Fischer. Platt planned to retire in September 1989. Three months after this announcement, the Arts Council ruled[116] that Kent Opera's Three Year Plan was 'too ambitious, expensive and ill-thought-out', and that 'its artistic standards had dropped' – though this latter accusation was subsequently retracted. Kent Opera's grant would therefore be withdrawn.[117]

There was a feeling of *déjà vu* over the way this harsh decision had been reached – it was taken as hurriedly as had the Arts Council's negative decision two years earlier. The Arts Council's music panel – an advisory unpaid group of people with musical interests – met regularly with a prearranged agenda. At the crucial meeting in December 1989, however, an item had been added to the agenda *after* it had been circulated. The single item was 'Kent Opera'. I believe there were no supportive papers available to the panel for reference. The panel were simply told that the Arts Council needed to make economies. The suggestion from officers of the Arts Council was that the Council's grant to Kent Opera should be cut. Sir George Christie of Glyndebourne – one of the seven companies – chaired the meeting and, as Platt said subsequently, was an interested party. The panel went along with the officers' recommendation. Robert Ponsonby was a member of that panel but, at such short notice, was unable to attend. Once he heard what had happened, he resigned immediately. He said: "*I am personally disillusioned about the Arts Council's advisory system. On this particular occasion, the Music Panel was not briefed at all about*

---

116. Ibid, pp107–110
117. In that same month, the Government gave the Arts Council an extra £20 million

a major item, it was not on the agenda…I don't really want any more voluntarily to give time and effort to the Arts Council when one is not properly briefed, one's advice is often rejected or ignored and one is misrepresented."

Former Arts Council music officer, Stephen Firth, wrote to *The Guardian*:[118]

'*As I attended meetings over the years, I frequently observed respected and knowledgeable representatives of the music profession being treated in what I can only describe as an off-hand manner and often lacking enough information to enable them to give informed, objective advice. This is in conformity with a trend in the arts bureaucracy towards what is quaintly known as 'generalism'; translated, this means that credence is given to those with minimal knowledge of the arts, but some skill in, for example, marketing, rather than those who have spent a lifetime working in the field.*'

Kent Opera's chair, Lady Northbourne, enlisted the help of the company's then patron, the Duke of Kent. They went together to the Arts Council to plead the company's case. They were heard politely but the Arts Council were adamant. The tone of the recent correspondence from Norman Platt had, she felt, stiffened the Arts Council's resolve and *"he* (Norman) *did not help matters at that meeting"*.

Norman Platt subsequently named Jack Phipps, Graham Marchant, the Arts Council's Director of Arts Coordination, and Anthony Everitt, its Deputy Secretary-General, as men who '*wanted to get rid of Kent Opera*'.[119] He had been forthright in his criticism of those he believed were resisting his pursuit of perfection. He named names and took no prisoners. Doubtless, he believed his strong feeling could best be communicated in this way. Equally beyond doubt is the fact that, politically, it was naïve.

---

118. Ibid p108
119. Ibid p103

It is difficult to resist the feeling that personalities played an important part in the demise of the company. Nicholas Hytner[120] spoke for many when he said:

"In the name of virtue he (Norman Platt) *sought out the best in the musical and operatic worlds, did battle with the funding authorities and even mortgaged his house. Never for him the cynical programming of a chic, new production of* Tosca *to pull in the crowds.*

"It is impossible not to share Norman's cold fury at the destruction of the company by precisely those who must have felt most undermined by its rigorous refusal to deal with what Norman calls 'the fading fad of relativism (ie, the view that everything is equally good, equally trivial, equally bad, equally valuable)'. Norman only cares for what is good. For too long now, we have been giving our audiences the popular and the successful, but we're in danger of forgetting that subsidised art is subsidised so that it doesn't have to worry about anything except excellence.

"During the twenty years of its existence under Norman Platt's direction, Kent Opera was like the city that is set on a hill. It could not be hid.

"Its resources were focused on truthful, musical and completely alive performances. It ruthlessly refused to have anything to do with the meretricious or the frivolous, either in its choice of repertoire or in the way it dealt with the works it chose to produce. It made no compromises with its audiences, still less with the authorities whose mission it was to dilute or eliminate the excellent, in the name of accessibility. But through its shining integrity, it made better opera more accessible to more parts of the country than anyone has managed since."

The company had indeed taken the experience of opera to many corners of Britain, even of the world. But Kent Opera's spiritual home was Canterbury and the Marlowe Theatre. The Festival Trust decided to support the company in its struggle to survive. It would

---

120. Now Sir Nicholas – theatre, film and opera director

hold a Gala Night to celebrate Kent Opera's successes and to raise funds. This was not as simple as it sounded, however. The event could not be billed as 'Kent Opera' because the company was in liquidation. The liquidators were consulted. The solution was to advertise it as '*a Gala involving former members of Kent Opera*'. As a charity, it was also necessary for the Festival Trust's directors (trustees) to avoid deliberately investing Festival money in a lossmaking enterprise. The event needed to make a guaranteed profit. As the Festival would be bearing the costs and expenses of the Gala, a limit of £7,000 was set on marketing, rehearsing and producing the show. Profits on takings, estimated to be £10,000, would go to Kent Opera while the Festival would benefit from any sponsorship. Our legal advisers were comfortable with the arrangement. The date for the Gala was set for September 30th, a week before the 1990 Festival would begin.

The Gala Night was a great success. Norman Platt later wrote a warm letter of thanks saying, 'the initiative we shall shortly announce has been made possible by the concert mounted by the Festival'.[121] Board members were pleased. Part of their minuted objectives in organising the Gala and paying the bills had been 'the building of bridges to heal the rift between Kent Opera and the Festival'. The initiative that Norman Platt then announced included three children's/community operas and a tour of Benjamin Britten's *The Prodigal Son*. We approved.

The 1990 Festival that quickly followed was also a triumph; Mark Deller produced a programme that included the Count Basie Band, the Royal Philharmonic Pops Orchestra, comedian Mel Smith, Judi Dench, Cantabile – The London Quartet, Sir Jeremy Isaacs, Elisabeth Söderström, Dame Vera Lynn, Mikhail Rudy, Nancy Wilson, John Williams and Ralph Steadman. Steadman had worked with composer, Jonathan Harvey, on a stunning production of the British premiere of the *Plague and the Moonflower* at the cathedral. Its message was way ahead of its time – a plea to conserve the world's rainforests. As Steadman wrote

---

121. CTFT minutes, January 29th 1991

in the programme notes: '*The very ground on which you stand is under threat...*' Steadman's illustration graced the front page of our souvenir programme that year.

The 1990 Festival made a small profit. It further reduced the deficit to £30,000. This was now, of course, covered by the loans for which some trustees had taken responsibility. The second £8,000 tranche to reduce that £40,000 loan from the city council would be made in December 1990 and the Festival had the cash to cover that. We now had a Festival programme that included walks, talks on a multiplicity of subjects, open houses, a street procession, competitions and a school-led initiative. Church halls, local galleries and churches themselves were used as venues.

We had reached out beyond Canterbury to initiate events in Margate and Broadstairs, Rochester and Westgate-on-Sea, Herne Bay and Whitstable, where the am-dram Lindley Players were of such a standard that their *Nicholas Nickleby* featured proudly in the Festival's main programme. Conspicuously, further down the Kent coast, one of the smaller theatrical jewels in the South East was showing signs of the return of a long-lost lustre. The Theatre Royal, Margate, closed since 1965, was reopened by a group of professional theatre people led by Jolyon Jackley, son of the late Nat Jackley. It was in 1786 that George III had granted the town a royal patent by signing an Act of Parliament for the building of a theatre '*in the Town and Port of Margate*', because the inhabitants had increased in number and it was attracting so many visitors '*on account of the Convenience of the Bathing and the Salubrity of the Air*'. The Theatre Royal on Hawley Square had originally opened its doors on June 27th 1787 with performances of *She Stoops to Conquer* and *All the World's a Stage*. It thrived as a playhouse and many famous actors performed there including Edmund Kean, Ellen Terry, Sarah Siddons, William Macready and Sarah Thorne, whose family ran the Theatre Royal for more than 50 years. The advent of the railways further increased the popularity of Margate as a seaside resort. The theatre's auditorium and stage were enlarged and improved in 1874 by Jethro T Robinson, architect of the Old Vic; it is said today that this picture-book seaside theatre has the oldest stage and auditorium in the country. During its 200-year existence, the building had served as a chapel and a cinema. It was closed during the two World Wars but it opened sporadically as a repertory theatre under a variety of managements until 1965 when it became a bingo hall.

As if he didn't have enough to do, the Festival Director saw in the Theatre Royal "*opportunities and a duty*". Mark had first 'discovered' the Theatre Royal in the 1970s. "*I was transfixed. A beautiful building, the only one of its kind outside London.*" When Jolyon Jackley reopened it once again as a theatre in 1988, Mark took a number of Festival productions there. Jackley's initiative failed but Trusts took over the running of the theatre and, in 1990, Mark promoted further Canterbury Festival events there, including Judi Dench and her husband, Michael Williams, and Timothy West and his wife, Prunella Scales. We were fulfilling our pledge to become an 'umbrella' Festival, showcasing other, smaller arts initiatives outside Canterbury. After the turmoil of the previous decade, we seemed to be entering a period of relative stability and calm...

*A Jolly Evening – (left to right) pianist Malcolm Binns,
Rona Lucas, Keith Lucas and Mark Rake.*

Mark Rake: the Trust's secretary

*Pat Ebden –
fund-raiser extraordinaire*

...some people can raise money...

US lawyer Bill Handel, a friend of the Festival,
with whom we filmed for an ITV documentary.

Chapter 9 – Giving

The constant that runs through the pages of this Festival book is the word 'money'. Set aside culture, talent and history and the lubricant of energy that keeps the wheels turning is the pursuit of cash to fund ambition. It's called 'charitable giving' or 'philanthropy' – and there is a clear difference between the two. Fifty years of seeking funds for community causes have taught me this:

'Charitable giving' is usually an emotional impulse in response to an immediate situation, often short-term and involving, primarily, a gift of time or money.

'Philanthropy' is usually directed at the root cause of social needs or opportunity, and requires a more strategic commitment by the donor.

One may argue that, in the end, the result is the same: the need is identified and met, the money is used positively and as it was intended. But the approach, from those who need the money to those who have it, must be tailored to appeal to both types of generosity.

This contrast has been emphasised in numerous conversations I have had over the decades with an American friend, William (Bill) Handel, a lawyer in Los Angeles. He and his wife, Marjorie, frequently visited us during the weeks of the Canterbury Festival and his observations were, to me, often revelatory. I recall one exchange after a particularly inspiring concert in Canterbury Cathedral; we had worked hard welcoming dignitaries and sponsors. As we left what was a buzzing, excited gathering to move on to another reception, Bill asked: "How much do they pay you to do all this?" "Nothing," I replied. He simply wouldn't believe it. He said, finally, "But this is a $75,000 a year job..."

We later examined the conversation. Bill said: "You have to realise that, in the States, much of 'giving' is associated with status. People vie with each other to support the major 'good cause' charities and the size of their donations is seldom kept secret. It's a highly-paid industry."

I must tell you about my friend, Bill. He is a big man in every way. Huge and generous with time and attitudes; Jewish and proud of it – "for the most part", as he would say. We first met in California when Jo and I were making a documentary on surrogacy, then illegal in Britain but available as a viable alternative to childlessness in the USA.[122] Bill Handel, never afraid of taking on a challenging brief, was a leading advocate of surrogacy. Through his regular drive-time radio slot, *Handel on the Law*, he was also a top shock jock on Los Angeles radio.[123] With this man of many parts, I explored the differences between generosity on both sides of the Atlantic. Bill gave me an example of giving that would not have happened in the UK; it illustrated a different attitude to the perceived responsibilities of state and citizen.

A stretch of new motorway near his home was welcomed as easing one of Los Angeles' many traffic problems. This would clearly have been seen, had it been in the UK, as the responsibility of local and/or central government. In Los Angeles, part of the deal was that the local Rotary Club had raised the money to clean and maintain that stretch of motorway. It is also fair to say, declared Bill, that much of US philanthropy, especially from the wealthy, goes to causes and organisations that lean towards benefiting the wealthy. *The Atlantic*, one of USA's oldest and most respected magazines, agrees with him:

'Of the 50 largest individual gifts to public charities (in the US) *in 2012, 34 went to educational institutions, the vast majority of them*

---

122. Babies by Mail. The Human Factor, ITV, September 1990
123. Regrettably, when we went together to a Festival performance at the Playhouse Whitstable in the 1980s, Marjorie tripped over a loose carpet and broke a bone in her foot. After she had been to hospital, Bill commented laconically: "Lucky that didn't happen in the States. The litigation would have bankrupted the Festival…" I'm sure he was joking

colleges and universities such as Harvard, Columbia, and Berkeley, that cater to the nation's and the world's elite. Museums and arts organisations such as the Metropolitan Museum of Art received nine of these major gifts, with the remaining donations spread among medical facilities and fashionable charities like the Central Park Conservancy. Not a single one of them went to a social-service organisation or to a charity that principally serves the poor and the dispossessed."[124]

In contrast, in Britain, support for smaller charities and causes is considerable, helped by nationwide organisations such as the Community Foundations.[125] These foundations handle and advise large funds from generous donors – and Britain is home to some of the most generous donors in the world. In 2014, 79% of its people gave to at least one charitable donation, raising a staggering £10.6 billion.

The UK government, through Gift Aid, can add 25% to a donor's gifts. This is less generous and certainly very different from the American tax system where individuals give mostly to recognised charities, itemise their returns and qualify for differing tax bands. The bigger the donation, the bigger the tax reduction. For the very wealthy American, philanthropy plays a key part in financial planning. *"And,"* added Bill, *"nearly 10% of the USA's wages and salaries go to those working in the non-profit sector. It's a huge business."* Which it is, of course, on both sides of the Atlantic. The truth is that, when seeking money for a cause, the appeal to the philanthropist is usually to the heart. To the businessman, it is primarily to the head in that, understandably, the gift is also an investment, part of the answer to the question: "What's in it for me, my business, my profile." The donation from a business executive is more likely to come from his or her marketing budget than from charitable funds.

---

124. The oldest surviving charity in Britain is the King's School, Canterbury, founded in 597
125. Kent Community Foundation acts as a one-stop shop for smaller charities, advising on governance, charity law and effectiveness

Those members of the Canterbury Theatre Festival Trust who were willing to canvass their friends and acquaintances for money – and many Trustees, in my experience, find it difficult to do so – were well-schooled both in the timing and the style of approach to each individual potential donor. Some Trustees were very good at it. Mark Rake was for many years the Trust's secretary. I was close to Mark, a man and a doctor for whom I had the highest regard. He was best man at my marriage to Jo and we had worked and played together these many years. Jo and I were able to help a little in his pioneering work on cancer care to reduce what he termed *"the white coat barrier"* between doctor and patient, by making a film for ITV on a club he had set up at the Kent and Canterbury Hospital. It was called The Chemoptimists.

He and 'matron' Sarah Walter, Andrew Jackson, nurse Wendy Hunt, Daphne Woodcock and so many others believed that medics and cancer sufferers could and should work and meet socially to reduce any emotional barrier between them, to lessen the fear and stigma associated with the 'c' word – cancer. The Chemoptimists held quizzes, competitions and parties and openly shared their joy and their sorrow. We called the film *Names on a Tablecloth* because the name of every member of this exclusive club was carefully and colourfully crocheted on to a bright, white tablecloth. The treatment they received was advanced and effective but it came at a cost to the doctors and those who ran the club for, in the end, most of the members died. As with all doctors who over the years have striven to 'beat' cancer, death is too often the end of each individual story. Mark once said, after a particularly harrowing few weeks: "*I don't know how many more defeats I can take*." When attempting to cure the frequently incurable, death may so easily become a personal defeat.

Mark Rake had always been interested in, and supported, the Festival. At dinner one evening with his wife, Patti, and Rona and Keith Lucas at our home in London Road, he was critical of the Festival and of its gaining an elitist image. He urged both Keith and me to "get organised". We assured him that was exactly what we were trying to do and, if he felt so strongly about the Festival's future, why didn't he come and help us? The next day he called and said he would be interested in doing just that. He joined the Board in 1988, became a leading member of the Trust and was subsequently appointed Secretary. He would come with me to negotiate the £40,000 loan from the city council and he was "known and trusted" by the city fathers. It was a good appointment.

In January 1988 when Mark attended his first meeting, the Festival faced a deficit of £38,000 and a possible total loss of £70,000. Beside the Four-Year Plan, a business plan needed to be developed. In the months ahead, Mark would become responsible for sponsorship and fund-raising and, later, for a speculation which became known as 'Golden Balls' and which would help, decisively and unexpectedly, to balance the Festival's books.

In the meantime, the skeleton of the 1989 Festival was in place but Robert Ponsonby, the Artistic Director who had constructed the programme, had just resigned amid a welter of recrimination... Or had he?

On December 12th 1988, we heard from Robert Ponsonby's lawyers. They were very clear. Mr Ponsonby, with one year of a three-year contract still to run, had *not* resigned and wished to be paid off with a full settlement of his contract. They argued that the Festival, in reducing its period from three weeks to two weeks, and in accepting the city council's offer to programme and pay for all the events held in the Marlowe Theatre, meant that 'there would clearly be no place in the Festival for Mr Ponsonby (nor for any Artistic Director at all)'. The Festival Trust had effectively and prematurely terminated Mr Ponsonby's contract. Bill Cotton, of Gardner and Croft, was our honorary lawyer, who gave us loyal and thorough advice over many years. He stressed that it was clear that the Marlowe events would be selected and scheduled in consultation with the Festival Director and that any sponsorships from those events would come to the Festival. It was a good deal for the Festival and there would be close consultation between council and Festival over all the programming at the theatre during those two weeks. Letters now flew between Bill and Messrs Iliffes, Robert's legal representative. Bill argued that Robert had resigned and quoted from a letter[126] from Robert to the President, Keith Lucas, in which he had written:

'The shortening of the Festival, the severe reduction in the artistic budget...the surrender of artistic authority in the Marlowe Theatre and my lack of confidence in the present Board structure make it impossible for me to continue as Artistic Director.'

In conversation with the Festivals' officers, he said Mr Ponsonby had reiterated these views "overlooking the benefit of a closer partnership with Canterbury City Council during the present crisis". In these conversations, wrote Bill Cotton, 'there was no opportunity to change Mr Ponsonby's position – he was utterly determined and emphatic about that'. Robert, he wrote, 'had resigned quite voluntarily'... an opinion which was 'shared by all other members of the Board taking a realistic view'.

Ponsonby wrote at the height of this verbal battle that he had 'no doubt that there is good will on both sides'. He was correct in that the Festival respected his experience and flair. But, ultimately, the words in the contract that Robert had signed brooked no argument. He had pledged to 'work to a policy and budget agreed annually by the Trust'. It could hardly have been clearer. The exchange of letters dwindled and ceased.

Once more, the Festival asked Mark Deller to step into the breach. This he did, but as Festival Director rather than Artistic Director. We had felt for some time that the roles of Artistic Director and Administrator should be combined. As Deller said: *'He who spends the money can also help to find it!'* so he took over the twin responsibilities of finance and programming. He had two handover meetings with Robert Ponsonby and took the hard decision of what would have to be cancelled. The London Mozart Players with Jane Glover had to go – 'there was insufficient money to pay the fee of £5,500'.[127] There *was* money, however, for a week

---

126. November 1988
127. CTFT minutes, January 13th 1988

of drama and a week of one-night stands at the Marlowe Theatre. With relief and gratitude we welcomed Mark Deller back to take us through the 1989 and 1990 Festivals. On his reappointment, *The Stage* reported that Canterbury would now adopt 'a more sensible attitude'. Mark Deller said:

"The amount of money spent on artists for the Festival has to be reduced. We can't be as ambitious or extravagant as we have been in the last two or three years. We can't risk adding to our debt. We need to make some money to pay off our debts for future festivals. I have already drawn up a new four-year plan for the Festival under which we hope to raise at least £500,000."

He saw the partnership with the city council as positive, not a threat. The council had guaranteed the Festival a grant of £45,000 over the next three years. He said of this:

"They (the city council) are showing a great deal of confidence in us. More than ever before. Now we must get our financial house in order, be more modest and sensible about how we spend money. This is probably our last chance..."

As part of the remodelling of the Festival's governance, a 'Festival Council' had been established. The Financial Board had been strengthened and the operational reins of the Festival were now in the hands of one person, the Festival Director. The Festival Council was intended to be a gathering where our members and supporters could have their say. It met for the first time on February 24th 1989. Its members represented those smaller groups in the city and East Kent who were interested in the arts and, importantly, representatives of all the political parties elected to the city council. Council leader, Jim Nock, attended the first meeting, as did many members of the Festival's Financial Board.[128] Mark Deller laid out

---

128. The Board held, and still holds, executive power in the Canterbury Theatre and Festival Trust (CTFT)

the shape of the 1989 Festival, including Benjamin Britten's *Noye's Fludde*, which would involve 500 Canterbury schoolchildren with Alan Wicks conducting, and was 'an integral part of the community spirit of the Festival'. Sponsorship opportunities were identified and, inevitably, the Festival's financial position was discussed. Pat Ebden was appointed to be in charge of sponsorship, an inspired choice as Mark Deller built a team around him that would serve the Festival well for many years. Our two-year contract with Mark was agreed in November 1988. It would be 15 years, in 2003, before Mark would retire, by which time the Festival was firmly established, both artistically and financially.

The Board, as I have indicated, was built around specialists. The members gave freely of their experience in business or their knowledge and enthusiasm for a particular strand of the arts. The most pressing area of concern was, and often is, finance and, with staff member, Pat Ebden, in place to seek sponsorship, a small group of the Board, led by Mark Rake, was set up as a finance sub-committee. We initiated a new position of vice presidents of the Festival, each giving an annual donation of £1,000, and we had an inaugural annual vice presidents' dinner, a tradition that has flourished ever since. It extended the 'family' feeling of the Festival. The 1989 Festival's theme was 'Sea Pictures; it would run for only two weeks rather than three and we launched the Festival aboard the Sally Line cross-Channel ferry, on September 19th. The weather was kind, spirits were high and Canterbury City Council's new chief executive, Colin Carmichael, carried out his first duty in that role by stepping aboard with us. The first tranche of our £40,000 loan from the city council was due to be repaid and he was kind enough not to remind us of that fact.

Mark Rake suggested a number of initiatives to raise money over and above sponsorship. The Festival invested in a high-profile, top quality raffle for prizes including a two-week Virgin Holiday, a weekend for two in Amsterdam, an original painting and copious amounts of champagne. It bombed – or, to quote our treasurer, John Round – it was "a great deal of hard work for the not-very-large amount of money raised."[129] But Mark Rake's finance sub-committee and Pat Ebden had done their jobs; sponsorship at £53,000, plus a huge rise in audience numbers, ensured that the 1989 Festival would be £26,000 to the good. I congratulated Mark Deller; there had been five full houses in the first week of the Festival and seven sell-outs in all. I thanked the newly constructed Board and the Festival team for the 'flair and discipline' they had brought to the running of the Festival. For the first time since the Festival was revived, it would go into the New Year with no overdraft. The first tranche of £8,000 would be repaid to the city council. The Festival, I reported, was on 'an even keel'. Our relief, however, was tempered by the fact that, across the county, Kent Opera had collapsed. The news was shocking and unfair but not unexpected, as I explore in Chapter 8.

The years 1989–1991 were a turning point for the Festival. Documents written at the time reflect that Mark Deller and Professor Michael Irwin produced a review and revision of the Festival's Three Year Plan. Mark Deller wrote:

'Since its beginning in 1984, the festival has suffered from a lack of continuity in funding and, in consequence, in its direction. Financial uncertainties have prevented sound long-term planning and the establishment of a permanent directorate.

'In 1988, the Board addressed the central problem of funding continuity and commissioned a Three Year Plan, as a basis for approaching funding bodies and particularly Canterbury City council...which provided core-funding of £37,000.

'Canterbury Festival accounts showed, at 31st December 1988, an accumulated deficit of £60,000. As a result of the new policy adopted by the restructured Board, and the successes of the '89 and '90 festivals, the current accumulated deficit now stands at £27,000.

'The Articles and Memorandum of Association of the Trust gives as the objectives:

---

129. CTFT minutes, November 21st 1989

'To promote, maintain, improve and advance the education of the public in the Arts, including the arts of drama, mime, dance, singing, opera and music, ballet, cinema and the visual arts generally.'

'To a large extent these aims have been successfully undertaken in the past two festivals. The 1989 programme with the theme of 'Sea Pictures' was hailed as an artistic and financial success. Events such as the spectacular production of Britten's Noye's Fludde in the Cathedral and The Burning Fiery Furnace in the Chapter House, the Ballet du Nord, the Lionel Hampton Big Band and Stéphane Grappelli at the Marlowe and Patricia Routledge and the Andy Sheppard Sextet at the Gulbenkian, all helped to achieve a working surplus of £28,000. (The year) 1990 was regarded as an even greater artistic success. Though less spectacular financially, the Festival nonetheless ended the year with a further surplus of £1,300.'

Michael Irwin wrote of the Festival's variety:

'In this country, Edinburgh provides the defining model for the multi-media festival. For the Canterbury visitor, Tuesday may offer a musical master-class followed by a lecture on local history, a play at the Marlowe and late-night jazz; Wednesday could begin with an art exhibition at Whitstable and proceed through a 'literary walk' to a Cathedral concert and a Fringe-conjuring show.'

Michael then argued the suitability of Canterbury as host to a Festival:

'If there is a tourist dimension to the arts – and no-one now doubts it – then visitors are surely more likely to be drawn to a festival, a feast, than to a musical hamburger here or a theatrical cheesecake there. The setting of the festival can itself be a significant entry on the menu. Thousands must have gone to see Edinburgh and found themselves enjoying the festival, while as many will have gone for the sake of the festival and found themselves rejoicing in the city. Perhaps a successful festival requires a beautiful setting; certainly a beautiful setting can offer a festival a flying start:

'A wide and cost-effective marketing programme has been established in the last two years. The Festival has been extremely successful in achieving a mass of national and local news coverage in print media as diverse as The Times, The Independent, the Radio Times and the Illustrated London News, plus free inserts in regional magazines and regular slots in local papers. In addition, TVS have given wide news and feature coverage including the filming of 'Creation', a black gospel musical, premiered at the Canterbury Festival and screened twice on Channel 4. Other broadcast media has included national television coverage on BBC News, ITV and Channel 4, plus wide news and feature coverage on regional television. BBC Radio Kent have, over the last two years, given regular prime-time slots to the Marketing Officer who has taken artists into the studio to publicise evening performances.

'With a strong PR effort, as exemplified above, the Festival's marketing budget has been left free to make maximum use of printed publicity and street publicity.

'Strategically, the festival will continue to match artistic and regional ambition with financial reality. Priority in 1991 and 1992 will be given to maintaining the quality of the festival, within the limitations of a tight budget, and to eradicating the accumulated deficit by the end of 1992.'

It was around this time that Mark Rake brought an idea to the Finance Sub-committee. Someone – a friend – while commuting to London, had seen an advertisement at Victoria station drawing attention to a lottery based in Ireland. It was open to charitable organisations and promised rich rewards. It was called the Golden Globe. We were sceptical. Even Mark Rake described it as 'a gamble' about which he was 'ambivalent'. We decided not to consider it further.

But the Golden Globe would not go away. Again, anecdotally, we heard that the Bath Festival and the Arts Council itself had entered and that it had the approval of ABSA, the Association for Business Sponsorship of the Arts. We reconsidered. We were tentative about buying lottery tickets with money given to the

Festival because the Festival was, and is, a charity and we did not want to risk our charitable status by breaking the Charity Commission's rules. We decided, then, to enter the competition with money given by individual members of the sub-committee. We paid up (the fee was quite expensive, £420 I think), filled out the entry forms – and more or less forgot about the Golden Globe.

This would prove to be the most profitable investment the finance committee ever made. Within three months, we had received £12,000 and by the end of the year a further £32,000. In two years, then, our deficit was reduced by £50,000. We renamed the lottery 'Golden Balls'. Mark Rake smiled quietly and Mark Deller reported, under the newspaper headline 'Lottery Luck':[130]

'With our winnings, plus a profit from the 1989 Festival, we wiped off our debt and had a bit of money in the bank. Prudent planning and good fortune overcame what could have been a serious problem for us.'

We had gambled and won.

---

130.   Kent on Sunday, October 5th 2003

PROGRESS
AND PLEASURE

Bloomers on the West Gate

Lady Moira Swire, a pencil sketch by John Ward

Christopher Gay, Canterbury Chief Executive, conducting the Christmans Eve carol concert in the City Centre.

Cleo Laine who had views on the Cathedral's 'echo'.

Max Wall 'Britain's greatest clown'.

Vera Lynn

Peter Williams and Timothy West – a shared experience

...with Harry Secombe in the West Indies.

...with Archbishop Rowan Williams.

Chapter 10 – Champagne and Chairmanship

The recorded minute of the Board meeting of the Canterbury Theatre and Festival Trust on December 3rd 1991, at Mark Rake's home at Pontus Barn, Molash, is quite specific. It reads:

'The financial report setting out the position as at 6 November 1991 was presented and received with acclamation (and a congratulatory glass of champagne).'

The minute continues: *'The chairman said that, having started the year with a £32,000 deficit – a deficit which had been £60,000 three years previously, arising from the original Marlowe refurbishment debt and the out-turn of earlier festivals – there was now the chance that the long-standing debt might be eliminated in the current year. The amount outstanding was £24,000, ie. three further annual repayments to the City Council of £8,000. The chairman congratulated the Festival Director on the box office surplus of £2,500 more than what was anticipated in the budget...'*

The 1991 Festival delivered exactly what the Board had hoped for – a positive financial outcome in an atmosphere of stability and calm. The result came at exactly the right time. It was rumoured the Festival would be assessed by South East Arts during 1991, an examination that would affect its future funding. We felt a little like students aware that A levels were looming in a few months' time.

The relationship with public funding bodies is interesting. Each has its own idea of the type of festival they would prefer to support. The overriding ambition common to all is that it should be successful, of course, but preferences vary – mixed arts or a bias towards music, themed or without a theme, tightly focused locally or reaching out across the county. The Board had clear views on each. We were determined that the Canterbury Festival should be mixed in its appeal; we liked a theme but were not slaves to the idea and, critically, though it was the **Canterbury** Festival, it needed to reach out to the rest of Kent, the South East and to Europe. Locally, as we had proved, an important part of the Festival's role was to act as an 'umbrella' for other initiatives in the county, to give advice and to encourage the growth of the arts at its grass roots. We produced a two-week festival once a year but the Canterbury Festival set out to be a presence in the county for 52 weeks of that year. All this was the basis of the Festival's then Three Year Plan.

Much of the above also applied to the preferences of businesses and personal sponsors of the Festival to whom we looked for financial support, though they were less likely to have detailed views on the content of the programme. They bought into the Festival because they liked its style and areas of influence and wished to be associated with it. The Festival offered profile for the company and happiness for clients in return for a donation. It was a business deal, just like any other.

The new, tightly drawn, 10-person Financial Board was working very well. Ginette Cobb, who had toiled so hard for the Festival since its inception, now resigned and became a vice president. Patrick Twigg, a lawyer with an international client base, filled her place. Patrick was a music lover and a fine pianist and he and his wife, Gubby, would make their home at Charlton Park generously and frequently available for many memorable Festival events.

Moira, Lady Swire, was a vital member of the team. Crucially, at both the moments of deepest crisis, when the future of the Festival was very much in doubt, she had thrown her support behind the hard-working Festival Board. The challenges, first from the Kent Opera lobby, and four years later, from those who wished to take over the chairmanship, were, she felt, destabilising and her confidence in the existing team and management structure helped to defuse difficult situations.

Moira championed the Festival. She also did what she could to secure its future and I don't just mean with the Swire family's consistent financial support over the years. When she left the Festival Board she ensured continuity by asking her daughter-in-law, Camilla, to take an interest in this community initiative. She handed the baton down a generation. Camilla remembers: "*It was something I hadn't really considered but the Swire family were devoted in their support of the Festival. The question I asked myself, and which I also discussed with Barnaby,*[131] *was whether this was the best use of my time. I decided it was and I have never regretted it.*"

Camilla Swire joined the Board of the Festival and brought to our discussion fresh, sometimes left-field opinions that reflected her interest in the community in which she lived. She also confirmed the Swire family motto *Esse quam videri*, 'to be rather than to seem to be' The Swire family support for the Festival has never wavered.

Most Board meetings began at 7.45am. The examination by South East Arts (SEA) also started early and spread over two days; it included visits to the 1991 Festival whose theme was *Relationships*. Chris Cooper, SEA's director, had already told me that the case for funding "mixed festivals" like ours was increasingly hard to make to his colleagues in the Arts Council. They preferred single-arts initiatives. After the SEA visit, Cooper wrote to us; his letter stressed that SEA were 'impressed and excited by the challenges you and your core team face in the future.'[132] The main points the letter made were that the Festival had 'rebuilt its strong and effective links with county, city, church and local sponsors' for which they congratulated us. They criticised, however, the 'lack of personal imprint' on the 1991 Festival; they stressed 'the flagship role' the Festival had to play and suggested 'part-time associates for the development of the artistic programme'. They urged us to 'secure extra income' to achieve these developments and to 'dictate the shape of the Festival'. It concluded: 'without the steady leadership

---

131. Barnaby Swire, chairperson of the Swire Group of companies.
132. Letter from SEA to Mark Deller and myself, November 1991

already demonstrated by yourselves, the whole enterprise could be overwhelmed by the (challenge of the) opportunities it faces'.

The Board did not take too kindly to some aspects of SEA's letter and I replied, the central section of which read:

'I think it is important to remember that we are still working through our 'period of financial regeneration', though we shall, with our next repayment of £8,000, reduce our debt to Canterbury City Council to £16,000. How far, then, we are in a position to 'dictate' the future role of the Festival, is debatable. The reality is that Canterbury City Council, Kent County Council and South East Arts have different views of what the Festival should be – some of the differences being of emphasis, others quite fundamental. We shall, then, continue to walk the tightrope, making our own decisions while listening to the preferences of our major funding bodies.'

The Board also felt that South East Arts asked a lot but contributed too little financially. The Brighton Festival consistently received a far higher grant than Canterbury. I went on:

'I must reiterate, as I'm sure you'll understand that, although we are grateful for the support given us by South East Arts, it continues to be apparent that both the City and the County more quickly and consistently contribute to the financial stability of the Festival. It is something you may wish to consider, particularly in the context of the (small) amount of South East Arts funding that comes to Kent – and East Kent in particular – relative to the other counties you embrace.'

But the greatest of the Board's displeasure was directed at SEA's criticism of our Festival Director. I wrote:

'I chose to answer your letter myself in the main because of the recurring theme of 'personal imprint'. I am genuinely puzzled as to the meaning of this phrase, for I cannot believe that this is meant as a criticism of Mark Deller's 'style'. Working on a very limited budget, he has produced clear and stimulating themes, to which, in

the opinion of the Board of the Canterbury Festival, he has adhered
with determination and ingenuity. More, he and his team have
simultaneously achieved financial stability after the excesses of the
recent past.

'Mark already informally consults experts and colleagues in each
of the artistic disciplines as he prepares each year's programme and
the addition of part-time associates (art form) posts (as you suggest)
would blunt, I believe, the essential direction and drive that the
Festival possesses. The Canterbury Festival, due in part to its simple
(not, with respect, 'complex') system and organisation, is one of the
few festivals to be consistently paying its way; if it works, don't mend
it, as my old mum used to say.'

And I concluded:

'We will do all we can to persuade the City's 'powerhouses' to remain
as positive contributors to the Festival though we share, with you,
disappointment at the relative paucity of sizeable, quality venues. In
conclusion, you know we are ready to grow, to form a focus for artistic
and community activities in the South East and we look forward to a
burgeoning partnership with our friends in South East Arts.'

As with South East Arts, so with many of the funding bodies we
wooed and on whom we relied. It was an important part of the
role of chairman to try to facilitate the relationship between the
Festival and those who might give it money. This applied to public
bodies such as Kent County Council, Canterbury City Council
and, of course, the Arts Council of Great Britain. Sir Sandy Bruce-
Lockhart at County Hall, was totally supportive. He understood
the 'flagship' value to Kent of a festival such as ours. Sandy
represented Kent but he always saw the big, national picture. He
would later chair the national Local Government Association.
His interests were broad and he argued hard the case for his
shire county. He got on with people; his friendship with Labour's
hard-line deputy Prime Minister, John Prescott, was invaluable in
guiding investment into Kent. We were fortunate, too, in having

Christopher Gay as chief executive of Canterbury City Council. Chris was himself a musician and, later, conductor of the annual open-air carol services in the city centre every Christmas Eve. A succession of the city's mayors became personal friends as they devotedly attended and introduced Festival and Festival-related, events. Jim Nock was the first Mayor of Canterbury to join the Festival Board and become one of our team.

The cultivation of these relationships had a second benefit. Mark Deller was very busy in the combined role of Festival Director, responsible both for artistic success and the administration. He, I think, welcomed some protection from the political manoeuvring that is an inevitable part of the job. It rapidly became apparent from the one-to-one meetings that regularly emerged in my diary, that the ability to discuss and answer questions about events in the Festival, was vital. This applied to sponsors as well as to public bodies. My wife, Jo, and I considered how best to go about it. We decided, if possible, to welcome every sponsor at their event and to attend as many performances as was humanly possible. From that moment, and for the rest of my 21 years as chairman, we seldom saw a complete performance. We attended receptions, joined audiences (sometimes for as little as 10 minutes), and warmly shook a multitude of hands in sincere gratitude. Without these friends, old and new, the Festival would not have survived.

Sometimes, new friends had curious needs to be accommodated. In October 1991, the Festival premiered the *Plague and the Moonflower* in the cathedral nave – music by Richard Harvey, words and paintings by Ralph Steadman with John Williams on guitar – cast of 30, plus the Canterbury Cathedral choir and the Finchley Children's Music Group. Ian Holm narrated. It was one of the Festival's 'Big Nights'. We welcomed the Brazilian ambassador, Paulo Tarso Flecha de Lima and his wife, Lucia Flecha de Lima, who was one of Princess Diana's closest friends. She was her confidante throughout the turbulent years leading to Diana's separation from Prince Charles in 1992. Jo was sitting next to her in the front row in the cathedral nave. Musicians, singers and soloists were in place. The nave was packed, expectant; a pre-performance silence had descended on the audience of 1600. It was then that the ambassador's wife leaned across to Jo and whispered:

'I need to leave for a moment'.

Jo rose to escort the ambassador's wife from her chair and the conductor delayed his entrance.

They left the cathedral through the martyrdom door and Jo said:

'The nearest loo is round the back and I'll come with you…'
'No, no', she replied. *'I'm just dying for a cigarette'.*

She lit up, puffed away and stubbed out. The minutes ticked by. The ambassador's wife and Jo then returned to their seats and the concert could begin…

Styles of chairmanship may vary. The method we chose gave rise to the privilege of meeting artists who are household names. I already knew actor, **Timothy West**, and his wife, **Pru Scales**, slightly; what we didn't know was that he and I had an intimate and painful connection dating back to our teens. One evening in Canterbury, I was alone with Tim in an upper room at the Mayor's Parlour near Canterbury's Guildhall, with time to kill before an official function. We had eaten well and were in contemplative mood. I knew that Tim had connections with Bristol, as had I. We had both spent our teenage years there, he at Bristol Grammar School and me at the newly named Cotham Grammar School (formerly the Merchant Venturers' School). We reminisced about our school days. He asked why I had left school at 15 rather than entering the sixth form. I confessed that part of the reason was that the then headmaster had told my father that his son was "*a quidnunc-ic*[133] *prig and a know-all*" and that he saw "*no future for him*" (me). Tim digested the information and asked: "*Was the headmaster called Woods?*"

He was indeed.

---

133. Quidnunc; Latin: busybody, someone seeking to know

"I knew him well. I moved to that school in the sixth form and I remember he beat me soundly."

Mr Woods was a master with a cane in every sense. So much so, that his nickname, 'Splinter' Woods, evolved from his ability to break a cane with the strength of his application to your backside. I confessed I was frequently beaten for alleged misdemeanours, a regular member of the small queue of boys waiting, it seemed daily, in the tight, dark corridor outside the headmaster's office. Tim and I compared notes over the various methods used to try to take the sting out of the strokes. We both favoured blotting paper inside the underpants – but care needed to be taken with the insertion because discovery would mean an extra stroke. A new and shared intimacy now established, we ambled over to the theatre, doubtless confiding in each other that, though painful at the time, *"it didn't do us any lasting harm – did it..?"*

Forces sweetheart, **Vera Lynn**, was one of the most charming stars to support the Festival. We met a couple of times and she gave a wonderful talk at the Methodist Church in St Peter's Street in Canterbury. She was a lady without any side or pretension. Her talents, she said, were God-given and she gave of them freely. She spoke to me only once of regret – that concerned the BBC's 18-month ban on her radio programme at the height of World War II.

For those who weren't alive at the time, it is hard to imagine the influence of radio during the war years. It was a most important instrument through which an entire nation could instantly be embraced. As Britain's men scattered around the world to resist and attack Nazi Germany, radio reached out to them. By 1940, Vera Lynn was an established solo act. Her singing of *'We'll Meet Again'*, which she had recorded in 1939 and which contained the nostalgic lyrics *'We'll meet again, don't know where, don't know when. But I know we'll meet again some sunny day,'* spoke to the hearts and minds of millions of servicemen. She became the 'Forces' Sweetheart'. Her 30-minute weekly radio programme, *Sincerely Yours*, crackled from battered Bakelite speakers in Burma and Benghazi, Murmansk and the Middle East. Then, in February 1942, the programme was taken off the air. The War Office felt that, because Vera's songs were by intention, sentimental, they might undermine the determination of the British troops who listened. Vera Lynn said: *"I didn't understand why? We knew the troops loved the programme – and so did their mothers and wives and girlfriends, because we always had a full postbag of requests."* She paused. *"It was my way of 'doing my bit' for the war effort."*

Forty years later, over a cup of tea in the vestry of St Peter's Church in Canterbury, the BBC's decision to 'cancel' her for more than a year still hurt. In the year 2000, Dame Vera Lynn was named the Briton who best exemplified the spirit of the 20th century.

An unwritten part of the contract between the Festival and author and lawyer, **John Mortimer,** was the need for an ice-cold bottle of champagne to be available in the dressing room – and I think I recall that it was necessary both before and after his performance. One evening in Canterbury, he confided that, on more than one occasion, the organisers of events who were "intent on indicating how tolerant and understanding they were prepared to be" had inquired whether he suffered from any addictions. Alcoholism, perhaps. *"Not really",* I tell them, *"except I do have my first glass of champagne around six o'clock in the morning".* He reported that, usually this would be followed by an awed, deeply sympathetic silence, *"then, the host says, 'Are you having counselling for that?' "No",* I have to confess, *"I'm not having counselling".*

"Well, how long has this been going on?"

"Ever since I could afford to have a glass of champagne at six o'clock in the morning."

I have always believed that there is more than a trace of Mortimer in his immortal creation *Rumpole of the* (Old) *Bailey.* Among the similarities, an appreciation of alcoholic drink. For the fictional Rumpole, it was claret. For Mortimer, it was always champagne. Certainly, there was a strong flavour of Mortimer the actor, in the career of Mortimer the lawyer. We once talked about timing.

Legal arguments could be won and lost, he insisted, through good timing. Identical words, identical phrases could sway a jury when delivered by a skilled lawyer, yet fall on deaf ears *"when used by a dunderhead"*. Mortimer remembered his lawyer father telling him that he had once appeared in court for a comedian, who had told him after the case was won that, above all, he had admired his father's timing both in his questioning of witnesses and in his opening and closing speeches. Mortimer said: *"I took a little while to realise the importance of this story. My father took his time in his arguments. Pauses, moments of pregnant silence that keep the 'audience' in court waiting, are extremely effective. My father used to count up to 10 before he asked his first question in cross-examination. So I thought that, when I got to court, I would try the same tactics."* As a callow defence lawyer, Mortimer remembered that, on his debut as a barrister, he had risen to his feet and slowly looked around the court. He had begun mentally to count; 'one, two, three...' but the carefully prepared train of thought was interrupted: "The judge said, quite crossly: *'Get on with it. We can't sit here all day, you know, watching you standing in silent prayer'."*

I think John lost the case...

It's not unusual for a performer to request a stimulating pick-me-up in his or her dressing room. The great jazz violinist, **Stéphane Grappelli**, would request a bottle of the best Scotch whisky to take its place beside the sticks of make-up and the tissues in the mirrored corner where he would prepare himself for an evening performance. Jo and I got to know Stéphane Grappelli only towards the end of his career. It was an acquaintance which had, at its heart, our respect for his music with the quintet he founded, the *Hot Club de France*, in the 1930s. Grappelli dispensed joy through his jazz throughout his life, either as a solo artist – as which he came to Canterbury – or with his four colleagues who included guitarist, Django Reinhardt. Grappelli was an outstanding musician. Anyone who doubts that should set aside an hour of their lives to watch the recording of a concert he played with classical violinist, Yehudi Menuhin. Listen to the flow of the music, the fluency with which they answer unfamiliar challenges in this collision of jazz and the classical – but, mostly watch the eyes of both men and see the mutual respect that each had for the other.

Grappelli and Menuhin recorded three albums together in the 1970s. They produced magical music but never lost the rivalry that propels many to greatness. Grappelli once confided: *"Yehudi had a wonderful violin, a Stradivari, dating back to 1714. (pause) Mind you, I was playing a violin made by…Goffredo Cappa, in 1695. It was 19 years older than his…"*

Max Wall was one of Britain's greatest clowns. He starred in our first Festival in 1984, in Samuel Beckett's *Malone Dies*. His career on stage, in films and on television spanned 70 of his 82 years. He was born into a showbiz family, son of Scottish music hall entertainer, Jack 'Jock' Lorimer, and his wife, Stella. For decades, Max Wall stood tall among Britain's leading entertainers, with his creation of the extraordinary character, Professor Wallofski, a grotesque he developed in the rubber-faced tradition of the French clown, Grock. Max had at least two careers: one in the nation's music halls as Professor Wallofski, clad in black tights, telling his jokes with a timing that is sublime, and two as a straight actor, conspicuously when he succeeded Sir Laurence Olivier in 1974 in the role of Archie Rice in *The Entertainer* at the Greenwich Theatre. That performance gained the review: '*Max Wall makes Olivier look like an amateur…*'

There is a 15-year gap between the two phases of his career and an examination of that gap provides an interesting insight into the moral barometer of British society over the last century. Max's mother, Stella, initially dominated him both personally and professionally. She managed his career. He set out to "escape in the conventional way by getting married". He did so, and he and his wife dancer, Marion Pola, had five children. In 1955, however, Max was asked to be one of the judges in the Miss Great Britain beauty contest. There, he met Jennifer Chimes. Miss Chimes became Miss Great Britain. Max married her in 1956. Those few words sum up a situation which, today, is not unfamiliar. In 1956, it was a major scandal. Tall headlines, week after week, condemned both Max Wall and his new love. The lexicon of invective was explored in a manner now familiar in social media but, then, quite unfamiliar. Whether or not this relentless criticism affected Max I don't know, but two years later he collapsed on stage, suffered a nervous breakdown and Jennifer Chimes left him. They divorced in 1962. He spent the next decade in his own personal wilderness.

I admired Max Wall as a highly talented artiste and he became a friend. I had first met him at the old Marlowe Theatre in Canterbury which, shaped like the interior of an old box Brownie camera, stood where now the Marlowe Arcade leads you from St Margaret's Street to Marks and Spencer. In the late 1960s, Max's career was on the rocks – but he got a booking through Bill Preston who was then responsible for programming theatre for Canterbury City Council and who was, like me, old enough to treasure a jewel when they saw one. I booked seats for the entire family. This man, I told them, is unique. When we arrived at the theatre, our footsteps echoed as if in an empty cave. Social separation would have presented no problem that evening. The entire audience, numbered about 40, and we were spread around the auditorium, balcony to stalls. My party probably accounted for a quarter of the occupied seats. But the show, of course, must go on.

Max Wall entered, stage left. There was a whisper of applause and a long pause. Max Wall said: *"Right. EVERYBODY down the front."* He waved his arms to embrace his scattered audience and, slowly but obediently, the patrons left their seats and resettled in the front two or three rows of the stalls. Max Wall played that evening as if it were a Royal Command Performance. He was hysterically funny and, afterwards, he was gracious and generous with his time for those who had come to see him. My children were deeply impressed.

It wasn't until 1982 that we talked about that evening and about the most turbulent period of his life in the 1950s and 1960s. By this time, Max was in his mid-seventies and had been 'rediscovered' as a serious actor. The rebirth embraced appearing in Samuel Beckett's *Waiting for Godot*, *Krapp's Last Tape* and *Ubu Roi*. He had succeeded Olivier, as I say, in the lead role as *The Entertainer*. In 1983, we made a documentary about him for Channel Four. Max was living in a bedsit in Hither Green, South East London. He still banged out his scripts and jokes for his one-man show, *Aspects of Max Wall*, on an old Olivetti typewriter, and a cigarette was never far from his lips. We spent much of that summer in his company. We went back with him to the house in Jersey where he had set out on a new life with Jennifer Chimes. When she left him, she also left a note telling him that he would die alone, an old man, and unloved. His attitude to women was bitter. He resorted to Genesis to describe it: *"It was the apple that was the problem. Man and woman were created, these two, but once the woman had plucked the apple, that's when the trouble started."*

He laughs often as he sits in the armchair in the house in Jersey that was formerly his. This is where he lived alone for three years when Jennifer left him. He laughs but, often, it is more a scream of painful punctuation. Relationships with women have dominated his life. His mother had controlled him and his wives had left him. His third marriage is dismissed in his autobiography with the single chapter heading: 'A Joke'. But strangely, he doesn't accept that leaving his first wife blighted his career or that it hurt him personally. *"No-one can hurt me, only God."*

In 1990, agile Max tripped and fell in the Strand in central London. The pratfall was a routine he had performed a thousand times to an audience of millions. This time, he fractured his skull. He never regained consciousness and died in hospital the next day, May 21st at the age of 82. He is buried in Highgate Cemetery. He was 'the greatest clown of his age'.[134]

Harry Secombe came to Canterbury to introduce the long-running series of ITV's religious programmes titled *Highway*, ITV's rival to the BBC's *Songs of Praise*. In all my years in the business, I have never heard anyone say a harsh word about Harry Secombe. What you saw on stage or screen was what you got across a table over a cup of tea. He was simply a lovely man, TVS brought *Highway* to Canterbury. It coincided with the day of my second

---

134. The Times, May 23rd 1984. 'Wistfully Watching the Sorrows of Humanity', Bryan Appleyard

marriage, to Jo. We were wed in a register office in the morning and we joined Harry for lunch at Waterfields in Canterbury before the filming began. Harry was an old friend. In my early days with Southern Television, we had taken the evening magazine programme, *Day by Day*, on location to the West Indies, Barbados and Antigua. We filmed five editions of the daily programme and one of them featured Harry, who was convalescing in Barbados after being forced to leave the musical *Oliver!* following a heart attack. In the circumstances, I was reticent about approaching him to take part. But, on the telephone, he professed to being "bored stiff" and would welcome "some light relief". We took him at his word and spent the morning with him, filming a long interview and then leaving him to rest as we assembled location shots to illustrate what we had talked about. It was a jolly day. We were in the West Indies for a week.

In those days, everything was shot on 16mm film, the interviews captured on a camera with 10 minutes of sound on each roll; the location shots were taken on a smaller, mute, wind-up Bolex camera. The only way of discovering the quality of what we had shot, was to develop the film. Prudently, we dispatched the first day's rushes back to London by air. By the Thursday of that week, we had finished the shoot. The material was in the can. As a crew of four, we looked forward to a day on the beach before flying back to Britain at the weekend. We went to breakfast and there was an urgent message from the UK at the desk for us. All the sound film was fogged. Useless. Light had got into the camera and ruined it. Camaraman, George Pellett, examined the sound camera. He discovered that the lens turret had shifted, most probably knocked in transit on the flight to the West Indies. Light had consequently penetrated directly on to the film as it ran through the sprockets, rendering it completely blank. That, then, was the fault. But was there a solution?

There began what was probably the most frenzied day of my career as the crew sprinted around the island of Antigua, reshooting as much as we could of the sound footage. But what about Harry Secombe, convalescing far from home? Without his sound interview, we had no item. I went to see him. Tentatively. He was already on the beach, same chair, same spot. I explained the dilemma. *"Don't worry, boyo; let's get it done again."* Within an hour, it was so.

That's the sort of man Harry Secombe was. His friends will testify again and again to his generosity, sometimes financial, always with grace and spirit. Harry died in 2001. That October, Jo and I went to his memorial service at Westminster Abbey. Jimmy Tarbuck gave the oration. He closed with this sentence. *"I have been privileged to know Harry Secombe and all that he stands for; they keep telling me Harry is dead – but I don't have to believe them."*

Freddy Kempf was always welcome at the Festival, both as one of the most accomplished pianists of his generation and as a local talent. Born to a German father and a Japanese mother, schooled at both King's Canterbury, and St Edmund's, he first played in public in a church in Folkestone at the age of four. He is both fiercely professional and lyrical in performance. He once told me: *"Music is the stage. I aim to reach out to the audience and give them as emotional an experience as I can. I need an audience – and I find a recording studio where I feel no-one is listening is…difficult."* I once asked him whether he ever found himself playing on autopilot, a piece so familiar that the mind wanders. He laughed: *"Not if I can help it. Mind you, I do recall playing one sonata and catching the inquiring eye of the conductor as he noticed that I had diverted off on to quite a different sonata…"*

I wonder if anyone noticed.

Cleo Laine was, quite simply, 'the best singer in the world'.[135] Her natural range was contralto but scat singing and high notes ('G above top C') gave her an international reputation. She came to the Canterbury Festival with her husband John Dankworth's band and, during rehearsal before their concert in the cathedral, made a comment that emphasised, for me, the challenge of singing in the cathedral's nave. She had run through one of her numbers when she stopped John and their fellow musicians in mid-note, it

---

135. Derek Jewell, Sunday Times

seemed. *"John,"* she said, *"we must sort this out. I don't know which echo I'm hearing."* I think they remedied this by a judicious use of microphones and working with the cathedral's own sound system. Anyway, the concert that evening by Cleo Laine and the Johnny Dankworth band was magical.[136] I never met an artiste who was not in awe of the weight of history and tradition involved in singing in Canterbury Cathedral. But, more practically, the acoustics in the cathedral nave are not the greatest. Mark Deller once described them to me as *"a nightmare. Not great, even for the audience. If I want to hear the best of a performance, I try to sit in the front three rows or, alternatively, in the back rows in the Nave nearest the West Door".* All singers, with modern equipment, cope with the acoustic challenge, some better than others. Saxophonist, **Jan Garbarek**, wandered around the cathedral extemporizing as he went as the Hilliard Ensemble sang Renaissance music from the nave steps. That was conspicuously successful, an ethereal moment. Garbarek was offstage for most of the performance but, acoustically, it was crystal clear.

And then there was **Marie Colvin** who so nearly graced our festival. Marie was a foreign correspondent for *The Sunday Times* with whom she'd been since 1985. I spent much of the summer of 2003 with her in Normandy, making a documentary film about another great war correspondent, Martha Gellhorn. We shared our admiration for Gellhorn who had impressed on me as a young reporter that *"the most important job of a journalist is to get it on the record. Otherwise they, the bastards, win".* Marie put it more simply: *"My job is to bear witness."* We called the documentary, which she introduced, *On the Record*.[137] Marie was a striking figure with a patch over her left eye, lost when she was injured while reporting the Sri Lankan Civil War two years earlier. She was twice married and embraced those 'failures' with the same sense of humour that she brought to her eventful life. She could also sink into a deep depression, driven by the experiences that went with

---

136. Later, Dame Cleo Laine and Sir John Dankworth, both, and unusually, separately honoured for their contribution to music
137. On the Record, ITV network, 2003

the job she was doing. But that was seldom and she was 'one of the boys' in the lengthy evenings on location during filming. She also found time to accompany me on a mission to choose a canteen of French, stainless steel cutlery that is still part of the everyday life of the Williams' household. This cultured, award-winning woman was fascinated by my connections with the arts and with the Canterbury Festival and she promised to come to Canterbury to talk about her life. She was killed before she could do that, blown up while covering the siege of Homs in Syria. She died while, as she once put it, "*shining a light on humanity in extremis, pushed to the unendurable*". She was a credit to her profession.

The years between 1991 and 2000 were conspicuous for the steady growth of the Festival. Mark Deller produced attractive programmes and, given that the Board at every meeting still dwelt on the inevitable problems of how to raise the money to pay for the events, the tightrope slung between artistic ambition and financial reality was safely walked. During these nine years we enjoyed the St Petersburg State Symphony Orchestra, Shobana Jeyasingh Dance, *The Damnation of Faust*, Kit and The Widow, Robin Knox-Johnston, Honor Blackman, Jenny Agutter, *Madame Butterfly*, *The Dream of Gerontius* – Archbishop George Carey's favourite music, incidentally – Johnny Dankworth and Cleo Laine, Jan Garbarek, Judi Dench, the Kyiv Chamber Choir, *Antony and Cleopatra*, *Tubby the Tuba*, David Hockney, Geraldine McEwan, Alan Price, the Richard Alston Dance Company, *Henry V*, the Jacques Loussier Trio, rabbi Lionel Blue, *The Marriage of Figaro*, Armando Iannucci, Brian Rix, The Sixteen, Robert Powell, Barry Cryer, Prunella Scales, *La Traviata* (in Margate), Freddy Kempf, Robert Cohen, and the Kent County Youth Orchestra, Michael Nyman, Trevor Pinnock, and the English Touring Opera. So many other talents graced Kent's stages in the years leading up to the turn of the century and beyond.[138] A flourishing programme of 'fringe' events took place in the city's and county's smaller venues,

---

138. An important aspect of the Festival's success was to include events to suit all possible tastes.

one of which gave me one of my more embarrassing moments. I'll let Mark Deller describe it:

"We had taken the Festival Fringe programme under our wing and there were two or three occasions when the Fringe contributions caused something of a stir. There was one exhibition – I can't remember the theme – depicting 50 penises in a shop window. This required the then Lord Mayor and Peter, our chairman, at the BBC's request to be interviewed live for the Today *programme at 6.30am."*[139]

I remember the incident well, though I can't recall the exact words I said: I think they included the phrase: *"art may take many forms"*. I *do* recall, however, that the Lord Mayor was a good sport during the whole affair. I also remember that not long after that, an enormous pair of bloomers was slung across the City's ancient West Gate. Canterbury chose stoically to take both incidents in its stride.

After the success of *Noye's Fludde* in 1989, Mark Deller was keen to come up with another similar community project, and in 1994 commissioned librettist, Michael Irwin, and composer, Matthew King, to write an opera based on the story of Jonah and the whale. Once again, it involved more than 300 children from 10 primary and secondary schools from Canterbury, Whitstable and Herne Bay, working with a professional director, choreographer, designer, conductor, orchestra and soloists. The project took three years in the making and *Jonah* was eventually performed in the nave of the cathedral during the 1996 Festival. We stepped outside Canterbury to London – twice – in the 1990s. In 1997, we performed Mahler's epic Symphony No 8 with the Canterbury Choral Society and the Royal Choral Society, under their conductor, Richard Cooke, with the Orchestre National de Lille, repeating our final night's cathedral concert in the Royal Albert Hall two days later, and again in Lille two weeks after that. And two years later, in 1999, we did a similar thing with our performance of Berlioz's *Grande Messe*

---

139. Mark, My Words, Mark Deller, 2021, p150

des Morts. Not only did these ventures to the Albert Hall make it financially feasible to programme these two great works in the cathedral during the Festival, but they were initiatives that took a positive profile of Canterbury's arts festival to the nation's capital.

The Board pursued its declared policies and, during these fertile years, resisted all suggestions by South East Arts to turn the Canterbury Festival into a 'South East Festival'. We moved headquarters from Ivy Lane to a suite of rooms above the cathedral's Christ Church Gate.[140] Appropriately, one of these rooms had been the office of the legendary Miss Babington.[141] Certain items consistently appear in the Board minutes of that period – frequent negotiations with SEA as we strove to increase their annual grant; the repayment to the city council of the final tranche of money they had loaned us (finally, £1,200 in December 1992); the regular organisation of fund-raising events with the help of our Friends organisation, at Leeds Castle, Godmersham Park, Lees Court, Charlton Park and other splendid venues. BBC Radio Kent moved into the highly successful Festival Club at St Alphege Church. David Cornett, as host, provided nightly coverage throughout the Festival. In 1993, Television South (TVS) lost the South and South-East ITV franchise to Meridian; the Festival had lost a friend. and we set out to woo the newcomers, Meridian Broadcasting, with mixed success.

Our core administration team remained much the same and we nominated Pat Ebden for the Garrett Award for initiative in funding the arts. My letter read:

'*Soon after I became chairman we, as a Festival, had a working deficit of £60,000. We have, due in no small part to Pat's efforts, cleared that deficit and more than broken even over the last six years.*

'*This, in itself, is fairly exceptional. We have, as a charitable trust, wooed funding bodies and formed vigorous Friends and Vice-*

---

140. Offices that could be reached only by ascending a stone staircase of 69 steps – not a journey for the faint-hearted and a situation that, because of the difficult/impossible access for the disabled, would not be acceptable today
141. See Chapter 3

Presidents organisations. But, conspicuously, we have formed warm and lasting relationships with businesses, both local and regional. Pat's record, not only of finding new sponsors, but hanging on to the established ones, is of the highest class. It is a compliment both to her style and her organisational ability – for to fail to discern and to satisfy a sponsor's requirements, is the quickest way to lose a sponsor.'

The Board unanimously supported the nomination. Pat's efforts, working with her husband Peter, were an illustration of the dedication of those who work, and have worked, for the Festival throughout my association with it. Mind you, not all our fund-raising initiatives were successful. We decided to raffle a top-of-the-range car in 1998. Tickets were, I think, £5 each and Peugeot gave us the best deal in town on their new model Peugeot 206 GLX 1.4 litre. We sent out the raffle tickets to our friends and supporters – and received a muted response. Many of them did not particularly want to sell draw tickets and sent them back, mostly with a polite note. We struggled to total ticket sales of £6,000. The car, on the road, was worth £10,000. We made the draw and the winner was a Canterbury resident, Susan Counsel. We informed her of her good fortune and she said she didn't want the car! It was 'not to her liking'. The cost of the car, to us, was £7,000. This was a tricky situation; even if Susan would take the car, we would still lose £1,000 – the difference between our ticket sales of £6,000 and the car's purchase price to us of £7,000. I went to see Susan Counsel. She already drove a Peugeot, she said, and was about to trade it in, but she didn't want the top-of-the-range GT speedster. She would, she added, welcome a cash offer. Letters on the legal position if we complied with her wishes flowed between Peugeot and Bill Cotton, our lawyer. The legal difficulties were solved – we didn't buy the car and Susan was kind enough to accept a cash offer from us of £6,000 – precisely what we had taken in ticket money. Our net loss was the £900 it had cost to arrange and administer the raffle.

Apart from fund-raising, one other item began to appear regularly on the Board agenda. It was 'A new theatre' and it was given fresh impetus in 1998 by an East Kent Cultural Strategy Report, commissioned by the six district councils of East Kent, plus Kent County Council and SEA. Its aim was to explain and highlight that the South East, and East Kent in particular, received less funding for the arts and culture than almost any other region of England.

This report set out policies to rectify the situation and suggested how the partners could work together to achieve those policies. The Festival Board welcomed the report by David Powell Associates as far as it went but felt it ignored the Canterbury Festival and its experience over the previous decade. The Board suggested amendments and the following addition to the report:

'The Canterbury Festival takes place every October and is by far the largest and most comprehensive arts festival in the region. It was revived, in its modern form, 15 years ago and, after a sticky start when it ran up a deficit of £60,000, it has balanced its books and now has a turnover of more than £300,000 a year. It has established itself, additionally, as an enabler for smaller developing arts groups. It has an all-year-round administration and now promotes events at times of the year outside its normal October slot. It has been blessed with good financial management and raised twice as much funding each year from the private sector as it obtains through public core-funding grants. Currently, the Director feels understandably constrained by a steady decline in funding commitment by SEA and a dramatic cut by KCC.'

It concluded: *'The lack of a suitable large-scale venue has long been identified as a hindrance to the Festival's further growth – and to the development of arts and audiences in the area.'*

The core of the Festival's concern was contained in that final sentence. If culture in East Kent aimed to flourish and make a significant contribution to the economy in one of the most deprived areas of the UK,[142] it needed a new, large venue. A 900-

---

142. Three of the ten most deprived areas in Europe were in East Kent at that time

seat Marlowe Theatre would not be big enough to attract the most lavish productions and remain economic. The report heard the message but warned against '*an overconcentration on larger venue provision...concentrating on the expensive and time-consuming process of trying to fund and launch such venues could detract from vital, smaller-scale work.*'

The Festival Board disagreed, so did the city council and the county council. The creation of a new, large venue in East Kent would now be explored with greater vigour. It would need all the partners who cared about the arts in Kent to work together, if the dream were to become a reality.

Vice Chancellors of the University of Kent: David Ingram and Robin Sibson.

Colin Carmichael, a key figure as the city's Chief Executive, in the campaign to employ culture in the regeneration of East Kent

*Councillor Marion Attwood – fired a warning shot
during the campaign to build a new theatre.*

*Allan Willett, Kent's Lord Lieutenant,
and an inspiration in all we wished to achieve.*

Chapter 11 – Grabbing the Nettle

In many ways, the University of Kent and two successive and supportive vice-chancellors, provided the key that released the energy to turn the concept of a new theatre in Canterbury into a reality.

Ever since the Canterbury Theatre and Festival Trust had come into being in 1979, a new theatre of up to 1500 seats had been part of its remit. The old tiny Marlowe Theatre, off St Margaret's Street, had been demolished to make way for a fresh commercial heart for the city, and the Odeon cinema had been converted into the 'new' Marlowe with the help of a donation of £20,000 from the CTFT. Its seating capacity was about 900. It was now owned and run by the city council. It was running at an annual loss of six figures – one estimate was £750,000 a year. One of a number of consultative papers at around this time advised Canterbury City Council that:

'The Marlowe (Theatre) has the potential to be one of Britain's leading touring theatres and the leading centre for the performing arts in the trans-Manche region. But at the moment, too many of the key attributes which are necessary for success are stuck in limbo... The Marlowe is depressingly average.'

The document titled 'The Marlowe's Renaissance' suggested an extension to the existing Marlowe or a completely new building. Whatever was decided, it warned:

'The upheaval in the short term will be uncomfortable for many; things may seem to get worse before they get better. But if the Marlowe does not go forward it risks slipping backwards until it

reaches a point where the Council feels it has no alternative but to wash its hands of it. That...must not happen. Grasp the nettle now and in 12 months time it could be looking more like an orchid!'

The report arrived amid a lively debate in the city over the alternatives Canterbury should pursue. Since 1994, led by the Festival, a committee had been set up to consider precisely that. Its members were the city council, SEA, the university, the Friends of Canterbury Cathedral and the city's museum. In its inaugural meeting, it identified a number of needs, including an increase in the number of venues in the city and the creation of 'a large venue for touring companies and large concerts'. It resolved to re-examine the potential of the Marlowe Theatre and the task was given among others, to a sub-committee of Mark Everett, the theatre's director; Malcolm Burgess, the city's Estates and Leisure Officer, and myself. Simultaneously, we would explore other possibilities involving the creation of a large multipurpose venue, embracing a theatre of more than 1000 seats. The three of us met separately and, as a committee, consulted others. At one such meeting in the summer of 1984, Kent University's Professor Robert Freedman drew our attention to a paper written to the Wolfson Foundation in September 1981 by the retiring vice-chancellor, Dr David Ingram. It suggested that 'a visual and performing arts centre' at the university might be... 'a fitting memorial to Sir Isaac Wolfson'. Nothing had come of the initiative, but the letter indicated that support for the arts through a major development could be part of the university's strategic planning. A two-acre site had been under discussion. I asked David Ingram if he would consider giving us that site as a possible home for a new, larger performance venue, which we were currently discussing. He agreed – but he was leaving his post that summer. It was important, then, to find out if his successor, Professor Robin Sibson, was of like mind. The contrast between the two vice-chancellors could hardly have been more distinct. David Ingram was, above all else, a diplomat. He steered the relatively new University of Kent judiciously for 14 years between 1980 and 1994. He was interested in the arts. Robin

Sibson was a mathematician professor of statistics at the University of Bath and, as vice-chancellor, was about to transform Kent's collegiate-based university into a more centralised establishment. This might not, we felt, make him popular with some academics – and so it proved. I went to meet him in November. He could hardly have been more supportive. He confirmed that the university would provide a site, free of charge, for a large performance venue and offered a 'structure of administration' as well as aid in seeking funding.[143] He offered to join our Venue Committee to pilot the initiative through. We accepted with alacrity.

This generous gesture by the university was important in two ways. Firstly, the site cost of a new theatre was removed at a stroke. Secondly, it moved the possibility of a new theatre in Canterbury from the 'pending' tray to 'action needed'. The Festival issued a press release:

'A new 1500-seat Venue for Canterbury

For the past five years, we have been trying to discover how to create a new, larger 1500-seat venue, in Canterbury, big enough to attract such talent as large scale symphony orchestras, pop stars and touring opera, in the knowledge that it must be an economic proposition.

The Festival and the University of Kent at Canterbury are now working together to explore the possibility of building such a venue on the campus of the University. There are two possible sites in mind. The building would:

a) solve a problem that is holding back the growth and development of the Festival, which has come a long way in the past 10 years.

b) be a world-class venue for concerts, say 50 times a year – or however many times demand dictates.

c) lock into an existing administration at the University, helping to meet the considerable running/administration costs that dog so many big arts venues.

---

143.   Memo, PW to Mark Deller, November 14th 1994

d) be a multi-purpose building, with an adjustable rake, whose adaptability would make it accessible to a range of university and community uses.

e) provide an architectural challenge, an opportunity to mark the turn of the century with a building worthy of the era.'

Both the city council and Kent County Council were aware of this initiative and we now sought their support. It became apparent that both were concerned about the impact the suggested building might have. Would its arrival jeopardise the viability of the Marlowe Theatre? Would it, with its mixed programme, draw audiences away from the traditional theatre? The debate, much of it reflected in the letters section of the *Kentish Gazette*, continued throughout 1995 and 1996. In September 1996, I was able to write to the editor of the *Gazette* that the Festival 'welcomed the letter from Councillors Iain Douglas and Ron Pepper[144] ('Residents have to come first')… and we are pleased to see the Labour pledge to market and expand festivals and events in Canterbury and the coastal towns (Whitstable and Herne Bay) and to seek the establishment of a conference centre/concert venue.' I went on:

'I was able to talk to the City Council Policy Committee this week about the importance of having time to think strategically – to dream, if you like. Currently, we believe that, as the Millennium approaches, one of the projects that should be considered is the building of a new world class 1500-seat concert hall and conference centre on land generously offered us by the University of Kent. It would be a truly regional asset which, through the medium of an architectural competition, could provide a building which would grace the city and show future generations the quality and breadth of our thinking and initiative.

'We currently need a Feasibility Study as the next step. What is absolutely certain is that, although we have the broad support of the SE Arts, Kent County Council and the University, this project will

---

144.   Members of the Labour opposition on Canterbury City Council

founder unless Canterbury City Council enters enthusiastically into the exploration of whether such a building makes sense.

'Opportunities like this do not come along very frequently. I urge our friends, inside the City Council and outside, to help us to grasp it.'

In October, the Canterbury Arts Council echoed our plea that 'STRONG local support from the City Council is vital'.[145] The following month, on November 15th, Councillor Marion Attwood told us that planning implications of the proposed new building would be considered at a site meeting at the university. But she added:

"I have to tell you that I am still deeply concerned about the effects your hall would have on our own Marlowe Theatre which is, as you are aware, very heavily subsidised by the City Council."

The Festival was deeply sympathetic with that view. But the Marlowe Theatre was too small and the university's portmanteau offer had obvious appeal. Our major objective, often stated, was to create a theatre large enough to accommodate large-scale productions; our reasons were both artistic and financial. Our immediate concern was to persuade *all* our partners to carry out a feasibility study to examine what would be best for the city and for Kent. This support was confirmed following a meeting with the city council's chief executive, Colin Carmichael, in November. His subsequent letter read:

'Although a number of reservations have been raised, we feel that, in principle, the proposal to construct a concert hall/conference centre/ hotel could have significant benefit to the local economy.'

The feasibility study would therefore take place, during which the views of all parties would be embraced and examined. The reaction of SEA was immediate. They were "very pleased" that

---

145. Letter from Alan Boniface, secretary, October 22nd 1996

an examination "of options, issues and solutions" could now be undertaken.

The campaign was given fresh impetus by the support of Allan Willett, soon to become Kent's Lord Lieutenant, Her Majesty the Queen's representative in the county. We knew Allan and his wife, Anne; they lived in the next village and he had always supported the Festival. Son of a tea planter in Africa, he farmed in Thanet and, after a military career, had become a market leader in electronic labelling through his business, Willett International Ltd. Allan was an innovator as he would later prove in his development of the Kent lieutenancy. A new, large arts centre/concert hall/theatre could be, he said, "just the shot in the arm that the development of the arts in Kent needed". He agreed to chair a task force to explore the alternatives. Colin Carmichael, Robin Sibson and I welcomed his input, his energy and his influence.

I had now lived in Canterbury for 20 years. When I first arrived from Wales and the West Country, I remember reflecting that, though there was a vigorous cultural and heritage centre in Aberystwyth, there was none at that time in Canterbury. Yet Canterbury had a history as rich as, perhaps richer than, any other city in the United Kingdom. Presumptuously, but seizing the moment, I wrote a paper[146] and sent it to Colin Carmichael in June 1997. Canterbury's tannery, which had brought prosperity and a noxious smell to the St Peter's area of the city for 200 years, was about to close. An arts development on this prime position, on the ring road round the city for those approaching from London, would make a captivating statement to mark the millennium. There would be space for all the possibilities being discussed – a concert hall/conference centre, a theatre, a visual arts centre – even a hotel. The Williamson family had run the tannery for six generations. In 1760, leatherworker, John Williamson, had married Susannah Row in nearby St Mildred's Church and a century later (1879) the tannery was opened and named St Mildred's Tannery. Despite 'the stink of the tannery process so close to the city

---

146.   See Appendix 3 for the text of the paper

centre,[147] the business had thrived and Canterbury's leather seats graced Rolls-Royces, Bentleys, Daimlers, Ferraris and Jaguars, as well as the House of Lords and the fearsome black chair of the television quiz programme, *Mastermind*. The Williamson family loved Canterbury and had made it their home. The company then expanded into a production relationship with Connolly Leather, a London firm which supplied leather to car manufacturers. In 1963, the Connolly family bought the tannery. The Williamsons had earlier given their former home and gardens, the riverside Tower House, to the city and this was now the Mayor's official 'parlour'. As we approached Connolly Leather, would they be as generous, as open to the community appeal, to support the creation of a Millennium Arts Project on the tannery site? We had several meetings with their representative over several years, but, in the end, the answer was 'no'. Several hundred houses now occupy the site behind a recreated, ersatz extension of the city wall.

This was a disappointment. But my paper contained a number of other suggestions including a plea that Canterbury, with its unrivalled history, might take a look at Colonial Williamsburg or Jamestown in the USA, or Ironbridge in Shropshire, to consider whether to create similar 'living history' complexes. They could be based on the theme of the Roman occupation or the martyrdom of Becket or even Rupert Bear.[148] Currently, it is good to see that the revitalisation of Canterbury Castle is being considered.

The debate over the shape, size and placing of Canterbury's new theatre would go on for a decade. I recall a morning spent with architect, Anthony de Moubray, not many weeks before the city council made its final decision on the site for the new Marlowe. With tape measure in hand, we paced the gardens of Tower House, near the West Gate, assessing whether a theatre could fit into this site beside the ring road. We thought it would be a squeeze.

As we approached the turn of the century, the Festival continued to flourish – Lord (Colin) Moynihan, a former Minister for Sport

---

147. The Williamson family papers, Canterbury Cathedral archives
148. Mary Tourtel (1874–1948), creator of the Rupert Bear cartoon character, was born and died in Canterbury

and Professor Robin Sibson joined the Board; socially, Jenny Bird, wife of our vice-chairman, James Bird – retired after organising a number of successful charity events for the Festival – and we reflected on how best to encourage performance in the city's smaller venues such as the Penny Theatre, now occupied by a local ironmongers. Our secretary, Mark Rake, resigned in 1999 and my response to his letter of resignation reflected our gratitude to him. He referred to the Board as a group who had "come through the fire". I replied:

'The parlous state of the Festival 12 years ago is now, thankfully, a matter of history but, as I said when we met at dinner, the rescue was made possible by relatively few people, many of whom put their own money on the line, as guarantors, indicating their confidence in the future, so that others could bestow theirs. Thank you for that and for your untiring work as secretary to the Board. The Festival would not be what it is today without your contribution.'

Mark referred to the successful 'Golden Balls' lottery adventure: *"I look back and know that we took risks to the point of personally guaranteeing losses…and gambled with those Golden Balls. But we won through and that is to our credit."* He was right, of course. Thankfully.

Then Brian Arnold died. He had been the Festival's vice-chair for a decade. Brian was, to all intents and purposes, Mr Music in Canterbury for more than 30 years. As a young man, he had been a tenor soloist, but it was as an arts administrator and entrepreneur that he was to achieve wide recognition. In addition to running the family fruit farm at Chartham, he managed to combine a career in music with work for the National Federation of Music Societies (now Making Music), of which he subsequently became national chairman. Brian was also chairman of the Canterbury Choral Society for 25 years. Brian's predilection was for fast cars and good food. He was genial, a true *bon viveur*; he was reliable and efficient. Somehow, he always seemed to be smiling.

In April 2000, we accepted the retirement of Keith Lucas from the Festival Board. He and Brian had been founder members of the CTFT. They had inspired the rebirth of the festival and had worked tirelessly to give that vision substance. The festival owes a huge debt to Keith and to his wife, Rona, for their energy and their vision.

At the turn of the century, the Festival was in a good place. It was successful but not complacent; we had, as my annual report said: '...*steadily increased our turnover over the last five years and retained our programming flair and loyal support. The Friends of the Festival, whose membership continues to grow, play an increasingly important role in our yearly balancing act, and our year-round profile. The Board join me in thanking them for their contribution and wish them well in their drive to achieve 1,000 members next year.*'[149]

The Festival was fast building a relationship with Canterbury Christ Church College (now University), which would pay dividends in the future; it was, as always, urging its Board members to redouble their efforts to recruit financial support. It was reaching out to Europe – the French ambassador, M. Bernard, had attended the Festival's production of Berlioz's *Grande Messe des morts* at the Albert Hall in October – and there was a unity among the partners in Kent as they sought how best to create a new larger performance venue in East Kent.

The Festival faced the new millennium with as much optimism as was wise to exhibit on any project involving the arts and the future.

---

149. The Friends of Canterbury Festival had flourished since 1989, led by Deborah and Jack Bornoff, Jenny Bird, Des Connolly, Rona and Keith Lucas, Peter Harris and Anthony de Moubray. The chairs of The Friends, and its annual contributions to the Festival, are listed in Appendix 6

Capital of Culture bid launched with a glass of pimms

Rosie Turner, Festival Director, in the Cathedral precincts, a far cry from the streets of Belfast

Rosie Turner came from Belfast with a quality reputation.

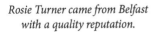

Chapter 12 – Ambition and Succession

The new millennium opened with a bid by Canterbury and East Kent to become Europe's Capital of Culture in 2008.

The region had never before pursued anything quite as ambitious as this and, inevitably, it involved a number of challenges, some anticipated, some rather more of a surprise. Seven local authorities in East Kent – Canterbury, Swale, Dover, Ashford, Thanet, Shepway and Kent County Council – forged links through which they talked to each other about culture and these links developed quickly enough to suggest that they would endure whatever the outcome of the bid. In addition, the exercise of putting the bid together served to emphasise what had always been a central tenet of the Festival – that Canterbury may lie in the South East corner of Britain but, more than any other British city, it stands as the gateway to Europe.

What came out of the bid was a sense of cohesion and optimism – a confirmation that 'culture' has significance for a community, which goes far beyond the enjoyment of top-class performers in concert for a few weeks every year. 'Culture' was increasingly identified as the cutting edge by which a regeneration of the whole of East Kent might be achieved, encouraging greater cohesion in local government; better communications, road and rail; fresh initiatives to ease life for the disadvantaged in East Kent and more inward investment attracted by a better and happier environment. The city council needed a headline for the Canterbury bid and someone found a quote from Virginia Woolf:

"There is no lovelier place in the world than Canterbury"

The supporting line was 'Odyssey: a journey from a great past to a greater future', and the five-word motto was 'In place, In motion, Inspired'. The city council, showing its consistent support for arts initiatives and well led by Janice McGuinness, proclaimed East Kent's past: Chaucer and Marlowe, Dickens and Conrad, Woolf and Turner. It also emphasised present strengths – a cathedral at the heart of the worldwide Anglican Communion; schools, colleges and universities; the solid private sector support from EuroTunnel, Pfizer, Saga, Land Securities Group, the Kent Messenger Group of newspapers and many others, and the links of friendships forged over the years with Europe. Tellingly, East Kent's population was polled to gauge local approval for the bid – and 83 percent of those asked, enthusiastically supported the idea of Canterbury as the European Capital of Culture. Canterbury, said the bid document, was 'a city for all ages'.

In the end, Liverpool won. But Canterbury's bid did not fail. At interview, we had impressed Sir Jeremy Isaacs and his panel of judges and Canterbury benefited by £150,000, which helped pay for some of the initiatives we had suggested in our detailed bid. In addition, the Arts Council awarded Canterbury £50,000 and SEEDA[150] £25,000.

The winners, Liverpool, invited me to join them as they celebrated their victory. Their chairman, Sir Bob Scott, recalled that the idea for the competition had been borne in a conversation between Melina Mercouri, film star and then Greece's Minister of Culture and Sports, and her French counterpart, Jack Lang. In his victory speech, Liverpool's chairman promised that his city would contribute vigorously to the declared aim of bringing Europeans closer together "by highlighting the richness and diversity of European cultures and by raising awareness of common history and values". He also said that he had been "confident of victory" because Liverpool was "the only city outside London, familiar to everyone, all over the world". I joined in the congratulations and applause but later, over a drink, I reminded him, that "Canterbury

---

150.   SEEDA – South East England Development Agency

would also fall into that category". We laughed, he agreed, and because this would be a speech well-worn as it was repeated throughout the year, he suggested that he remove the reference to Liverpool's uniqueness. I thought that an elegant reaction.

One of the side-effects of Brexit is that British cities may no longer enter this European Capital of Culture competition. Though no doubt absent from politicians' lists as they argued during Britain's referendum about the pros and cons of being in or out of Europe, this is an outcome to be deeply regretted. Brexit encouraged, and still propagates, insular rather than international thinking. As Britain's 'International Festival', this did not chime with the Canterbury Festival's ambitions for the future. We agreed with the Government's 'deep disappointment' at the European Union's decision, pointing out that, though the UK was leaving the EU, "we are not leaving Europe." Britain's exclusion seemed a spiteful reaction, a fit of pique by the EU, particularly as other non-EU cities including Istanbul, Reykjavík in Iceland and Stavanger in Norway, had competed in the past. The uncompromising letter to the British Government from the European Commission simply ruled that any UK application would be 'discontinued'.

The Festival was entering a period of change. It welcomed new directors: Darren Henley from Classic FM; theatre and opera director, Richard Jarman and singer, Kate Lewis. We developed a warm relationship with Roger Reed, now chair of South East Arts. But we also prepared to bid farewell to Mark Deller, Festival Director since 1988, and willing saviour and caretaker in the four troubled years before that. Mark had successfully combined the twin roles of Artistic Director and Administrator for 14 years. His calm and his contacts, his sheer talent and dedication to the job had been particularly valuable in the early years of the Festival's revival. His record spoke for itself and an extract from his 1998 report, when he looked back over 10 years, is included in Appendix 4. It is there to indicate the breadth and complexity of the responsibilities he assumed.

In 2002, Pfizer were persuaded to become the Festival's lead sponsor with a grant of £50,000 and EuroTunnel also agreed to sponsor an event. Financially, it was a good year. During 2002, the Festival began to look for Mark's successor. We advertised – and the response was enormous – more than 80 applications. The Board felt they must be doing something right because the job seemed so desirable to so many. Either that, or it was so obviously a shambles that every man and his dog felt they should be able to improve matters. In the meantime, Mark produced a programme for the 2002 Festival that opened with a spectacular South American carnival procession of 300 people swinging through the city's streets and included a performance of Elgar's *The Kingdom* performed in the cathedral, Evelyn Glennie with the world première of a new percussion concerto, The King's Consort with their celebrated re-enactment of the music for the *Coronation of King George II*, the Courtney Pine band and the Rambert Dance Company at the Marlowe, the Henri Oguike Dance Company at the Gulbenkian and an all-Russian final night concert in the cathedral with Prokofiev's *Alexander Nevsky* and Rachmaninoff's *The Bells*. There were events featuring Tony Benn, Mike Atherton, Rolf Harris, Tony Hawks, Mary Black, The Blockheads and, as Mark wrote, 'much, much more...' Willard White's stunning concert in the cathedral the previous year, when he had performed an *Evening from Paul Robeson's Song Book*, was broadcast on Christmas Day on BBC4.

The Festival's profile was high, the cash books were balanced – if ever there was an ideal time for a change, this was it.

In April 2002, with Mark Deller's help, we whittled down the applications for Festival Director and set aside a day for interviews, which, as reported to a Board meeting later that month, was "a good day". The panel was made up of Board members, plus John Brazier from Kent County Council and the Marlowe's director, Mark Everett, from Canterbury City Council. The applicants offered us a complete spectrum of skills, from the young but inexperienced, to men and women who would be leaving established jobs in order to join us. One or two felt they might be able to combine their current job with the position of Festival Director. The attraction of this approach was that they would bring their reputations, experience and contacts with them. We rejected this, however, because we knew that the commitment necessary to carry the Festival into the 21st century would need to be total. At the end of the day, our verdict was unanimous. We would offer the job to Rosie Turner, then Deputy Director of the Belfast Festival at Queen's University where she had worked for the previous 11 years.

Conversations that take place across an interview table should be privileged and subject to Chatham House Rules, but one exchange during Rosie's interview must go on the record. She had talked about her experience with the Belfast Festival, first as a volunteer in 1981 and then as a core member of staff. One member of our interviewing panel began his question to her: "*Now, Mrs Turner, if we offered you the position, you realise that it would be politically demanding. You will have to balance the demands of a number of supporters we need to keep on board – Kent County Council, Canterbury City Council, South East Arts – and each has a different agenda. It's a tricky business to balance...*"

At which point, a fellow member of the interview panel burst out laughing. Here were we, in the secure calm of the precincts of Canterbury Cathedral, with a woman who had successfully worked professionally for 11 years amid the turmoil of a city gripped by bomb and bullet during The Troubles between Republican and Unionist, and we were warning her about political complexities in the arts in East Kent. I think Rosie replied that she thought she could manage it.

We offered Rosie the job and she accepted. Within a week, she called me. She was, as we knew, married to Mark Dougherty, musical director of *Riverdance*, the iconic Irish dance theatrical show. She said that *Riverdance* had, that day, finalised an agreement for a world tour to Australia and China, where they would perform in the Great Hall of the People in Beijing.[151] Though she 'loved Canterbury and the people I might work with', this was a once-in-a-lifetime chance and she would really like to accompany her husband. So, "regretfully..."

---

151. In the event, the China leg of the *Riverdance* world tour was cancelled at the last moment because of an outbreak of the SARS virus

We had planned a short transition period during which Rosie would 'shadow' Mark during the 2002 Festival, working together. I asked her to give me a couple of hours to consider this latest development. Two facts were apparent: one, that the interviewing panel unanimously wanted Rosie Turner as the next Festival Director; two, that we did not want to go through the interview process again, if it could be avoided. I called Rosie back: If we held the job open for her, when could she join? She was flattered, I think, and a little relieved. She said that the world tour would begin the following January and finish in June. She could start in Canterbury in August 2003. I said, again, I would call her back. It was now May 2002 and the Festival had a vital gap to fill lasting 14 months.

I telephoned Mark Deller, explained the situation and asked if he would postpone his retirement for a few months and Mark, being Mark, agreed. Thus, the smooth transition we had planned and sought was accomplished, though lengthened and slightly delayed. To be mercenary for a moment, I had long felt that those who make their living in the world of the arts musicians, actors, administrators, were underpaid for their talent and skills. Understandably, if Rosie were to join us, she did not want to earn less than her salary in Belfast. That was just over £30,000. If Mark was going to do the job for a further year, I recommended to the Board that his salary should be raised to that level. The Board unanimously agreed.

The 2002 Festival was successful, both artistically and at the box office and, as we looked ahead to changeover, we produced a paper for the record that summarised the governance and administration of the Festival. Part of it read:

'In many ways, the Festival Board is the engine room of the Festival. They handle and supervise an annual turnover of more than £½ million. They have created six full-time jobs, which enables the Festival to fulfil an 'umbrella' role throughout the year to many smaller arts and community organisations in East Kent who approach the Festival Office in the Canterbury Cathedral Precincts, for advice and guidance.

'As Alan Boniface, chairman of the Canterbury Arts Council,

says: *"The Festival works for us in a number of ways. First, it enables our members to be bolder with their programming than they might otherwise be, because of the larger audiences drawn to Canterbury, Whitstable and Herne Bay during the Festival fortnight. Second, the Festival's publicity machine gives a huge and added profile to the events. And, third, after consultations, we often experiment with new venues – this year alone, our members have used the Steiner School at Garlinge Green, Wingham Church, and Ickham Church."*

'To give them their full title, Festival Board members are actually directors of the Canterbury Theatre and Festival Trust, a charitable trust born in 1980 to help the fight to retain a theatre in Canterbury. The result was the Marlowe Theatre, converted from the old Odeon Cinema in 1984; some current Board members were part of that successful campaign, as was the outgoing Festival Director, Mark Deller.

'The spread of the Board's interests is impressive. Katharine Lewis is a professional singer, who teaches at the King's School, St Edmund's and the University of Kent. Trust Secretary, Dr Kate Neales, is a consultant gynaecologist in the East Kent Hospitals Trust, and sings in the Canterbury Choral Society. Vice-Chairman James Bird, a company director and business consultant who lives in Deal, is a deputy Lord Lieutenant of Kent. Sir Geoffrey Chipperfield, a former Whitehall mandarin, is the University of Kent's Pro-Chancellor, chairman of the UK-Europe Gas Group and director of South-West Water. Peter Harris is chairman of an arts consultancy and trustee of the Wapping Arts Trust. Darren Henley is Managing Editor of Classic FM and a director of the Broadcast Journalism Training Council. Richard Jarman is General Director of the Britten-Pears Foundation in Aldeburgh and was a director of Scottish Opera and Artistic Director at Covent Garden. Brigadier, John Meardon, is Receiver General of the Cathedral and a member of the Kent Tourism Alliance. Accountant, David Pentin, is a former Lord Mayor of the City and a former Leader of the City Council; he is the board's treasurer. Anthony de Moubray is one of the most respected architects in East Kent. Solicitor, Richard Sturt, was until recently HM Coroner for East Kent and is Registrar of the Canterbury Diocese and a director of a number of companies and public utilities. Accountant, Hugh Summerfield, from Ashford, is a director of Finn-Kelcey and Chapman Trustees and newcomer, Simon Backhouse, is a partner at estate agents Strutt & Parker. Chairman, Peter Williams, a television producer who is also Freeman of the City of Canterbury and Chairman of Canterbury's KMFM radio station, says:

"The value to the city of the spread of experience represented by the Festival Board is immense. Each director gives freely of his or her time, and time is one of the most valuable of gifts in this hectic world. Most of our Board meetings are at 7.45am because this is often the best and only time to get busy people together in the same room. I am hugely grateful for their advice over the 18 years I've been chairman."

Mark Deller explained:

"'As Festival Director there are two things, above all else, that I look for from my Board of Directors: one is to provide me with a secure financial base from which to operate (however modest that may be); the second is to give me, within that framework, the freedom to exercise my artistic judgement when it comes to programming. In both these areas I have been wonderfully supported throughout my time as Festival Director. Experience tells me that this is by no means always the case, so I'm well aware that both I and Canterbury are immensely fortunate.

"In addition, during the past year, the Festival was at the heart of the city's bid to become European Capital of Culture. Joining a number of other voluntary, educational and charitable organisations, they made up the Working Party which contributed to and vetted the much-praised Bid document produced by the city council. Chairman Peter Williams says: *"There is a very British tradition of voluntary work which often makes the wheels go round in some of the most difficult and delicate parts of our society. The Festival identified very early on that culture could and should be at the cutting edge of the regeneration of a region which is perceived as being prosperous but in fact has areas of huge deprivation...If the Festival is a success it's also because of a myriad of voluntary contributions made by men and women all over East Kent".*

While Mark Deller assembled the programme for 2003, the Festival also prepared to bid him farewell. The parting would take place at the cathedral's International Study Centre. The Festival's friends and advisers gave generously so that a cheque for £2,500 would be presented to him. We wanted to give Mark a personal gift that would remind him of his inspirational years as the Director of the Canterbury Festival. We felt that, had he not been such a talented musician, Mark Deller would have loved to have played cricket for Kent. Alas, Kent missed their chance, but, as a second-best, we bought Mark a life membership of the Kent County Cricket Club, giving him access to home matches and privileges at away games – plus, of course, as with all cricket watchers, the freedom and ability at close quarters to give wise advice on the state of play to anyone who cares to listen...

In the event, there were three farewell presentations to Mark and he pronounced himself "overwhelmed...by the generosity... and by the warmth and affection of all those who so kindly attended the occasions".[152]

I was sad to say goodbye on behalf of the Festival, but immensely grateful to him for his part in what had been achieved in the past 20 years. I was also moved to reveal a significant truth that evening: debates we had had in plenty, but neither of us 'did' arguments. We had, as I recall, never exchanged a cross word. That year, my chairman's message read:

'It is 15 years since Mark Deller became Director of the Canterbury Festival. This is the last Festival he will arrange and nurture into life and a string of clichés flash through my mind – among them *"this is the end of an era..."* and *"...things will never be the same again..."*, both of which thoughts are undoubtedly true because that is the overriding characteristic of all the best clichés.

'Over the last 15 years, and on a number of levels, my friend Mark

---

152. Personal letter, November 25th 2003

has been a brilliant Festival Director. First, and most obviously, the programmes he has put together for our pleasure have been so innovative and attractive that our box office takings and our audience figures have gone up and up and up. Second, the Festival has grown and flourished during his dedicated stewardship. Our turnover in his first year was just over £200,000; this year, it is close on £600,000. Third, he has fostered relationships, not only with our friends in the community, in business and in local government but also within the Festival itself. He has confirmed for us in the Financial Board that it is possible to satisfy artistic ambitions while recognising financial realities, and he has led an all-year-round Festival administration with drive and understanding.

'Fourth – but by no means the least important of his achievements – Mark has understood his audience. It was an American advertising executive who used to say when assessing the potential of a show or a product: "*Yes, but will it play in Peoria, Illinois?*" Mark's concerns have been less the taste of middle America and more what plays well in East Kent, from Broadstairs to Herne Bay, Whitstable to Faversham and, of course, in Canterbury itself. He loves this corner of England, which is hardly surprising because, as schoolboy, chorister, conductor, counter-tenor and Festival Director, he has given so much of his life to the well-being of our community. We thank him for the dedication from which we have all benefited.'

The Festivalgoers who examined their programmes before the curtain rose that year, read:

'As we sit here tonight, the Festival is in the middle of a handover period. Mark leaves at the end of the year; Rosie Turner, who was deputy director of the Belfast Festival, is already organising the 2004 Canterbury Festival, and has been '*shadowing*' Mark since August. We are delighted that Rosie has agreed to join us. We looked for quality and we know we have found her.

'Nothing, however wonderful, stays the same for ever. We must move on because to stand still is to stagnate. Yes, it *has* been good over the past 15 years. But we believe it's going to get even better. And, in wishing Mark Godspeed, we know you believe that too.'

Chilham Castle – where the Festival welcomed the Globe Theatre on its national tour, with the support of Stuart and Tessa Wheeler.

Festival Team 2012, Sylvianne Martell, Alison Chambers, Sarah Passfield, Amanda McKean, Rosie Turner, Stephanie Klinge-Davies, Kerry Barber

Rosie Turner, an inspirational Festival Director.

Festivals are fun!

Amanda McKean – at the heart of the Festival.

"Lean, mean Amanda McKean's" radio show

Rosie Turner Deputy Director Belfast Festival

Queen's University Belfast – home of the Belfast Festival

Chapter 13 – Team Rosie

Rosie Turner is a force of nature. From the first day in the job she led from the front and, like Mark Deller, she has the ability to survive nasty shocks while keeping her principles intact. It's called flexibility and, without it, the Canterbury Festival would not have survived.

There are other important attributes in a Festival Director that make the wheels turn smoothly – loyalty, dedication and flair, for instance – but flexibility minimises challenges that could become terminal. Rosie had not led a choir or formed a dance troupe, but she had run a festival in one of the most testing and turbulent environments one could imagine – Belfast. She had studied drama at Aberystwyth University in Wales and, born in Ireland in 1981, she had become a volunteer for the annual Belfast Festival. She had lectured on drama for 11 years before joining the Belfast Festival staff in 1992, rising to become Deputy Director. All this amid the troubles that blighted Northern Ireland for decade after decade. In short, she had been there, seen it and done it.

This was a woman who had had to work amid all the sectarian pressures in Belfast, in the knowledge that many of the disagreements in everyday living were settled by violence. Relatively speaking, the politics of Canterbury must have seemed a doddle. Much later, I asked Rosie how she had coped during her Belfast years with that extra, unique pressure. She said:

"We didn't avoid the controversy and we were helped because all sides throughout The Troubles seemed to accept that The Arts were above the conflict, that at least one aspect of life, if possible, should go on as normal. Only once can I remember being afraid and that was

when folk music became a political issue. Folk music and the stories it told, were history and heritage, and that was obviously a sensitive area. We ran a folk club throughout the festival. I remember sitting in the club one morning and watching the people come in to buy their tickets and realising how vulnerable we all were. Artists and audience. We had no security, no protection against men with guns. Keeping the club open was the right decision, by the way – but one man, one gun and, in seconds, a lot of people could have died. They never came, thank God."

The Belfast Festival was, in Rosie's words, *"a cultural beacon in very dark times"*. It was bigger than the Canterbury Festival; it had high-profile launches in London at the Post Office Tower (now BT Tower), in Belfast and in Dublin and Glasgow. It had an international reputation. It was, after all, one of the few shafts of good news to emerge from Northern Ireland for decades. Two years before she wrote to Canterbury, as deputy director she had applied for the position of Director in Belfast. She didn't get the job. She was hungry for a chance to develop her own ideas. Her research would have indicated that, paradoxically, the Canterbury Festival was more vulnerable because of uncertain finance than what she was used to in Belfast. There, the Festival was run and protected by the university. In Belfast, she enjoyed the comfort of a budget built on donations of £150,000 a year from the brewers of Guinness and £50,000 a year from British Telecom. This was an enviable certainty that she would miss in Canterbury. Rosie's first impressions of Canterbury are enlightening:

"I remember, in those first few weeks, realising that the Festival in Canterbury operated in a cocoon – cathedral, history, university. It was like All Gas and Gaiters, *all very English; cucumber sandwiches and a stroll on the Deanery lawn. I knew nobody here – but supporters opened their homes after concerts and, quite early on,*

I met the Great and the Good at Audrey Eyton's house.[153] *There were no huge companies giving large sponsorships and expecting, demanding a marketing return on every pound they committed. Canterbury seemed to rely on philanthropy, a community eagerness to make the Festival work, whereas in Belfast philanthropy was virtually non-existent."*

Rosie's second impression was that, in Canterbury, the Festival, though important, was not seen as pivotal. In Belfast, it had been literally vital; it was tangible evidence to the world that the Belfast community was still alive, still functioning. Rosie says:

"I realised that, in contrast to Belfast, in Canterbury every pound of sponsorship was a minor victory. I remember in a conversation quite early on, asking a Board member what we did if, after all our financial forecasting, we made a loss. He said: 'Go to the bank and see if we can get a loan'. That required, from me, a different mindset as we considered our programming."

And thirdly, as she considered this different way of operating, *"I realised that one of the major avenues I had always used to achieve success, was closed to me. The media had always given the Belfast Festival a high profile. We had a radio slot every day, our press conferences were televised, there was constant press activity. That wasn't the case in Canterbury. However hard we worked and however cooperative the* Kent Messengers *were,*[154] *there simply weren't the outlets. However famous Canterbury was for being Canterbury, it was not 'national' in the way that Belfast represented Northern Ireland."*

Rosie assessed the audience she was now serving. It was predominantly elderly. She set out to attract younger supporters,

---

153. Audrey Eyton, author of the best-selling *The F-Plan Diet*, lived in Blackfriars Street on the banks of the River Stour. A Festival Vice-President for many years.
154. Kent's local newspaper group of weekly and regional editions, which supported the revival of the Festival from the outset through Edwin Boorman, Bill Dorrell and, later, Geraldine Allinson.

family groups and students, even though, as she said, all the evidence from previous years was that "*they were not our natural market*". And, if the Festival could be accused in any way of being elitist, she pointed out that, in sporting terms, 'elite' was a compliment. Why should that positive interpretation not also apply to the arts? The description '*Kent's International Arts Festival*' was Rosie's invention, seeking to spread the Festival's wings and to draw interest (and funding) from the city council and Kent County Council. The tag line '*Bringing the World to Canterbury and showing Canterbury to the rest of the World*' was calculated to reassure local artists and performers that the Festival was not turning its back on them.

It was also obvious from the outset that Rosie believed in the team ethos. Her team, when she took over, were Sylviane Martell, in charge of the office and The Friends; Bob Messer, finance; Jo Tuffs, marketing and publicity; Jessica Healey, Festival assistant; Peter Cox, technical matters, and Amanda McKean, who was responsible for fund-raising and sponsorship.

Jo Tuffs soon left after 11 good years with the Festival, to become director of the Broadstairs Folk Festival and Rosie, in a mild reshuffle, widened Amanda's brief by promoting her to Development Officer. The Festival has benefited hugely from this working relationship between Amanda and Rosie. I recall an early conversation between Amanda and Jo Tuffs before she left. Amanda asked Jo how long she had been working for the Festival. She replied: "*Eleven years*". Amanda raised an eyebrow: "*How have you managed to work in the same place for so long?*" As I write, Amanda is now on her 19th year devoted to the Canterbury Festival. Her reaction simply reflected the peripatetic nature of her earlier life. She had worked in Saudi Arabia, France and the USA. She had run her own T-shirt business, recruited students for language schools and, in France, had had her own radio show, Riviera Requests, with '*lean, mean Amanda McKean*'.

Amanda's French connections pursued her to Canterbury. One of her initial challenges was to be interviewed for radio by a representative of Découverte Mutuelle Artois-Kent. She was questioned about the transition from Mark to Rosie as Festival Director. Of Mark, she said: *"We still see him regularly for lunch. He has so much musical knowledge...he's well loved and he had just become a grandfather for the first time so he visits baby Ben and family in Bath"*. Of Rosie, she said: *"She's a very dynamic lady. She brings with her from Belfast a wealth of knowledge and experience. She has settled into her life in Kent with great ease, making a lot of friends in a short time"*. How had the transition been accomplished? *"Smoothly"*.

In South Africa, where she lived for a while when her mother was ill, Amanda had run a two-day arts festival at Marionhill, near Durban, from a big top. *"We broke even..."*, all of which prepared her for a key role in the development of the Canterbury Festival. She had learned of the vacancy in the team through Sheelagh Deller, Mark's former wife, with whom she had made friends when they had both worked at a Canterbury language school. Rosie interviewed her for the job, I met her, and the job was hers. The team ethic has always been vital to the Festival's success; Rosie and Amanda regularly visit other festivals to spot emerging talent and, on one occasion, the entire team went with them to Edinburgh – accountant, John Biffen; programme assistants, Meg Williams and John Prebble, and Amanda and Rosie. They stayed in student accommodation at the Kenneth McKenzie suites and met at breakfast each day to review the acts they had watched the previous day. The very first report that Rosie gave to the Festival Board on April 28th 2004 foreshadowed the success she was to be as Director at the Canterbury Festival. It outlined a further step towards forging a long-standing relationship with Canterbury Christ Church University and it contained her first thoughts on commissioning a community opera from scratch. Both these initiatives would have a profound impact on the growing reputation and the stability of the Festival. Rosie wrote:

'The community opera will be called The Promised Land[155] and will be based on the story of the Kent coalfields, an extraordinary sociological experiment which, in the 1920s and 30s, brought to Kent thousands of miners and their families from Scotland, Wales and Northern England. The first New Town in Britain, 'Aylesham', was built to accommodate them, and its streets rang with their music, dance and accents for sixty years. In 1987, the collieries were shut – leaving a population of four thousand people displaced, disenchanted and devastated. The tragic story of their odyssey to "the promised land" and its subsequent destruction is uplifted by the feisty, indomitable spirit of this unique community and robustly celebrated through music, song and archive footage by their descendants and those throughout Kent who remember them.

'The opera will involve a mixture of 300 professional, amateur and community participants. An accompanying Education and Outreach programme will support the performance, which will run for one week of the Canterbury Festival in the Marlowe Theatre. An audience of over nine thousand is anticipated.'

And that was almost exactly how it would turn out in the Marlowe Theatre, nearly two-and-a-half years later, as I will detail in the next chapter.

Rosie has vivid memories of the "scramble" to get together a concept and a budget for the opera:

"We had about a week to give a fairly detailed outline to the city's Capital of Culture bid. Peter put forward the idea of the Kent coal mining community in a wartime context and I remember thinking: 'What coalmines… where?' I didn't even know there was a coalmine in Kent!"

Rosie's second observation in that report would foreshadow the Festival's burgeoning relationship with Canterbury Christ Church

---

155. Promised Land, DVD, is available from the Canterbury Festival Office or from Peter Williams Television (peter@pwtv. co.uk) at £10.00

University. This would, she said, become the Festival's "first Artistic Partnership". It was strengthened when Rosie was invited to open the University's new art gallery in March 2004. Six years later, largely due to the link with Christ Church, the Canterbury Festival would move into a home of its own at 8 Orange Street next to the city's new Marlowe Theatre. It would be called Festival House. But, again, we're getting ahead of ourselves...

This key partnership with Canterbury Christ Church developed quite quickly. This was a university, perhaps seen by some as the also ran or new university, eager to establish itself a base for artistic excellence in the city and to associate itself with a more youthful, artsy, risky festival to attract more students. This brought much needed funding to the Festival and, I believe, the first five-year partnership between an English university and an arts festival. Queen's in Belfast had given Rosie the model and the experience and the Arts Council were quick to recognise the potential of this university partnership. Rosie believes *"they were also keen to support 'the new girl' in her plans to reposition and democratise the Canterbury Festival"*. Regular funding followed and support to restructure and professionalise the Festival team led to the development of a staff of seven working year-round, delivering projects for young people and communities, as well as the annual Festival. The Festival fortnight is 'the engine' which drives the year-round work of free arts in the community; it is also perhaps the most fundable part of what the Festival does.

Rosie also set herself a target to reposition the Festival among its peers. She joined the board of BAFA[156] and, after a couple of years, became its first female chair. The annual conference brought festival directors and staff from all over the UK to the Canterbury Festival and, as Rosie noted, *"put us firmly on the map"*.

She produced an excellent Festival in 2004, with a Hungarian flavour. Victor Orban, the President of Hungary, which had joined the European Union the previous year, attended a Balla Demeter exhibition and the Festival's closing concert in the Cathedral. Alex

---

156. British Arts Festivals Association

de Gelsey, who lived in our village[157] and was Hungary's attaché in the UK, helped to broker the visit, and Rosie wrote: *"It is important that Canterbury is recognised as an important cultural centre where exciting and newsworthy events take place...this is an important international partnership and it will spotlight us in the national press in a positive manner."* It did. In addition, the Hungarians made substantial financial contributions to the events in which they were involved, buttressing the Festival's economic stability.

The Philharmonia Orchestra returned to Canterbury after a gap of 20 years. This, too, presaged a lasting partnership between the city and one of the nation's leading orchestras, so much so, that it would lead to the Philharmonia embarking on an annual series of concerts at the Marlowe Theatre and to their treating Canterbury as their second home. The link with the University of Kent flourished through the relationship with its inspirational Director of music, Sue Wanless, and through the Festival's music bursary scheme. A second Artistic Partnership was formalised with the Dean and Chapter of the Cathedral. In June 2004, a new Festival Foundation was set up 'to give the Festival a firmer financial base, with funds provided from legacies and large donations'. The Foundation would be a charitable trust, separate from the CTFT, and the incorporation of The Friends organisation into the Foundation would enable The Friends also to have charitable status. Richard Sturt and David Pentin had worked hard on this amalgamation and the Foundation's aim was agreed as being *'to promote and support the charitable purposes of the Canterbury Theatre and Festival Trust'*. The cheque signatories were Friends chair Alan Bull, John Harris, Rosie Turner and Sylviane Martell, the Foundation's secretary and treasurer, whose links with France had been so valuable both to the Festival and to The Friends organisation. The Foundation would prove, years later in 2010, to be the avenue through which the Festival would secure a permanent home.

We held confidential meetings that summer with Allan Willett at which he made an annual three-year commitment to

---

157   Boughton-under-Blean, Kent

the Festival of around £20,000. When the city council team of Colin Carmichael (chief executive), Janice McGuinness (arts and culture) and David Pratley (architect) joined that meeting, Allan agreed to give £40,000 over two years to fund the feasibility study to explore the possible sites of a new theatre/concert hall. I reminded that meeting that it was the Festival Board's unanimous view that, in seeking a solution to this ongoing debate, "*it was vital for Canterbury to retain its theatre*" and that "*the opportunity for this development could be lost if there were wrangling over which site and which option should be chosen*". We were fortunate that the city council were as eager as we were to keep a theatre in the city. The meeting agreed that a "*strategic view of how the city should move forward...was needed*" and as quickly as possible.[158]

Hungary joined the European Union in May that year and, to mark the occasion, we welcomed the Hungarian ambassador, Ferenc Mádl, to the final concert, Magyar Magic, with the Budapest Tomkins Choir, the Canterbury Choral Society and the Canterbury Philharmonic Orchestra, conducted by Richard Cooke. Rosie produced an excellent programme for that year's Festival, including the world première of Maha Maya, a concert of Sir John Tavener's music, in the cathedral quire. The Festival celebrated 10 years since the return of democracy to South Africa with the European première of *Cry, the Beloved Country*, graced by the Soweto Gospel Choir. It also embraced the Cottle and Austen Circus with its big top and high jinks. The Trust's annual report praised the new Festival Director and noted that the 2004 Festival had produced '*a working surplus which will enable the Festival Trust to achieve a number of ambitions*'. For Rosie Turner, in her first year, it was a triumph.

The advantage of having bid to become the Capital of Culture was becoming more and more apparent. The consolation prize for each of those cities which had failed – there were 11 of them – would be an award from central government of a total of £11 million. The winners, Liverpool, would receive £4 million. But

158. CTFT council, November 24th 2003

the judges were so impressed by the initiatives put forward by the 11 losers, including Canterbury, that they wished to encourage them to go ahead with some of their plans. The community opera, *Promised Land*, was firmly on that list. The Festival felt there was 'a good chance (financially) of receiving something',[159] and held its breath.

Rosie Turner reported to the Board on her first year. She felt that the previous year had marked a pinnacle in the Festival's achievement. Turnover had reached an all-time high of over £1/2 million, and, due to two sell-out concerts by Van Morrison, box office income had totalled £180,000. The 2004 Festival had achieved a surplus of £95,749. It was a comfortable and unfamiliar position for the Festival to find itself. Rosie reflected:

"As a new Director, following Mark Deller's retirement after twenty years in post, I felt it was important to review and restate the Festival's mission and aims, in pursuit of which all our practice flows. It is against these, and the objectives set out in the Three Year Plan, that I evaluate the 2004 Festival. Unexpectedly, within months of my arrival, the anticipated level of sponsorship had plummeted by almost 40%. That, coupled with an artistic refocusing on new work, and events for younger audiences, dictated a more restrained approach to expenditure, and although support from core funders showed a slight increase, and the Festival was successful in attracting finance from two significant new sources, Creative Partnerships Kent and the Allan Willett Foundation, the anticipated growth from the 2003 position was not possible. I felt I had to be extremely cautious in programming. Not only was I unfamiliar with the audience so I could not confidently predict the box office, but we were also striving to achieve a number of risky goals – commissioning new works, hosting world premieres, attracting national interest and appealing to younger and more diverse audiences."[160]

---

159. CTFT minutes, November 29th 2004
160. Conversation with author, November 2004

The goals for the 2005 Festival remained much the same, she said, and she cautiously forecast a small surplus.

Rosie and I were both members of the local Arts Steering Group and we agreed the importance of continuing to give priority to the future of the Marlowe Theatre.[161] It would also be the year in which the Festival became committed to the community opera, *Promised Land*. Janice McGuinness, the city council's arts officer who would become the council's assistant director of all its commissioned services, brought the significant news that the Festival would, after all, be granted from the Capital of Culture funding, £100,000 towards the cost of producing the community opera, as well as £27,000 to support a composer's competition. The city council would financially support 19 projects in all with the money resulting from Canterbury's unsuccessful bid to become Capital of Culture, and the Festival was one of the major beneficiaries. But the financial challenge to the Festival Trust of these two projects was enormous and our treasurer, David Pentin, fired a warning shot:

"It seems we have been offered a total of £127,000 (£100,000 + £27,000) from the Culture and Communications Division of CCC[162] towards these projects. However, am I correct in assuming that the Canterbury Festival's own projected contribution to both projects is estimated to be £180,000 (£153,000 + £27,000)? Also, do we hope to raise all this in sponsorship?

"If so, this looks to be a very tall order indeed. I know we have set aside £20,000 from the 2004 profits to put towards the Composer Competition just in case our sponsorship for this event does not materialise. If everything goes to plan, this would leave us with the balance of £7,000 for this event but nothing to go towards the remaining requirement of £153,000 by 2006. As our total sponsorship income for the whole Festival was £97,000 last year, it will obviously

---

161. A working group from Canterbury visited a number of different theatres in the UK to inform views on what the new Marlowe Theatre could and should provide

162. Canterbury City Council

need a lot of productive work on Amanda's[163] part to reach the target figure required of £180,000, in addition to a 2005 Budget figure of £140,000 for sponsorship to back our normal activities."[164]

It was a timely warning intended to focus the trustees' minds on their responsibilities when supporting the Festival Director in this ambitious programme. It was also typical of David who, more than anyone else, was always very clear about what trustees in positions of authority in charitable organisations can and cannot do. I took David's concerns to the Board:

"The community opera is a huge commitment for 2006, and the Marlowe Theatre has been booked for three performances to launch the 2006 Festival. As you know, we are taking the story of the East Kent coalfield as our theme and there are a number of issues I need to share with you. One, the project is understandably home-based – librettist Michael Irwin, composer Mark Dougherty, and myself. Rosie has a rudimentary budget, for your information.

"In detail, I shall receive no money for the work I do because to do so would potentially infringe my status as a trustee. Mark is Rosie's husband but, though we need to note this, I do not believe that it should affect our desire to embrace him in our creative team; musically, we are fortunate to have him on board – which, of course, also applies to Michael Irwin, an experienced librettist and translator and a long-time friend of the Festival. I am happy, however, to hear your views on this…"

I was asking the Board whether the arrangements for the community opera were too cosy. They approved the arrangements.

The underlying theme of the 2005 Festival would be war and peace, *"explored in an uplifting and inspirational way across the art forms"*. It reflected the anniversaries of Tallis, Tippett, the Battle of Trafalgar and the end of World War II in Europe. However, the

---

163. Amanda McKean is a brilliant fund-raiser; she would become Deputy Director of the Festival
164. Confidential letter to Festival Director, copied to me

programme's accent was on having fun and the Festival began with singing in the streets on the opening Saturday and finished in true Irish style with a ceilidh on the final night. Jo Brand and Chris James made us laugh; George Melly, Ray Davies and Michael Nyman brought their different musical talents to entertain us and, in the tiny St Mary's Hall studio theatre in Northgate, Michael Morpurgo's *Private Peaceful* moved us to tears. The Festival also managed to avoid a court action when one of its banners fell on the roof of a car. The settlement involved a 'without prejudice' payment of £500 to the victim.

The 2005 Festival made a surplus yet again. Nevertheless, throughout 2005, two major themes dominated – the need for a clear decision on the future and siting of a bigger Marlowe Theatre and the Festival's ambitious commitment to produce the *Promised Land* community opera.

In the autumn of that year, a commitment by members of the city council clarified the debate over the Marlowe. The new theatre would be on the site of the current theatre. All interested parties met and gave their support, both implicit and explicit. The cost of the new theatre was estimated at £24 million. Canterbury City Council, who owned the site, unanimously committed £8 million to the development of the theatre, which was a huge and brave pledge for a district council to make. Harry Cragg, a member of the Festival Council and a leading city councillor, reported that SEEDA[165] had offered "up-front support" and he hoped that "building land could be acquired so that the new theatre would be alongside the River Stour". The Marlowe Theatre would be closed for 18 weeks while the adaptation and renovation took place.[166]

The Festival had been at the heart of these discussions for nearly 10 years. It was a major step forward. We maintained the strength of our financial voice by appointing accountant, David Pentin, as vice-chairman to succeed James Bird, who had served the Festival loyally for many years. Camilla Swire and the cathedral's receiver

---

165. South East England Development Agency
166. CTFT minutes, annual meeting, April 26th 2005

general, John Meardon, were now members of the Board, as was Professor Keith Mander from the University of Kent, who would go on to chair the Trust for many years. John Harris succeeded Alan Bull as chair of the Festival Friends organisation. It seemed like an adjustment of governance; in fact, it was a rearrangement of trusted friends who shared a unity of purpose.

The Festival continued to flourish. In 2008, it went back to its roots, reinvigorating its links with the cathedral with a new work by Sebastian Barry titled *Dallas Sweetman*. It told the story of a pilgrim driven to justify the actions of his life. It attracted national praise and, overall, more than 75,000 people attended Festival events. Rosie describes the commissioning of *Dallas Sweetman* as *"possibly the most exciting time artistically for me. The Cathedral Plays tradition was a deciding factor in my choosing to apply to Canterbury Festival and I came with the ambition to revive the practice. All my skills in raising money, generating national interest, drawing on my theatre and literary experience and contacts, and exciting the local audience were needed to get the project funded and up and running and I was extremely proud of the result. It wasn't a perfect piece of theatre – it was very wordy and lacked visual splendour – but it helped that the playwright was simultaneously nominated for the Booker Prize and attracted our longed-for national press coverage. Cathedrals are not theatres – and despite state-of-the-art sound enhancement and the staging, I felt the drama would have been better served in a conventional theatre space than in the cavernous nave.*

"That said, Barry's work was poetic, it was brilliantly acted and directed, and the fact that the story referenced Canterbury Cathedral as a location made it very special. A career highlight for me occurred when one of the shepherds at the Cathedral told me later that a visitor has asked for directions to the final resting place of Dallas Sweetman, not realising that he was, in fact, entirely fictional!"

What Rosie Turner said about events in the cathedral echoed the views that Dean George Bell had expressed 80 years earlier, and this was the beginning of a period of spectacular progress. In 2010, we welcomed the Moscow Radio Symphony Orchestra (now Tchaikovsky Symphony Orchestra) and, in 2011, the Soweto Gospel Choir entranced a packed cathedral in the Festival's opening concert. The following year, the traditional Opening Day parade successfully moved to midday, which met with Canterbury's approval, and a returning Van Morrison was again a sell-out. A new venue, the Spiegeltent on the Kent County Cricket Club ground, added excitement to the 2013 Festival – attracting a fresh, younger audience – and the balance between this and the fine arts in the rest of the Festival worked very well. Customers always write and, in 2014, we received the following:

'I can't quite put my finger on it, but my impression of this year's festival was that it had significantly grown in maturity, stature and presentation. To say that the Canterbury Festival punches above its weight would be an understatement. The breadth and quality of performance that I saw/heard during the fortnight was staggering, and emotionally powerful.'

Rosie summed up the 2015 Festival as "vintage" and, in achieving a surplus of £30,000, confirmed the success of her policy of placing one key event each night to "avoid conflicting with ourselves as we have sometimes done in the past". The Festival played a key role in bringing the Globe Theatre company to Chilham Castle in 2016 and the Director's report stressed the work the Festival did with the younger generation through school concerts and its bursary scheme that encouraged budding musicians.

The following year in 2017, the Festival welcomed Tasmin Little, Mary Black, Imelda May, Freddy Kempf and the Tenebrae Choir; it was a joy. Partnerships flourished with Canterbury Christ Church University, Tony Pratt at the Canterbury Auction Galleries, Kent College and Paul Roberts, and in 2018 a star-studded Festival included Sir Bryn Terfel, Sophie Ellis-Bextor, the King's Singers and Evelyn Glennie. This was the year however, when the world was again gripped by financial crisis. Nearly $7 trillion was wiped off stocks in the financial markets.[167] The Festival lost core funding from the Arts Council, Canterbury City Council and Kent County Council. Major stores in Canterbury's High Street closed and the Festival suffered a small deficit for the first time in years. The speigeltent would later become a casualty of the necessary economies and funding now depended entirely on the attraction to sponsors of events and projects; it was an unexpected and unwelcome challenge. The Festival decided on a fresh venture to open its own box office to sell its, and others', tickets. It was to prove a great success.

Despite the financial difficulties, the Festival's involvement with youngsters was maintained. One of the Festival's goals is to see that *'every child and young person has the opportunity to experience the richness of the arts'*. To that end, access to the Festival events has been enhanced on its new website, optimised for tablets and phones.[168] Audio and digital versions of the brochure have been produced since 2017. The Festival has granted 100 arts awards a year across 41 Kent schools, many of them in the most deprived sections of the county.[169] It encourages young talent in drama and comedy, promoting art exhibitions and engaging teachers in propagating the arts. The endorsement from those taking part is, and has been, encouraging: *'A fantastic experience for the children...they loved working with the artists and were so proud to be part of the Festival's opening parade'*, to quote a letter from Petham Primary School.

In a single year, Festival funding enabled six primary education degree students at Canterbury Christ Church University to train as advisers for 'Discovery' certification. Finances may have been tight, but the encouragement of young people, the next generation of audiences and, we hope, festivalgoers, will always be a priority.

Covid struck in 2020, but the Festival followed the adage 'the show must go on' and produced a pared-down programme which was loyally supported, to the extent that it broke even financially. At the end of it, Rosie Turner thanked the Festival 'family' of

167.   Reuters, December 20th 2018
168.   In its first year, visits to the Festival website increased by 10,000
169.   Eight of Kent's most deprived wards are in the Canterbury district

volunteers, staff and patrons: "*You have proved your loyalty, your bravery, your generosity and your sheer determination to enjoy yourselves by donning masks, forsaking interval drinks and keeping your distance to support the Festival.*"

Festivals during the pandemic were tough to organise and an act of faith, for both the Festival team and for those who trod softly, breathed carefully and sat separately to enjoy and ensure the survival of something they loved. Nor was there a loss of quality – how could there be with the Tenebrae Choir, Joanna MacGregor, Barbara Dickson and The Kingdom Choir on the cast list? The Really Promising Company came together again to produce *The Parting Glass*, a tribute to Mark Dougherty, musical director of *Riverdance* and composer and MD of *Promised Land*, who sadly died in 2020. It was a bittersweet evening. It took place in Kent College's Great Hall, a magnificent 550-seat addition to the venues now available to the Festival. It revived in a completely new setting memories of a past triumph. We also welcomed and used The King's School's beautifully built Malthouse Theatre in the heart of the city on the former site of Barretts motor company, now relocated to the city's industrial suburbs. Technology enabled the Festival to reach those supporters unable to attend events. The Tenebrae Choir's concert was beamed on-line from the cathedral's nave,[170] as was the Young Musicians' Bursary concert, a talk by Bettany Hughes and the adult poetry competition.

The Festival's determination during the COVID-19 crisis did not go unnoticed. Arts Council England commented "*how brave*" the Festival was to keep going amid the COVID-19 restrictions. As its president, and therefore no longer involved in decision-making, I was more than happy to agree with that assessment. It was typical of the reasons why the revived Canterbury Festival had flourished under Rosie and her team and the chairmanship of Keith Mander.

---

170. With 2-metres of social distancing necessary, the audience that could be accommodated in the cathedral was reduced from more than a thousand to 200

Director Syd Ralph – "It was one of the most satisfying and moving experiences of my life."

Michael Irwin, professor, librettist, and in at the birth of the modern Canterbury Festival.

Mark Dougherty leads a rehearsal for Promised Land.

*Promised Land – rehearsals for an inspirational community opera,
set in the heart of Kent.*

Chapter 14 – Promised Land

The idea for *Promised Land*, the community opera commissioned and performed in the Canterbury Festival of 2006, was 40 years in its gestation. I came to Kent in the 1970s and during the first six months, I clearly remember noting that the unique story of the Kent coalfield had never been properly documented. On reflection, that is an understatement because, at first, I was completely unaware that a coalmine even existed in Kent Throughout a long career making documentaries for the major networks in the UK and overseas, I tried from time to time to persuade the major channels – BBC, ITV, Channel 4, Discovery and others – to commission a film on a century of coal in Kent.

There were no takers.

But the idea, the conviction that this was a story that needed telling, never went away. The talk of a community opera provided an opportunity to pitch it again – and Festival Director, Rosie Turner, liked the idea. The title *Promised Land* metamorphosed from a number of fledgling identities. Its first title was *When the Dust Settles*. Then it became *The Black Hut*, to be centred on a multipurpose building in the heart of a Kent community, which would alter its shape as the action on stage dictated. Strategically, however, the direction of the piece never wavered. The original brief I sent to Rosie, read:

'*There, amid the hops and fruit of East Kent, were accents that echoed my childhood in South Wales. Voices from the Rhondda, in conversation with others from Nottingham and Scotland, Durham and, of course, Kent.*'

Promised Land emerged quite early on. It had community and biblical connotations and echoes of Lloyd George's pledge at the end of World War I, to create a land fit for heroes. The uniqueness of Kent's mining community, centred on the village of Aylesham, provided the context and the tension that drove the plot. Here was a group of people, gathered from every corner of industrial Britain, trying to settle in a predominantly agricultural county. Setting the story during World War II added to that tension. The partnership on which the creation of the opera rested was that between composer, Mark Dougherty, and librettist, Michael Irwin. Mark Dougherty said:

"The mystery surrounding the creation of a piece of music is something many people regard with awe. But really, like a chef, a potter or a carpenter, I find that the essential starting point is with the raw ingredients. The stricter the parameters imposed by the commission, the easier I find it to generate material, and therefore to get the ball rolling. So when writing a piece for the theatre, on a specific subject and for a cast of 100 people from East Kent, there were several obvious places from which to start. There is a story to be told, and it is the job of the music to steer the emotional journey of the piece. The production's budget will largely determine the size of orchestra, and therefore the limitations on which combination of instruments to choose.

"One of the most important requirements of a community project is that it creates opportunities for all of the participants to be challenged. Some people will have experience of performing, others will not – and so in discussing the libretto with Michael Irwin, I want to make sure that there are plenty of individual parts, plenty of solo lines and enough to keep the wide variety of performers engaged. We want both big epic pictures of Kent featuring the full cast, and more intimate scenes where we can explore specific relationships and personal opinions."

Michael Irwin said:

"East Kent has been home to a number of working communities, often mutually suspicious as they strove to make a living from the same patch of land. *Promised Land* will be a dramatized account of two such occupations – hop-growing, a local tradition for hundreds of years, and coal-mining, which was introduced only in the 19th century. It will follow the decline of both ways of life, as technology changed and the economic winds shifted.

"In their different ways, both involved immigration. The Kentish coalfields drew recruits from older pits in Wales, Northumberland and elsewhere. The hop-harvest depended on an annual influx of cheap labour from London. Although the in-comers contributed a good deal to the local economy they often felt themselves to be unwelcome – as is true of their successors today."

My contribution was pretty much what I wrote at the beginning of this chapter. I added a quote from Richard Church:[171] "Everything that has happened to the English people has happened to the people of Kent first...Kentish folk have been the watchers at the door."

We had a series of meetings, the three of us. I still have the note from Mark Dougherty who, knowing my inexperience in his specialist field, sent me a paper entitled 'How to Write a Musical'. It made excellent sense, as the following extracts illustrate:

'Good songs are not enough. Is your story compelling – and how compelled are you to tell it? Do you care deeply about it, so deeply that you must tell the story, or die?...Show, don't tell – please don't tell me what your characters are; let their actions show us!...Cut everything that is not essential...kill your 'darlings',[172] because every character, song, word and gesture has to serve a clear, dramatic purpose...open the show with a 'kick-arse song'.' The note ended with a quote from Patricia Routledge about what we were trying to create:

"It's a risk...but once you're willing to risk everything, you can accomplish anything."

---

171. Portrait of Canterbury, Richard Church, Hutchinson, 1953
172. 'Darlings' – favourite character or language

We considered inserting a real-life hero into the script – Bob Stanford Tuck, a British ace Spitfire pilot in the Battle of Britain who destroyed more than 30 enemy aircraft in combat. He had survived the war despite twice being shot down and had settled into life as a farmer near Deal. It was a seductive thought – and we rejected it. Better to go with characters who represented the story line. There's a signpost near Betteshanger indicating the way to two adjoining villages, Ashley and Studdal. 'Ashley Studdal' became one of the opera's draft protagonists.

In the months that followed, Mark and Michael Irwin honed and polished words and music to produce an opera that spanned more than half a century, embracing the influx of miners to Kent, World War II and the fear of invasion, the Battle of Britain, the miners' strike against the Thatcher government and the closure of all the Kent pits. At the end of the process, Michael Irwin said:

"*Promised Land* is founded on a fictitious family saga that draws locals and newcomers into an uneasy tangle of relationships. It spans a period from the Second World War to the late eighties and is bracketed by two strikes, one in 1941, in which the miners prevailed, and the other in 1984–5, which proved no more than a prelude to the closure of the last of the Kent coalfields. Through the same period, the old hop-growing traditions were superseded and our summer landscape changed. There was a need for new modes of employment, new ways of life, new 'communities'..."

Mark Dougherty said:

"I like melodies and tunes that people can hum; I make no apology for this. Luckily, the elitist view that once existed in academic circles – that a good tune relegates a composition to the shabby world of *entertainment* rather than the boundary breaking world of contemporary (or '*important*') music – seems to have somewhat diffused.

"Like a good film score, the essence of a project like this community opera is that music supports the action on stage and complements the moods, feelings and characters of the piece. If it doesn't do this, then the composer has failed. I have intentionally incorporated a variety of styles into this score – from the folk tune pastiches in Act 2, to big romantic melodies in the arias, to the use of a more musical theatre 'groove' against which the dialogue and story can be conveyed in the form of a sung conversation – traditionally *recitative*. Michael's wonderful rhythmic writing at times almost sang itself, so while the compositional process was a long one – it was never arduous."

I observed, quite objectively of course: "It's bloody marvellous!"

The concept was now a structure, but it had to be delivered. Syd Ralph, talented and experienced, was chosen to direct *Promised Land*. She had worked with Mark Deller in previous festivals; we admired her work with youth theatre musicals in Kent.

Syd, now living in Northern Ireland, has warm memories of *Promised Land*. She has a DVD of it and, every so often, watches it even now because it was "such an extraordinary experience". For a woman who has directed at the Young Vic Theatre, the Savoy Theatre and the Royal Opera House and, in 2016, was awarded the MBE for her work as a writer and director of youth theatre musicals, this is a considerable accolade. I asked her what made *Promised Land* so remarkable. "It was terrifying...exciting...and warm. It was the warmth that permeated the production that made it stand out – so many people working so hard for me."

Why 'terrifying'? "Well, I had read the script, come to Canterbury and climbed hundreds of stairs to the Festival office above the Christ Church Gate and been interviewed by you and Mark and Rosie, and then realised the size of the cast, the hundreds of people, amateur and professional, who were going to have to make this thing work. That was terrifying."

Nor did she know anything about coalmining. Because she felt she needed to understand better the life in a mining community, both below and above ground, she went down The Big Pit in South Wales. She suffers from claustrophobia. "Dropping down in the cage, I felt we were on our way to the end of the world. That was terrifying too." But rewarding. "I got an inkling of what these men went through to bring us warmth and prosperity."

She built a team around her – choreographer, Paul Madden, with whom she had worked on a production inside Wandsworth

Prison; designer, Gary McCann and lighting director, Colin Grenfell. There were production meetings and script conferences, in London and Canterbury: "I felt it was important to emphasise the humanity in Michael's script, so that the audience cared about the Bateson family and the Joneses, as well as following the story line of the plot."

The opera, set in 1942, spans more than 50 years. The tension in the plot centres on the relationship between workers in the 'new' industry, coal mining, and those who traditionally made their living from the land, particularly through cultivation and the gathering of hops.[173] Kent, like the rest of Britain, is under siege. A nurse and a wounded fighter pilot fall in love, but they do so across a divide because he is a farmer's son and she is a miner's daughter. The resulting family entanglements and hostilities take place during a period in which the established industries of coal mining and hop farming fade in importance. Through war and peace, changing technology and shifting politics, the characters strive to dig out a decent living from this tip of England, in the sunlit hop gardens or the dark industrial world of the coalmine.

The cast would number more than 100. Syd and Rosie pondered how best to recruit them. Syd says: "in the end, we decided that anyone who wanted to be in it, could be in it." They held auditions; seeking talent in singing, dance, comedy and sheer presence. More than 200 people turned up. Among the cast chosen were our treasurer and later, chairman, David Pentin, soon to become the city's mayor, and John Brazier, Kent County Council's arts officer. They began to rehearse in St Peter's Church hall. The devotion of the cast to the opera was total. Their ages ranged from three seven-year-olds to 11 members who were between 70 and 88. This is how they spent a typical Sunday, March 5th 2006, to be precise. Auditions were still ongoing:

---

173. The details of Promised Land are set out in Appendix 7

9.00am:	Practitioners and Canterbury staff arrive
9.30am:	Applicants arrive to be registered
9.50am:	Rosie to address everyone
9.55am:	Michael to address everyone
10–11.30am:	Mark to work with everyone in main hall
11.45–12.30pm:	Paul to do movement warm-up with everyone in main hall (*Mark doing pm solo audition rota*)
12.30–1pm:	Syd to work with everyone in main hall
1–1.45pm:	Lunch break
1.30–2pm:	Syd to work with all 14-yr-olds and under in upstairs room
1–1.45pm:	Everyone else to gather in main hall for announcing afternoon timetable
2–2.50pm:	Group A (with Paul – main hall)
	Group B (with Syd – upstairs room)
	Group C (with Rich for data + N/A gathering Mark taking individual auditionees from this group)
3–3.50pm:	Group C (with Paul – main hall)
	Group A (with Syd – upstairs room)
	Group B (with Rich for data + N/A gathering Mark taking individual auditionees from this group)
4–4.45pm:	Group B (with Paul – main hall)
	Group C (with Syd – upstairs room)
	Group A (with Rich for data + N/A gathering Mark taking individual auditionees from this group)
4.45pm:	Announcement of rehearsal and performance dates
5pm:	End of day

In the summer of 2006, they rehearsed twice a week. The principle singers, the professionals, were now on board – John Upperton, Trevor Alexander, Ian McLarnon, Liza Pulman, Richard Morris, Anthony Hawgood and Peter Cox. Former cathedral chorister, Jacob Austen, was plucked from Canterbury's St Edmund's School to play the youngster, Sam. Syd says: "This melding of professional and amateur was, potentially, a difficult time when much could have gone wrong – but the professionals and the amateurs respected each others' skills."

One tricky scene depicted the miners emerging from the pit and taking a shower before leaving for their homes. One does not shower fully clothed and the men playing the miners were informed that they would have to strip for the scene. They would, however, be able to wear flesh-coloured jockstraps. In a mixed group, this caused considerable hilarity. One 'miner' immediately stripped to his underpants, and did so for every rehearsal thereafter. The scene, in performance, raised an eyebrow and numerous questions at the Marlowe Theatre. We reassured the questioners that, as the miners scrubbed each other's backs to remove the ingrained coaldust, jockstraps were firmly in place!

The opera's dress rehearsal took place early in October. Syd remembers:

"I took up my usual place, sitting on the floor so that I don't interfere with sightlines. I started to make notes. It was a good rehearsal. Then I realised I had put down my pencil and stopped scribbling. I was enjoying it too much...

"How that had happened, I can't really tell you. It just happened. I try to make a cast feel safe with what they're doing. They need to feel confident that they know the material and that they have worked as hard as they can, so that they *know* that they can do it. This cast gave me everything. They believed in each other and in the production.

"They would do anything for the show – and I can't give them higher praise than that."

Promised Land was performed in the Canterbury Festival on Friday October 13th and twice on Saturday October 14th. It was a triumph. At the end of it, with the audience on its feet, Felicity Harvest, then director of SEA, reached across a row of seats, hugged me and said: "That was the best community opera I have ever seen..."

Rosie Turner remembers sitting behind the then Lord Mayor, Councillor Pat Todd, as the final curtain fell, and watched as he stood to applaud the cast. He was weeping. Pat told me, later: "I was a policeman at the time of the strikes and it was rough out there. It brought it all back to me. This was a community fighting for its life; it was very emotional."

We went backstage, Rosie, my wife Jo, and I. It was a unique moment; these people, this team, had exceeded any expectations we had of them. I told them what Felicity Harvest had said and they cheered. We clapped them and they celebrated.

Promised Land was never performed again. Sadly, there was nowhere to store the costly and magnificent set, which was a vital part of the production. That, in itself, was a tragedy because, as Syd later told me, she had watched from the stalls beside her partner, Paul Tingley, and, as she held his arm in her nervousness, he had said: "This is West End, Syd." It was that good.

So many things resulted from the production of *Promised Land*. The team of amateurs enjoyed each other's company; they knew they had contributed to something special. They formed a new drama group, The Really Promising Company, and went on to make *Kentish Tales*, again with Mark Dougherty and Syd Ralph, and to stage other productions. Mark Dougherty died on Christmas Day 2020 and The Really Promising Company came together again a year later for a special celebration of his life, to sing and perform extracts from *Promised Land*.

For Syd, the opera introduced her to Mark Dougherty and they worked together frequently for the rest of his life. For Rosie Turner, for me, for the Canterbury Festival, the success of *Promised Land* raised the Festival to fresh heights. It renewed its credentials as a 'producing' festival, inspiring quality material that reflected the community it served. I recall an earlier leader column in the local newspaper, the *Kentish Gazette*. It read:

'The Canterbury Festival and Theatre Trust was formed by a handful of people who could see a day when Canterbury would become a showcase for the arts. Some would say that they had to have a lot of

vision to jolt the city out of its artless rut. But they have done it and it is our pleasure to salute their success.'[174]

Promised Land, the result of a profound and committed community effort, was a confirmation of that assessment.

174. Kentish Gazette, October 27th 1989

Chair David Pentin and his wife Alicia present the farewell portrait to my wife Jo and me.

John Ward, at work.

Home at last – Roddy Loder Symonds, Rosie Turner and chair of the Festival Trust, David Pentin open the Canterbury Festival's new city centre headquarters.

Chapter 15 – Farewell...

The front cover of this book is a portrait by my late friend, artist John Ward. It was exhibited in 2007 by the Royal Society of Portrait Painters and John simply titled the painting: The Chairman. The portrait was presented to me by the Festival at a ceremony at Broome Park on Friday, May 11th, 2007.

It is precious for two reasons; firstly, because it recalls 21 years of my life during which a community initiative flourished into a thriving festival, and secondly, because of the man who painted it. John lived at Bilting. He had always found pleasure in recording the image of his fellow man – and woman, come to that. We first met when I discovered that his house and grounds had been the birthplace of a secret army, a group of men who, in 1940, at the behest of Winston Churchill, trained as saboteurs, willing to lay down their lives in defence of their country if Hitler's armies had invaded Britain. They were known as the Auxiliars they wore ordinary Home Guard uniforms and, cloaked in anonymity, they learned to kill and demolish. They practised hiding in their underground bunkers from which they were trained to emerge, strike and then run, to live to fight another day. John was amused by this connection. He had spent part of this war building concrete defences along the Kent coast as a member of the Royal Engineers. Later, he was part of the Allied army that landed in France on D-Day. The first dead person he saw *"was a child, in a village we were at. He'd been killed by shellfire. Since no-one possessed a camera, the relations asked me if I could make a drawing of the boy. Which I did. I sat and drew the child while the rest of the village came and dipped sprigs in holy water and sprinkled him..."* This experience in the war, "*the war of timid men*", he called it, influenced the whole of his life, taught him so much:

"*The ability to draw men's faces, to draw a man's portrait, was a great asset. I was an 'entertainer' and wonderfully looked after, and you became their artist... there was this thing about living in a slit trench. I loved seeing men paint their faces with a shaving brush – little bit of mirror and then they would shave. The way they pulled their faces – one side and then the other, I loved all that.*"

Conversations like this were a vital part of sitting for John Ward while he created the image on canvas; just the two of us in the airy studio beside his home, so light and bright that birds flew in to share the experience, their plumage vying with the colours that John magically moved from palette to portrait. It is a special place, almost sacred, a museum of materials and passions past, a gallery of places and faces, many of them women of unquestionable beauty. John's wife, Alison, confided that the fact that he had included his own image in my portrait was "unusual and a compliment". It was an experience I will never forget and which I owe wholly to the generosity of the Canterbury Festival and its friends and supporters. John was much loved and respected by his peers, by those who sat for him and by royalty; he was the official artist to record the Queen's wedding dress in 1947. I wrote of him, in 2004: "My personal image of John always starts with his eyes. They twinkle. They reflect his acute, often amused, always interesting observation of life in all its forms." John was a great painter.

I chaired my last Festival meeting, the 30th Annual General Meeting of the Canterbury Theatre and Festival Trust, on Monday April 30th 2007. I said it had been "a privilege and a pleasure to work with such a terrific team – the council, the Board, the Friends and the administrative and artistic talent in the festival". No-one had the right to expect such flair and dedication over 21 years and "these years as chairman have truly been a labour of love".

The Festival asked me to become its president and I succeeded Keith Lucas who retired after so many years' service to the Festival he helped create. As president, I watched from the middle distance as Rosie Turner and her team unfolded festival after festival, which were always interesting and frequently ground-breaking. Over the years, David Pentin, Michael Wright of Canterbury Christ Church University and Keith Mander, from the University of Kent, became chairs of the Trust, each with their own effective styles.

Rosie Turner has introduced a number of 'firsts' to Canterbury in her time in charge. She brought together all three Canterbury universities to support a Fringe Festival for students; she negotiated a Three-Year Partner and Principal Sponsor agreement with Canterbury Christ Church University; she and the team mobilised restaurants to offer the "Big Eat Out" scheme, and the hotels in the "Big Sleepover", part of the Festival's "Big Day Out". She has looked to Europe with "Kent's International Arts Festival" – and, under her guidance, the Festival linked with Kent County Council's trade delegation and Canterbury City Council's twinning arrangements with Hungary. She sustained the link with the Philharmonia Orchestra and, conspicuously, the Spiegeltent became part of the Festival, attracting with its cabaret approach, a new generation of festivalgoers.

I once asked Rosie if, among the festivals she had organised, she had a favourite; she picked 2007. She gave three reasons; first, it had broken new ground with site-specific commissions such as a drive-in theatre at Dreamland car park in Margate, dinner theatre in an Italian restaurant, Mirandolinas, and the Noise Ensemble, which was a Festival commission by Ethan Lewis Maltby; second, it was studded with stars – tenor Alfie Boe, Humphrey Lyttelton, Courtney Pine and Don McLean; comedians Michael McIntyre, Alan Carr, Ardal O'Hanlon and Jenny Eclair; folk singers Seth Lakeman and Altan and violinist, Nicola Benedetti. Newsreader John Sergeant, Clarissa Dickson Wright, Robin Knox-Johnston and Roger McGough gave talks; third, there was a host of international stars – Blake, a sculptor from Monte Carlo with 'Fragments,' his memorial to the landmine victims of war; Moscow Radio's Tchaikovsky Symphony Orchestra; the Chilingirian Quartet; Heinavanker, a vocal ensemble from Estonia; the

Chamber Orchestra of Europe, with Mark Simpson (clarinet); Los Excéntricos, clowns from Barcelona; comedian Ennio Marchetto and *Slava's Snowshow*, which was an interesting experience for those enveloped as they sat in the stalls at the Marlowe. The Really Promising Company stepped out once more with *Kentish Tales*, directed again by Syd Ralph, with music by Mark Dougherty.

Conspicuously, while Rosie was in charge, the Festival has found its permanent home. The initiative grew from the relationship that Rosie had pursued with Canterbury Christ Church from her first year as Festival Director. It was delivered largely through the efforts of the late Roddy Loder-Symonds, chair of the Festival Foundation throughout the campaign, helped by his friend and lieutenant, Evelyn Wright, and the staff of The Friends. Roddy was an effective and determined leader. He set a timetable for his objectives and he delivered ahead of time. Just before his death in 2021, he summed up the campaign:

"I was asked to become a Trustee of the Canterbury Festival in 2009, but said that I did not in any way want to become involved in fund-raising. Almost immediately, I was asked to be chairman of the fund-raising Foundation! We launched the Building for the Future appeal in October 2010, to provide long-term financial stability, and secure the Festival for future generations. We were concerned at the time that an appeal for just bricks and mortar would not be appealing to donors and so we had a twin aim of finding a permanent headquarters for the Festival and inaugurating an annual bursary scheme to support the development of talented young local musicians. The appeal's target was to raise £400,000 by July 2015."

Roddy and the Foundation pursued that target with commendable vigour. He summed up the campaign perfectly:

"From October 2010, we were very active in organising many fund-raising events including a golf day at Prince's, an opera evening at the Marlowe and a cricket day at the Spitfire St Lawrence ground, as well as numerous smaller events. We had a very hard-working

committee, particularly *Evelyn Wright who raised £20,000 from the golf day. We also received support from the Bernard Sunley Charitable Foundation, the Beerling Foundation, the HR Pratt Boorman Family Foundation, the John Swire 1989 Charitable Trust and the RG Hills Charitable Trust. We raised a very large percentage of the total from the Festival's Vice-Presidents, who were very generous.*

"Canterbury Christ Church University, an organisation with an established track record in delivering large-scale capital projects, was our Partner and Principal Sponsor. In 2011, they purchased the property 8 Orange Street, and let it to the Festival at a peppercorn rent. The property was in a perfect location between the cathedral and the Marlowe Theatre. At the time, the Festival office was in Christ Church Gate which was quite unsuitable, as there were 69 steps and no disabled access.

"Canterbury Christ Church gave the Festival a fixed purchase option expiring in 2015 to acquire the freehold of the property at market value, which we were able to do by the deadline, having raised £280,000 from donations and £150,000 from the Arts Council a year ahead of the appeal target date. In addition, the Festival funded a major refurbishment project over a six-week period costing about £80,000 in 2012 to create a sustainable, future-proof office, with new energy-efficient double glazed windows and daylight interior lighting."

As a result of this very successful project and Roddy's efforts, the Festival has a home in central Canterbury and has become a highly visible and accessible year-round resource, helping East Kent's young musicians of the future to develop their talents. Festival House in Orange Street was officially opened on September 30th 2010.[175]

When I look back over the 50 years in which I've been involved, the loyalty, initiative and sheer hard work shown by Board members, vice-presidents, who give their time and money year after year, the entire staff and the legion of The Friends of the Festival, has

175. See also Chapter 13

been remarkable. We have been fortunate in our choice of Festival directors whose devotion has been both admirable and profoundly moving. So, when an individual falls below these standards that, too, is remarkable. Such was the case in 2019 when Mark Burford, the Festival's financial director for three years, was convicted of defrauding the Festival's charity of £80,000. He forged signatures and faked invoices to siphon cash into his own bank account. A team is a family. If one member fails, all suffer. When the size of the theft was discovered, a number of members of the team feared for their jobs because, as I said at the beginning of this book, the battle to find sufficient money every year to fulfil artistic ambition is incessant. Today, and tomorrow and tomorrow... The loss of the money was hard. Just as hard was the feeling of betrayal by *"one of the gang. He was a quiet worker, a man of few words. He had baked us cakes; he was one of us"*.[176]

In contrast, it was at about this time that we said farewell to another family member, Cynthia Hawes. Cynthia was the Festival Board secretary for decades. As chairman, I had inherited Cynthia from her previous role as secretary to the University of Kent's then vice-chancellor. Tiny, punctilious and energetic, Cynthia kept me on the straight and narrow and brought with her a wealth of knowledge on how meetings should be run. She never lost her love of the Festival and she supported it throughout her life.

As with so many of the Festival's supporters, she never benefited from that relationship by a single penny.

---

176. Conversation with a fellow member of the Festival team

THEATRE MATTERS

Dr Paul Bennett, who has spent his life delving into and recording Canterbury's history.

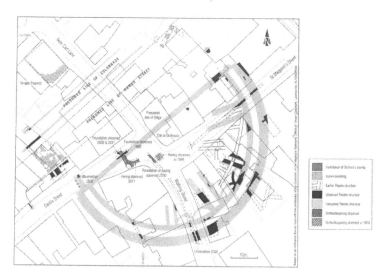

Fig. 1: Plan of the Roman Theatres at Canterbury (drawn by Simon Pratt)

*Fig. 2 Artist's impression of the second theatre in c. AD 300.
(drawn by Gill Atherton)*

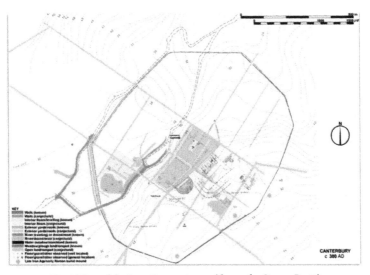

Fig. 3 Plan of the Late Roman town. (drawn by Simon Pratt)

Illustrations in this chapter copyright Canterbury Museums and Galleries

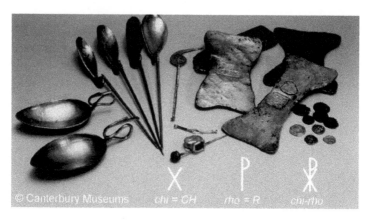

Fig. 4 The Canterbury Treasure

Fig. 5 Artist's impression of the Roman theatre in the later fifth century.
(Gill Atherton)

Illustrations in this chapter copyright Canterbury Museums and Galleries

Fig. 6 Plan of the earliest Anglo-Saxon town.(drawn by Simo Pratt)

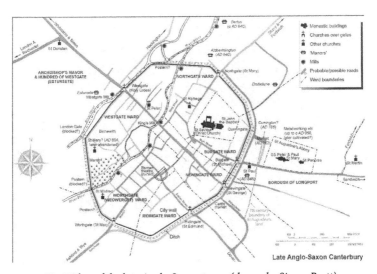

Fig. 7 Plan of the late Anglo-Saxon town. (drawn by Simon Pratt)

Illustrations in this chapter copyright Canterbury Museums and Galleries

Fig. 8 Artist reconstruction of the late Anglo-Saxon cathedral, Archbishop Cuthbert's baptistry and cloister. (drawn by Ivan Lapper)

Fig. 9 St Mildred's Church from the south-west. (photo Andrew Savage)

Illustrations in this chapter copyright Canterbury Museums and Galleries

Chapter 16 – An Anatomy of a Theatre

There has been a theatre in Canterbury for 1900 years. In considering the history of the Canterbury Festival, theatre is embedded in the heart of its genesis and its success. Certainly, throughout the challenging yet successful re-establishment of a modern festival in Canterbury, the Marlowe Theatre and its future has been an ever present consideration and concern. Where would it be and how could the community afford it?

Theatre has always been important to Canterbury's prosperity. Today, the Marlowe Theatre contributes £30 million every year to the economy of East Kent. This importance, both culturally and economically, is no new development. So, as we examine the history of the Canterbury Festival, it is appropriate to record the part theatre has played in the story of Canterbury.

I asked my friend, Paul Bennett,[177] to trace this relationship between city and theatre back to its beginnings. He extended his brief and embraced the significance of theatre in Britain. I learned a lot more, and what follows reflects Paul's knowledge and research.

The first theatre in Canterbury (of which we know little) was constructed in c., AD 80--90 for the early provincial Roman town. A second theatre was built on the same footprint a century or so later but on a grander, classical scale, reflecting the impressive wealth of Roman Kent and underpinning the status of Canterbury as a civitas capital of significance *(Durovernum Cantiacorum)*. It was this later theatre that dominated Canterbury's skyline throughout the later Roman and Anglo-Saxon periods and which

---

177. Professor Paul Bennett was a member of the Canterbury Archaeological Trust for 45 years and was its director for 35 of those years

played a pivotal role in a period of transition; it was a place of security, commerce, public meetings, ceremony and jurisprudence during the formation of the Kingdom of Kent in its 'golden age'. Over time, this great, decaying structure dictated the development of a post-Roman street grid, which influenced the present map of Canterbury. By the mid- to late-Anglo-Saxon/early Norman period, the theatre became an enormous 'quarry' for building materials. So extensive was the quarrying of Roman stone that nothing of the theatre survives above ground today and all knowledge of it was lost until it was rediscovered by archaeological excavation in the 1950s.

Greek and Roman Theatres

The Roman theatre at Canterbury, like other theatres across the Roman world, was based on a Greek prototype dating back to the 8th century BC. The earliest theatres were of wood, almost invariably built into a hillside, with wooden seats placed in the natural slope of the hill to provide an elevated view of an orchestra and stage. By the 7th century BC, the stage area was raised and rectangular, with wings of seats extending on either side, beyond the chord of the stage, forming a plan describing three-quarters of a full circle. At this time, stone seats were introduced for important patrons in the front row adjoining the orchestra. By the 6th century BC, most seats were of stone and the stage acquired a backdrop of stone, often including columns and other architectural conceits.

These basic components were shared centuries later in the design of the Roman theatre. Perhaps the biggest difference between the two is that most Roman theatres were built freestanding and not into a hillside, with the overall building forming a D-shape. The backdrop to the stage *(scaenae frons)* became far more elaborate and was often built to two storeys, with openings and doorways flanked by columns, joined to stepped seating which did not extend beyond the backdrop to the stage. Other modifications included the paving of the performance, semi-circular orchestra areas and the provision of stone seats. The stage was raised in both forms, but the front of the stage in the Roman theatre, like the *scaenae frons*, was often decorated in stone or marble with niches containing statues, plaques or dedicatory inscriptions to make the performance area even more impressive to the viewer. Provision was also made for permanent seating space for high officials and priests at the base of the raised seating and sometimes inside the orchestra retaining wall. There was reserved seating at a high level for officials, guests or benefactors.

Performance

The performances held in the Greek and Roman theatres were quite similar. Comedy and tragedy dominated and both encouraged drama competitions and festival events at different times of the year. Masks, costumes, props, singing, mime and dancing all had a place, with actors connecting with the audience directly or indirectly. With a few exceptions, Greek tragedies and comedies were performed by up to three actors with some doubling-up of characters. The masks took on a life of their own, possessing personality and character attributes that were well known to the audience. As such, stock characters would have been immediately recognisable to knowledgeable patrons, but it was up to the play and the performance to dictate successfully the personality of the characters. Apart from the actors, Greek dramas made use of a chorus,[178] distinct from the stage action and spatially separate, as they stood against the circular orchestra in front of the stage facing the audience or facing other characters, and sometimes as a removed viewer of the action on stage, as distant voices.

While taking their themes from Greek myths and topics, Roman dramas gradually established their own themes of Etruscan and Latin origin. Choruses in Roman tragedies were incorporated into on-stage action, an aspect that differed from Roman comedy where the Greek chorus model was retained. Roman comedy was either adapted from a Greek model or was entirely Roman in a Roman setting. There were also more actors involved, often again wearing make-up or masks. In the Greek theatre, all actors were male. In

---

178. See also Chapter 1.

the Roman theatre, although the majority were male, women also appeared. In Canterbury, the theatre and the temple precinct were on opposite sides of a major street and closely associated, following a Gallic model. The theatre was used for a wide variety of religious festivals involving priests, processions and even the setting up of an altar. As a place of congregation, it was almost certainly used for important political meetings, perhaps during local elections or public speaking competitions. In addition, it was used for nude dancing, acrobatics and boxing matches and even, on occasion, gladiatorial combat.

Theatregoers in towns such as Canterbury or St Albans would probably find a pantomime on the programme, with players representing stock characters to act out well-known stories from mythology. The performances were probably by troupes of travelling actors touring Britain from one centre to another. A typical show might open with a mixture of music and dancing, followed by a pantomime, with masked artists acting out a tragedy based on well-known mythology. This might be followed by mime performed by stock characters cavorting on stage in a form of slapstick or ribaldry based on local people or prominent events, to roars of laughter, applause and shouted comments from the audience. Not too different from a current Marlowe pantomime!

The raised rectangular stage was constructed with an ornamental façade and a permanent structural, decorative backdrop and the performance was flanked by storage rooms for props and a greenroom or changing room for the actors. While the stage area may have been provided with an awning, the rows of seats were open to the elements, sweeping in a great arc from one side of the stage to the other and separated from the stage by an orchestra. Although state sponsorship might have funded the building and rebuilding of the theatre at Canterbury, it was far more likely to have been paid for by wealthy and influential townspeople and the tribe *(Cantiaci)* who built the theatre and supported the institution in the longer term, as an outward expression of *Romanitas* (of being civilised). Seats were free; the performances being paid for by senior magistrates or other benefactors.

Theatres in Gaul and Britain

Roman theatres occur all over the Roman Empire. Some exceptional examples had seating for 20,000 patrons, but most had a capacity of half or one quarter of that size or even less. Theatres of this type in Britain are rare. The closest parallel to the theatre at Canterbury is the Romano-Celtic theatre at *Verulamium* (St Albans), a building with seating for perhaps 2,000, carried on earthen ramps, similar to the earliest theatre at Canterbury. We know there was a timber theatre at Gosbecks[179] near Colchester, destroyed by Boudica and her followers in AD 60–1, and there was a later masonry version at *Camulodunum* (Colchester). A theatre may have existed at Bath *(Aquae Sulis)* and another at Brough-on-Humber *(Petuaria)*, the civitas of the *Parisi*, known only from a dedicatory inscription mentioning a new stage building. There were a far greater number of amphitheatres in Britain indicating the more widespread popularity of public sports.

The second theatre at Canterbury, built in AD 210–220, was of classical type with massive external walls and seating carried partly on the earlier gravel bank but also on substructures of masonry. This building, four-fifths the size of theatres at Arles and Orange, three-quarters that at Lyon, but larger than the theatres at St Bertrand and Paris, is evidence of the impressive wealth of Roman Kent. When related to the wealth of the respective provinces, towns such as Canterbury with an impressive civic centre (containing theatre and temple complexes, a forum/basilica and public baths) were not notably inferior to those in Gaul in the scale of their public buildings or in the considerable investment that such buildings represented. The building of both theatres, one replacing the other, represented not only significant investment and reinvestment of resources by the townspeople of Canterbury, but a key symbol for the *Cantiaci* of their acceptance of a Roman way of life, their cultural links with the Roman world and of pride in their city.

---

179. Gosbecks is an Iron Age and Roman archaeological site in Essex

The First Theatre: What Remains Now?

Only a few elements of Canterbury's first theatre are known, found during the formation of the city's sewers in the 1860s beneath the intersection of Watling Street and St Margaret's Street by the city engineer, James Pilbrow. It was not recognised as such until the 1950s when excavations by Professor Sheppard Frere and the Canterbury Excavations Committee allowed a better interpretation of the early observations (Fig. 1).

The first theatre was constructed in Flavian times, perhaps no later than AD 80–90. It was of Romano-Celtic type, its seating formed over banks of gravel retained by a substantial curving outer wall 1.20m in thickness. An inner wall for the orchestra retained the toe of the gravel bank which may have been 25m wide. Few details survive but it must have been a substantial structure with a half-elliptical rather than a semi-circular plan, an orchestra describing a different radius from that of the outer wall (perhaps semi-circular) and a stage aligned north-east to south-west, built against a wide street positioned to the north-east of the theatre. This was one of the earliest Roman streets, laid in around AD 70–80 over the remains of the Iron Age town, perhaps in preparation for the building of the theatre and temple complexes. It became the *cardo* of the town, separating the four central insulae containing the principal civic buildings. The theatre was therefore one of the earliest civic buildings constructed for the early Roman town. While several early roads and timber buildings were constructed at this time, the development of the town's orthogonal street grid did not take place until the beginning of the second century.

The Second Theatre

Our knowledge of the second theatre is rather more detailed, benefiting from the trail-blazing work of Sheppard Frere and the numerous observations of below ground fabric over the past 50 years by Canterbury Archaeological Trust.

The theatre, built in the early third century, was a massive structure resting on mortared flint foundations of great depth. The outer curving wall 3.25m in thickness formed a D-shaped structure approximately 78m in diameter, built against a pre-existing major street aligned north-east to south-west, with the rear wall of the theatre approximately adjoining the street. The full depth of the theatre from the back of the stage to the external face of the outer curving wall measured 57m. A second inner curving wall 2.25m wide was located inside the first to form the internal wall of the *cavia* (the retaining wall for the banked seats) and an ambulatory (walkway) 2.2m wide between the two walls. The main internal features comprised three pairs of symmetrically placed passage walls leading from the inner curving wall to the position of a D-shaped orchestra wall. The central pair of radial passage walls, aligned north-west to south-east, divided the internal plan into two symmetrical halves with each half subdivided into two segments, one twice the size of the other. The passage walls were cut through the gravel bank of the early theatre with the bank reused for theatre seating. Associated with the wider segments either side of the central passage walls, were contemporary curving walls or caissons (shaped like a flattened apse)[180] formed at the same time as the *cavia* to strengthen and support the upper tiers of seats. Although this device may have extended into all four segments, the caissons may have been restricted to the area either side of the central passage where symmetrically placed pairs of short passage walls perhaps marked the position of stairs, giving access to upper levels of seating. The outer curving wall suggests it was formed with an open arcade at external ground level or with multiple entrances symmetrically located, opening on to the ambulatory. Larger openings may have existed in the external curving wall close to its termination on-line with the front of the stage, for rapid exit at the end of a performance (the aditus or so-called 'vomitaria'). It is equally possible that to make full use of the banked seating adjacent to the stage, egress from the theatre may only have been through the radial passages and the ambulatory.

The seating, resting on the early gravel bank strengthened by caissons, was flanked by passage walls in each of the segments,

---

180. Apse – a curving recess

with the largest number of banked seats located either side of the central passage, with stair access to the highest seats. Access to the lower seats in all four segments and to higher seats to the north and west, would have been from openings at the junction of passage and orchestra walls. The orchestra was paved in large slabs of dressed ragstone, discovered during service trenching in 1868, 2000 and 2011. The most recent observation was of an expanse of 15 in situ slabs of differing sizes, but on average 0.23m thick, aligned to the presumed axis of the stage. We know little of the stage building, but the position of front and back walls is known, indicating a rectangular structure measuring approximately 70m by 10m internally. The stage would have occupied most of the central area, but a prop store and greenroom would have formed parts of the complex; these facilities perhaps located at either end of the stage building. The stage was raised and probably fitted with wooden boards supported on masonry cross walls.

The front wall of the stage between the orchestra curving walls may have been decorated with niches containing statues or simply plastered and painted for decorative effect. The rear of the stage would have been decorated with architectural devices and may have been of more than one storey.

It is difficult to determine how high the theatre would have stood and to do so is pure speculation, but the foundations of the *cavia* are of substantial width and depth, sufficient to carry significant load. The walls of the *cavia* may have risen to a height of 20m (more than three times the height of the Roman city wall). Although much of the standing fabric would have been built in mortared flint, Roman brick would also have been extensively used for decorative and structural string courses, with Roman brick used for supporting walls and the turning of arches. Stone would have been extensively used for structural and decorative components, particularly quoins for corners and openings, and columns, column bases and capitals for the stage and other parts of the complex. Local greensand from Reculver, Folkestone and Hythe, lightweight tufa from local chalk valleys (mainly used in the construction of vaults) and ragstone from the Maidstone area, together with imported stone from Gaul, all formed the palate of building stones.

As with other buildings in the Roman civic centre, particularly the temple precinct and the forum/basilica, parts of the theatre, notably the front and rear of the stage and perhaps the greenroom, may have been decorated with imported marble veneers and paving from many parts of the Roman world. None of this now survives. Taking speculation to the level of raw guesswork, the Canterbury theatre may have accommodated up to 3,000 people (Fig. 2).

Four insulae of different size occupied the centre of the Roman town (Fig. 3). The largest, to the north, contained the forum/basilica with principal market, administrative offices and a law court. The smallest, to the east, was for the public baths. To the west was the temple precinct, flanked on all four sides by a portico with perhaps a centrally located classical temple and smaller shrines set within a paved courtyard. Adjoining the temple insula, separated by a wide, early street was the theatre, within its own insula. The theatre appears to have occupied most of the block with domestic buildings known against the south-east and north-east sides, but at some remove from the theatre itself. Much of the ground east (and perhaps south) of the theatre was gravel paved, suggesting that the insula was open and a place where people could congregate before or after performances. At other times it may have been used as a marketplace.

The Role of the Theatre in the Post-Roman Period

Sub-Roman occupation of the town, albeit in greatly reduced numbers, may have continued into the 5th century, with evidence for some building work in stone as late as c., 370–380, and in timber into the early 5th century. While there is some evidence of epidemic and illegal burial within the town walls in the last decade of the 4th century and perhaps a short period of abandonment, several of the extra-mural cemeteries remained in use into the 5th century, clearly suggesting reoccupation and adherence to Roman law, with some late interments suggesting the presence of long-distance travellers from beyond the Rhine frontier.

That a proportion of the early 5th century population of Canterbury was Christian is perhaps indicated by a group of mainly silver objects (the Canterbury Treasure) found outside the walls by workmen building the Rheims Way roundabout in 1962, close to the site of the Roman London Gate (Fig. 4). The hoard, comprising mostly silver spoons but also three silver ingots and gold and silver jewellery, was perhaps the property or stock of a silversmith, buried for safekeeping with the intention of retrieval in the first or second decade of the 5th century. One spoon displayed a Chi Rho symbol, while others featured Christian iconography, and one was inscribed 'VIRIBONISM', perhaps 'viri boni s[v]m', meaning 'I belong to a good man'.

Quite how the theatre was used during this period of economic decline, epidemic and a growing threat from overseas, is impossible to determine. But, archaeological evidence from elsewhere in Canterbury suggests that abandonment of the town may have taken place in the second or third decade of the 5th century at the latest, when the earliest Anglo-Saxon migrations of people from northern Germany and southern Scandinavia took place. By this time, urban life in Canterbury was no longer tenable and most inhabitants lived off the land. In the middle of the 5th century, individuals or families, either indigenous or migrant, probably squatted in the ruined town for short periods. As coins were no longer minted and readily identifiable mass-produced pottery was no longer in circulation, it is difficult to date so-called dark-age deposits with any accuracy. Nevertheless, what *can* be seen across Canterbury is a carpet of dark loam that seals the latest Roman levels, this generated by vegetation, decaying and collapsing buildings and generations of industrious nematodes (worms), recycling leaf litter and compost to create a mantle of soil. The earliest traces of Anglo-Saxon occupation have been found cutting through the dark loam or in later layers, capping it. Unfortunately, these deposits have not survived within the footprint of the theatre and there is little in the way of artefacts to provide a clue. What we *can* be sure of, however, is that the vast mass of the theatre survived as a conspicuous ruin, standing well above decaying buildings within the city wall and visible from the old Roman approach roads, still in use, and the ridges of the Stour Valley overlooking the town (Fig. 5). Those passing through the town would have visited this great ruin, and who could have resisted it?

In the second half of the 5th century, in periods of stress and perhaps conflict, the interior of the building and particularly the paved orchestra and stage, could have been used as a place of refuge and congregation, perhaps even a redoubt. Such an edifice would have provided shelter for those in need, despite the risk from collapsing inner walls and decaying high-level stonework.

The earliest phase of Anglo-Saxon reoccupation of the city may be dated from the last quarter of the 5th century and into the early 6th. It is from this time that we can see metal objects, mainly brooches and identifiable handmade ceramics in the archaeological record, with some of the earliest Anglo-Saxon timber buildings constructed from the early 6th century onwards. The greatest number of early timber buildings of the period have been found near the theatre – under the Marlowe Arcade, the Hilton Hotel on St Margaret's Street and in the back garden of No 16 Watling Street. This is partly a consequence of the presence of open ground around the theatre, but also the role of the theatre as an important nodal point within the developing early Anglo-Saxon town.

The Map of Canterbury

Although there is no reference to the theatre in Anglo-Saxon documents, early or late, the relationship between the theatre and a developing grid is self-evident, with three early streets meeting in the orchestra. There are few roads within the walls that follow a Roman line that suggest an abandonment of the Roman grid in the 5th century and the formation of a new, irregular network of streets evolving over time thereafter (Fig. 6). The earliest of these streets may owe their genesis to the theatre. The present line of Castle Street (named *wistraet* in later Anglo-Saxon documents) extends from Roman Worthgate (Anglo-Saxon *weowerget* – 'the gate to the men of Wye'), to the south-west corner of the theatre, possibly entering the theatre through, or close to, the south-west *vomitaria* into the orchestra. The present line of St Margaret's Street extends from the orchestra, possibly leaving the theatre through the north-east radial passage exit in the *cavia* and continuing to the north-east (along Mercery Lane). This joins the south-west corner of a possible early inner burgh and an important intersection with Burgate Street (*burhstraet*), the possible site of an early market. A third early street, Watling Street (*ealdenstraet*) extends from the orchestra to Roman Ridingate – the red gate – from the use of Roman brick in its construction. The present line of this street now enters the orchestra in its southern corner, but perhaps originally entered through the south-east radial passage halting in the orchestra. In a later period, this road was continued to the north-west (Beer Cart Lane) to cross the stage, exit the rear wall of the theatre through a new opening and extend across the former temple precinct to meet an early ford, crossing the River Stour.

Eighth and 9th century charters indicate that the land beyond the ford was pasture, flood plain and largely uninhabited. These three early roads then, suggest that the theatre was not only an important landmark but was used in the early Anglo-Saxon period and formed with the early burgh (flanked by a road linking Northgate and Burgate), an important nodal point during the rebirth of the town.

The theatre and its relationship with the grid road indicates that the huge structure, the largest single building in Kent, with perhaps intact entrances and significant elements of its internal plan, performed an important function during the early development of Canterbury and the Kentish Kingdom as a meeting place for the people of Kent, the *Cantware*. With the old town still served by Roman roads, radiating out from the city into East Kent like the spokes of a wheel, those entering the town through old Roman gates, would have seen the great theatre at the centre of a small community, living within the decaying vestiges of the past. Even though Canterbury was not a place to find shelter in, it was perhaps an important destination and the theatre a meeting place for the upper echelons of society living in East Kent and perhaps in a kingdom extending from the Thames to the Isle of Wight. It was perhaps within the theatre at Canterbury that the first kings of Kent met the *Cantware* at certain times of the year, to be seen by his ranking subjects for ceremony and procession, to reward good service, to settle matters of warfare, politics, marriage and trade, and to dispense justice. The theatre, then, was perhaps the initial secular and royal centre of the early Anglo-Saxon town, called *Durobernia.*

Before the Augustinian mission of AD 597, Anglo-Saxon occupation of the old Roman town may have been low-key and perhaps focused on the theatre. Canterbury was not a 'metropolis' at the time of Æthelbert, as suggested by Bede (writing in the AD 730s) but, once established after AD 600, the religious houses of St Peter and Paul (St Augustine's Abbey) and St Saviour Christ Church (Canterbury Cathedral and Christchurch Priory), both with royal patronage, acted as a catalyst in the development of the town. In Bede's day, *Cantwaraburgh* (the stronghold of the men of Kent) may well have been a flourishing urban centre, but not at the time of the Christian mission.

At the time of the conversion and for some time afterwards, the theatre remained important as a meeting place for the people of Kent and a fitting seat of Æthelbert's imperium, in 'the golden age' of Kent, when he was *Bretwalda* and Kent was the oldest, most influential and most continental of the earliest English Kingdoms. Indeed, the wholesale conversion of the Kentish people, following the rapid baptism of Æthelbert in December 597 (according to Bede), may well have taken place in the old theatre.

These early monastic establishments acted as a bridge linking Anglo-Saxon society and institutions with the late antique world, not just in monastic life and liturgy, but in the development of new architecture, in music, the arts, learning and in education. Anglo-Saxon society at this time was rife with feuds and it is likely that the monks helped Æthelbert to establish a new set of written laws, thereby encouraging literacy and stable government. The law code compiled at this time (before AD 616) promoting social harmony through a system of compensation and arranged according to social rank from king to slave, is the earliest in a Germanic language and the theatre at Canterbury may well have been the location where the *Laws of AEthelbert* (the root of English Law thereafter) were enacted for the first time.

Over the course of the next 150 years or so, new roads were added to the city's grid, the ecclesiastical houses flourished and an important school was established in the monastery in AD 669 by Archbishop Theodore of Tarsus and Abbot Hadrian. There is increasing evidence of domestic Anglo-Saxon occupation, for industry (outside the walls), churches associated with some of the gates, manors within and outside the walls and a Canterbury mint – all of this underpinned by 8th and 9th century charters (Fig. 7). The Kingdom of Kent was eclipsed, however, in AD 726 and made subject to kingdoms of Mercia and then Wessex, changing the dynamics of power and the need for a place of assembly in Canterbury for Kentish kings and their people.

The significance of the theatre gradually diminished throughout this period, but it remained a vast ruin at the intersection of major streets and a spectacular centrepiece of a processional route from the Worth Gate to the inner burgh and gate, opening on to a major lay cemetery south of the mid-8th century St Saviour Christ Church. It was at this time that Archbishop Cuthbert (d. 760) constructed a baptistry to the east of the cathedral church, almost certainly using local stone and brick gleaned from Roman ruins.

Surviving this long period of use during the development of the road grid are three wheel ruts, found cutting into and across orchestra paving outside the Three Tuns Public House in 2011. The ruts, formed by the repeated use of iron-shod cartwheels over an extended period, continuing the line of Castle Street across the former orchestra, testify to the survival of the theatre as a nodal point during the development of a processional way and the longer term formation of a new road grid for Canterbury.

The Theatre as a Quarry for Stone

In the early 9th century, Archbishop Wulfred (805–32) rebuilt the cathedral church on a massive scale (from 808–13), with a crypt at the east end under a raised sanctuary – later described as 'like the ring-passage at St Peter's in Rome' – a central tower and an extended nave with aisles and narthex, inspired by early Carolingian churches on the continent. Later, Archbishop Oda (942–58) raised the height of the church by 29 feet. In 978, following St Dunstan's reforms (d. 988) at the abbey of St Peter, St Paul and St Augustine, new buildings were being constructed to the west and north of the abbey church. By the 9th century, standing Roman buildings were probably in short supply and it is from this time onwards that the theatre may have become a quarry providing stone for major building projects, churches and work requiring masonry or brick on the city walls and gates in the 10th century.

In September 1011 following a three-week siege by an army of Yomsvikings from the River Oder led by Thorkell the Tall (a mentor of Cnut the Great), Canterbury was sacked. Archbishop Alphege was taken captive and murdered at Greenwich the following Easter. His body was transported from London to Canterbury Cathedral for burial in 1023. At this time, the cathedral was extended probably by Archbishop AEthelnoth (1020–38) with a massive *westwerk* on two floors, which contained a chapel dedicated to St Mary, flanked by polygonal turrets and a western apse with raised platform supporting the *cathedra* of the archbishop. Transepts were added at this time; the tower of St Martin to the north containing the novice school and the tower of St Gregory to the south containing the south door to the cathedral.

On completion, the cathedral was probably the largest Anglo-Saxon building in England and a rival to some of the greatest Ottonian and Romanesque churches in Europe (Fig. 8). A huge amount of stone was required for the project and much of this will have been taken from the theatre. The theatre may well have been visited again by quarrymen seeking stone and brick for several new churches built perhaps in the 1030s (St Mildred and St Dunstan and perhaps St Peter and St Alphege). Of this group of churches, St Mildred is a stunning survival, with a nave near completion and chancel containing massive stone quoins in marquise, greensand and ragstone that can only have come from the theatre (Fig. 8). Late developments at the abbey by Abbot Wulfric II (c., 1047–59) saw the building of a cutting-edge rotunda linking the church of St Mary to the nave of the early abbey church; a tomb chapel with western tower to the west of the abbey church and a freestanding bell tower to the south-west of the church. All this was a huge undertaking demanding significant quantities of stone, flint and brick, much of it sourced locally, and probably from standing elements of the theatre.

A final phase of quarrying in the early Norman period saw the removal of all above-ground elements of the theatre and the quarrying out of foundations. Canterbury became an enormous building site in the aftermath of the Norman Conquesta new cathedral and Archbishop's Palace (1070–80), a new priory with cloister and claustral buildings (1070–80), a new abbey church and buildings (1071–85), a royal castle precinct (1084) and keep (1100), two new churches (St Mary de Castro and St Andrew), St John's Hospital (1080), a leper hospital (St Lawrence) at Harbledown and a nunnery (St Sepulchre). Although new building materials were sourced from abroad or from local quarries, local stone and brick from Roman buildings, including the theatre, were mined to their foundations. In the case of the theatre, all the robber trenches that have been excavated in the past have contained Norman pottery. We can therefore be sure that by the late 11th century the theatre had vanished and all that survived of its presence were four streets forming an important intersection.

On the Ground

Today, the south-west corner of the early theatre's stage building lies between Nos 79 and 80 Castle Street and the north-east corner, to the rear of Nos 37 and 38 St Margaret's Street; this leaves the centre of the stage beneath No 5 Beer Cart Lane. The orchestra falls at the intersection of these three streets, with modern buildings at the junction of Beer Cart Lane and St Margaret's Street overlapping and intruding into the footprint of the orchestra. The junction of the great *cavia* (the inner and outer walls of the theatre) with the south-west corner of the stage building, lies in the courtyard of the Three Tuns Public House against the frontage of Castle Street.

The *cavia* extends beneath Nos 25, 26 and 23 Watling Street and to the rear of Nos 4–6 St Margaret's Street, extending under St Margaret's Street at the north-west corner of No 7. The *cavia* meets the north-east corner of the stage building to the rear of No 38 St Margaret's Street.

Fragments of the theatre's curving walls survive in the cellars of Nos 23 and 24 Watling Street and can be seen in the cellars of Nos 7 and 38 St Margaret's Street (the Hilton Hotel and Alberrys Wine Bar, respectively).

Conclusion

The story of the theatre at Canterbury is a remarkable one, spanning a millennium, from the end of the 1st century AD to the opening years of the 12th century. Rediscovered by archaeological excavation in the 1950s, nothing survives in epigraphic or documentary sources recording its mighty presence, and yet its role in the development of *Durovernum* and *Cantwaraburgh*, was pivotal. In the Roman period, it represented strong cultural links with the Roman world, forged by the *Cantiaci* as an outward sign of civilisation and civic pride. Its reuse from the late 5th century onwards repeated that continental connection, but between the *Cantwara* and the late antique[181] world. The high points for its use in the latter period may have been during a frenetic mass conversion to Christianity, and the theatre may well have played a vital role in enacting *the Laws of AEthelbert* for the first time, the foundation of jurisprudence today.

The theatre was also important in the development of a new road grid for Canterbury and supplied building stone for a significant number of internationally important buildings, some of which still stand. For a great building that disappeared nearly 1000 years ago, the early theatre remains at the heart of the Canterbury story.

---

181.   Late antique (AD 284–700)

Glossary of terms used in this chapter:
Ambulatory: processional path often encircling an apse or cloister in a monastic foundation
Civitas: a favoured Roman provincial town
Cantiaci: the dominant late Iron Age tribe in Kent
Insula: measured and regular block of land in a Roman town
Cardo: an axial street in a Roman town, usually north-south, at right angles to the *decumanus*
Cavea: walls supporting the banked seats of a Roman theatre
Quoins: stones forming the corner of a building
Redoubt: a fortification or place of refuge
Vomitaria/vomitory: slang Latin word for a main exit from a theatre or amphitheatre
Nodal: a key location
Cantwara: the people of Kent in the later Anglo-Saxon period
Imperium: the absolute authority (of the king)
Narthex: a vestibule or porch
Claustral: pertaining to a cloister in a monastic foundation or buildings associated with such a foundation

Prime Minister Margaret Thatcher, flanked by Sir Geoffrey Howe, sign the Channel Tunnel Treaty, in 1986, in Canterbury Cathedral, with French President Mitterand.

Director Mark Everett, on the steps on the new 1200-seat Marlowe Theatre.

Councillor Hazel McCabe – a lone voice against the new Marlowe Theatre, an admirable councillor who stuck to her principles.

The Eight o'clock Club – Members of the New Marlowe Theatre Development Trust, who raised £5 million to help build the new Marlowe theatre: Stephan Kingsman, Charles Villiers, Clive Relf, Paul Barrett, Ian Odgers, Michael Head, Sir Graeme Odgers, Peter Williams, Nigel Beevor, James Bird, Vyvyan Harmsworth, Roger Mitty (consultant), Graham Sinclair, Sir Michael Bett and Andrew Clague

Keith Williams (right), the architect and designer, celebrates.

The new Marlowe Theatre

Prince Edward, The Earl of Wessex, surveys the new theatre.

Opening Night

Chapter 17 – A New Theatre

The Roman theatres in Canterbury functioned as centres of the community until the beginning of the 4th century. Thereafter, no new theatre was built in Canterbury until 1789. For a city with such a cultural tradition, this hiatus of 1400 years appears truly staggering until one realises[182] that professional drama and theatregoing were not part of daily life in England during that time.

Though both Shakespeare and Christopher Marlowe had been born in 1564 and the Globe Theatre had opened beside the River Thames in 1599, the rebirth of theatre in England was a slow affair. Cromwell, after King Charles Stuart was beheaded in January 1649, gave little priority to such fripperies as theatre and the next decades were dominated by intense political argument over an important issue: Should Britain be a monarchy or a republic, a parliamentary commonwealth or a military protectorate? The impact of the civil war was long-lasting and all-consuming but, happily, the settling of old disputes was frequently less bitter than could have been anticipated. The parliamentary victors sought little vengeance on the defeated Royalists. Similarly, when Charles II returned to the throne in 1660, he showed admirable clemency to his late father's enemies. Even Cromwell's sons, Richard and Henry, went unpunished. Perhaps King and Commoner both realised they claimed the same God as their champion – though one of Cromwell's prayers recorded in the 1640s confirmed the clear contrast in the objectives of the two men:

---

182. See Chapter 2

"*Strengthen us, O God, to relieve the oppressed, to hear the groans of poor prisoners, to reform the abuses of all professions, that many be made not poor (in order) to make a few rich – for Jesus Christ's sake.*"[183]

The 17th century, then, was unexciting from a theatrical point of view; it was as if the whole nation was exhausted by the years of civil war and cherished the chance to live together once more in peace.

During the 1730s in Canterbury, a theatre began to operate out of the upper floor of a market building close to the cathedral. It was known as Buttermarket House, but the building was demolished in the 1780s and the city was again left without a theatre until the emergence of a genuine theatrical impresario named Sarah Baker. She was born Sarah Wakelin into a travelling family and inherited her parents' troupe of wandering performers – dancers, clowns, jugglers, even Punch and Judy puppets. She was herself a puppeteer, but she had theatrical ambitions – she admired Shakespeare, Sheridan, Marlowe – and it is recorded that, in the 1780s, she brought her *Sadler's Wells Diversions* company to play at the Buttermarket Theatre. When it closed, Sarah Baker had no playhouse in Canterbury in which to perform. So she built her own theatre and home in Prince of Orange Street (now Orange Street) and named it The New Theatre or, unofficially, The Canterbury Theatre. This was noteworthy for two reasons; firstly, Sarah Baker was a woman active in a man's world and, secondly, she revealed that she was both able and obsessive in her love of theatre. She managed to succeed by using a combination of innate business acumen and a full-on, fairground approach to the job in hand. The New Theatre opened on August 24th 1789 with a performance of *Twelfth Night*, in Canterbury's first purpose-built theatre for more than a century. Sarah Baker led from the front. She took the money at the door and regular theatregoers became used to her shrill cry. "*Box or pit? Box or pit?*" and "*Pass on, pass on...*"[184] An actor recorded in his

183. Oliver Cromwell 1599–1658. A Time to Pray, Philip Law, Lion Publishing, 1997, ISBN 07459 3910 4
184. Seat prices were Box: 3 shillings, Pit: 2 shillings, Balcony: 1 shilling

diary: "*She owned an excellent heart with much of the appearance and manners of a gentlewoman…but occasionally her language was more forceful and idiomatic than tasteful and refined.*"

The indomitable Mrs Baker built a circuit of 16 theatres for her companies in Kent and Sussex – at Maidstone, Rochester, Faversham, Dover, Royal Tunbridge Wells, Folkestone and Hastings. She used local actors and international stars such as the clown Grimaldi; artist Thomas Sydney Cooper painted scenery flats for her. Hasted[185] described her New Theatre as '*elegant… handsome…and far and away the best of her theatres*'. On her death in 1816 the theatre passed to her son, William Dowton, and was completely refurbished. The New Theatre finally closed in 1859, condemned as unsafe. The premises were then converted into a warehouse, a use that continued for 100 years until the 1950s. It was then transformed into a grocery store and, in 1955, into offices of a television cable company. In 1984, the building was bought by a local developer, Colin Tomlin and was converted into the retail premises of Merchant Chandler who operated there for 30 years until 2014. Despite its illustrious history, there is little physical trace today of what went on at No 4 Orange Street during the 70 years from the turn of the 18th century.[186]

A new, smaller theatre in Guildhall Street, funded by Thomas Sydney Cooper, opened in 1861. A plaque on the old Debenhams building records that Charles Dickens gave readings there, describing his audience as '*the most delicate…I have seen in any provincial place*'.[187] This 'Theatre Royal' closed in the 1920s as cinemas became more popular.

A number of Victorian halls were used occasionally for theatrical productions and, in Northgate, The Penny Theatre[188] appeared. Tiny, but as atmospheric as its name implies (18 feet wide and 35 feet long), it opened between 1750 and, perhaps as late as

---

185. Edward Hasted, historian (1732–1812)
186. My thanks to Clive Bowley and Doreen Rosman for information on early theatres and Dr Sheila Sweetinburgh
187. Written City, Brown, Hutchinson and Irwin, 1986
188. Dover Kent Archives, Public Houses, Paul Skelton

1903, when it was known as the (Princess) Alexandra Music Hall. The legendary reggae and ska singer, Judge Dredd, died there from a heart attack in 1998. I knew it as a fascinating ironmongery shop with a bizarre balcony filled with lawnmowers, but it subsequently had a number of incarnations as storage space, a restaurant, an amusement arcade and a pub. There is still a small theatre at the rear of this Grade 2 listed building, large enough to host live bands.

* * * * * * * * * *

The building of the new Marlowe Theatre in Canterbury early in the 21st century is perhaps the finest example in the city's history of community and philanthropy working constructively together with the city fathers.

On Friday April 27th 2007, a group of nine people gathered at the Westgate Hall in Canterbury – the city's chief executive, Colin Carmichael, its theatre director, Mark Everett, and fund-raiser, Jane Redman, from Canterbury City Council; businessmen Michael Head, Michael Bukht, Ian Odgers and myself, and fund-raising consultant, Roger Mitty. There were apologies from other businessmen, including Paul Barrett, Stephen Kingsman and architect, Anthony de Moubray. The city council had, in 2005, decided to support the development of a new, larger Marlowe Theatre on the site of the current Marlowe Theatre, which it owned, and in the two years that followed, a steering group had explored the ways that development might take place. All the people I have named had been members of that steering group. There are a number of Canterbury families that traditionally wield a benevolent influence in the city – some more than others. The Barrett family is one of them. George Barrett, founder of the Barretts motor company, was the son of a Canterbury Town Sergeant and Sheriff's Officer at the end of the 19th century. One hundred and twenty years later, Paul Barrett would become High Sheriff of Kent and a Freeman of the City for his services to the community and his activity as a fund-raiser for charity. His contribution to the campaign on which we were about to embark would be considerable.

As a group, we knew what was wanted but we didn't have the money to pay for it. Fund-raising is an art. It needs, above all else, organisation. Like all the best achievements, it needs a beginning, middle and end. Each stage is crucial, but the beginning is probably the most important. The key to starting successfully is to obtain a commitment to a big financial donation, even before the appeal is launched. This matters because, obviously, it is a major contribution to the final target total. But it also matters because, however large the target figure, the existence of the big initial donation indicates, to the world at large, that this is a project worthy of support. There are also political factors to be considered. The collateral for a big donation for a capital project such as the Marlowe is that the donor usually seeks a high-profile 'naming opportunity'. It is part of the deal.

Increasingly, in recent years, patterns of approval in British society have changed. All careful charities now periodically question the source of the money they are being offered. They do not want to risk tarnishing their image or their cause with a *post-facto* explosion of negative publicity. An association with tobacco or fossil fuels may create protests. The many projects which have benefited from the Sackler millions have been embarrassed because members of the Sackler family own, or have owned, interests in Purdue Pharma LP, a company that is facing hundreds of lawsuits in the United States over its alleged role in the opioid crisis. The war in Ukraine has meant that all Russian money is potentially tainted. Over the years, fashions change and professional fund-raisers have to be quick-witted. Thankfully, we would face none of these potential traumas; local businessman, Michael Head, would pledge £250,000 to the campaign, a crucial commitment that grew solely from Michael's love of the community in which he lived.

The city council had hired the experienced Roger Mitty as a fund-raising consultant. After further interviews, Jane Redman was chosen as campaign co-ordinator. The target figure for the campaign was £6 million.[189] Roger Mitty had done his homework. He and his team had assembled a list of 175 'high-value, Kent-based individuals', 196 employees and 242 trusts, which might support the campaign. He had interviewed '32 individual prospects' and the bosses of six major companies and, as he presented his plans he thanked the city council's Hazel Levy for 'ensuring the smooth running of the interview process'. He produced a summary of comments made and advice given, by those he interviewed. They had variously declared:

'I need to be convinced that this will be a stunning project...you need to stress the economic impact a successful theatre will make on the area....it must have easy access because parking in Canterbury is a persistent problem...we could and should be much bigger in the arts...does a theatre really have to be this expensive?...this project needs to be free from political interference...I am concerned about the costs; where does all the money vanish?'

Looking back nearly 20 years at his thoughts on that day in 2007, Roger Mitty says that he was 'confident in recommending that the campaign should go ahead'. The estimated cost of the work (the adaptation/rebuilding of the Marlowe) was £23 million at 2008/9 prices. He went on:

'I believed it would be possible to raise £6 million, through the formation of a charitable trust, provided that:
- *the Marlowe had a positive image in the community*
- *the need for the Theatre, both artistically and in its financial contribution to the economy, could be supported*
- *the City Council was dedicated to the new theatre and the campaign*
- *the volunteer campaign leaders were dedicated, vocal and well-organised, and*
- *all involved showed a vital sense of urgency, to argue the use and need for a theatre.'*

---

189. Fundraising Planning Study Report to Canterbury Council, August 2006

In financial terms, the council's support for the adaptation of the Marlowe made sense, though the sums involved, for a relatively small district council, were large. The fact was that the Marlowe Theatre, the old Odeon Cinema, was falling down – the roof leaked and there were other structural problems. The décor was tired. Failure to act would mean that the theatre would have to close. To repair and refurbish it would cost around £13.5 million. For an additional £13 million, then, the city could have a totally new, state-of-the-art theatre. Of that sum, the city council reckoned that half would come from the public sector – Kent County Council and SEEDA. They agreed that that would leave around £6 million to be raised in a public campaign. Mitty said he was confident that could be done.

Members of the Steering Group, which I chaired, had worked closely with Roger Mitty throughout these months and knew that one of his priorities was, as he put it, *'access to leadership which could influence and motivate others at the higher levels'*. He had seen that the city council were firmly dedicated to saving a theatre for the city. One of the most impressive aspects of the debates over many years had been the consistent determination shown by successive sets of councillors that the Marlowe Theatre should not become a party political issue. Ron Pepper for Labour was an early champion. Like Michael Dixey, Alex Perkins and Nic Eden-Green for the Liberal Democrats and Harry Cragg and Rosemary Doyle and, of course, David Pentin for the Conservatives, they became deeply involved in the discussions; always optimistic, their support consistent. They were our champions.

The support from the city council was total – well, virtually total. Throughout the campaign, one city councillor had her reservations. Hazel McCabe was a diligent and admirable councillor. She represented the people of Canterbury for almost half a century. But she would not be persuaded to support the building of a new theatre. She was twice Mayor of Canterbury and much respected, not least because she declared her principles and held to them. One of them was that public money should not be spent on the arts and entertainment. Four or five times over the years, a commitment to build the new Marlowe was considered by the council. Hazel either opposed the proposition or abstained. Those who knew her were fond of her, knew that to try to change her mind was a waste of time. In 1986, when Prime Minister Margaret Thatcher and French President Mitterand had met in the Chapter House of the Cathedral to sign the Treaty of Canterbury that authorised the building of the Channel Tunnel, Hazel had refused to attend. She was then Mayor of Canterbury but, while Thatcher and Mitterand put pen to paper, Hazel sat in mute protest in the Mayoral car, parked in the cathedral precincts. Chris Gay, then the city's chief executive, remembers that there were numerous opponents of this link to France. They resisted any closer relationship with Europe, citing what they termed 'the garlic factor'.[190] Julian Brazier, soon to be elected Canterbury's Member of Parliament, feared the economic and environmental impact the tunnel would have on Kent, and says: *"Hazel was not alone in her opposition to it. The Dean's position was not filled at the time and the Cathedral Chapter met and requested that the signing of the treaty should not take place in the cathedral. I think the Archbishop, Robert Runcie, who was abroad at the time, had to be contacted to overrule them! Otherwise, the signing could not have taken place in the cathedral."* Hazel McCabe stuck to her principles then and throughout the Marlowe campaign – a lone voice among 48 committed supporters on the city council.

The chief executives of the council, firstly Chris Gay and, throughout the fund-raising and development campaign, Colin Carmichael, could not have been more accessible and positive. Colin would subsequently tell me:

"It is fair to say that, without either the city council or the fund-raising trust, the theatre would never have been built, particularly not to the design and standard that we eventually achieved.

---

190. Chris Gay was instructed to write to the Prime Minister objecting to the decision to arrange the signing in Canterbury Cathedral. Ironically, he was himself in favour of the Treaty and the creation of the Channel Tunnel

"The trust influenced the council, and the council influenced the trust in our joint objective to build a theatre of which the city could be proud."

The relationship between the council and the Trust was constructive and friendly. The scope for confusion and misunderstanding was considerable, but friction was rare and used positively. Decision-makers from the council were members of the Board of the Trust. Colin Carmichael was one of its Trustees. The primacy of the city council was always acknowledged but the debate over the project ranged across the spectrum. We were, together, asking a community to give us millions of pounds to fund our dream. Pragmatically, residents are unlikely to give money to a council, which was why the charitable trust had been set up in the first place. Members of the Trust were very aware of the challenge that faced them. However perfect the fund-raising plan, however wide the net cast, there would come the moment when they would have to ask a potential donor to commit money to the project. People do not like asking other people for money. It is not easy. We agreed that the public appeal needed a high profile and an instantly recognised attraction that would loosen purse strings.

The make-up of the Trust's Campaign Board was a broad church. Together (and in alphabetical order), Paul Barrett, Nigel Beevor, Sir Michael Bett, James Bird, Michael Bukht,[191] Andrew Clague, Vyvyan Harmsworth, Michael Head, Ian Odgers, Sir Graeme Odgers, Clive Relf, Graham Sinclair, Fiona Sunley and Charles Villiers were energetic and generous with access to their contacts and acquaintances. During the years of early-morning meetings, colleagues became friends, so much so that we still meet once a year as The Eight O'Clock Club; those who don't wear the orange and black tie bearing the letter 'M' are chided for their forgetfulness.[192]

The leadership of the fund-raising campaign was crucial. Roger

---

191. Sadly, Michael died before the new theatre opened
192. Our Royal Patron, Prince Edward, is an exception to that rule

had, in early conversations, asked whether I would be interested in chairing the Trust. I thought not, for a variety of reasons which included a feeling that, having been involved so closely for so many years in the battle to save the theatre – and to launch a festival – in Canterbury, I was simply a familiar part of the furniture. In addition, the leader of the campaign should have influence outside Canterbury and its district. I was, I told Roger, willing to be vice-chairman. It was agreed that Sir Graeme Odgers should be invited to become our chairman – and it was hinted that his brother, Ian, should whisper in his ear.[193] Sir Sandy Bruce-Lockhart,[194] leader of Kent County Council, agreed to become our president. Roger had advised we needed a strong leadership. This *was* a strong leadership.

Graeme Odgers and I had never met. He came with an impressive CV after a long career in South Africa and in British industry. He had chaired Kent County Council's investment arm, Locate in Kent, for seven years and had also led the Kent Economic Board for a similar period. He was wise and well connected and we became friends. He recalls the reasons why he joined:

"The Trust at that time had been ably driven by you, Peter; it was a group of prominent Kent individuals and it had strong support from the council and its chief executive. All that was very important, I felt."

Graeme became one of the new theatre's most generous benefactors, over many years. His initial financial contribution to the campaign was in memory of his daughter, Victoria, who, at the age of 14, had been tragically killed in a motor accident. He told me why, at a time in his life when he was shedding responsibilities, he had decided to support the theatre. *"It seemed worth doing. I was particularly drawn by the ambitions for outreach, new writing, new productions. That was where I hoped my funding would make a difference."*

The road to success can be bumpy. The financial crisis of

---

193. Sir Graeme accepted the invitation
194. Later, Baron Bruce-Lockhart

September 2008 was a period when the whole project might have been abandoned. News of the financial crash coincided with a scheduled meeting of the Trust. It was a day when captains of industry all over the country held their heads in their hands, when contracts were torn up like confetti in a May Day parade. The city council embraced the Trust in its deliberations; should they call a halt to the project or should they go ahead? With so deep a financial crisis and with the construction contract not yet signed, the option to call a halt was on the table. Overwhelmingly, the feeling was to keep going. Colin Carmichael again:

"We were helped, it has to be admitted, by the fact that the tender for the construction works coincided with a downturn in the construction industry economy, allowing us to get a reasonable price for the rebuild and to allow many of the architectural highlights of the building which had otherwise been removed in the interests of economy, to be restored to the design."

We reckoned the project saved £2 million that day. There had been a lively debate over the style of seating in our new three-tier theatre. Cloth seats were serviceable but would wear out relatively quickly. Red leather seats, made in Italy, would last longer and, we felt, would make a statement of vigour and confidence, but these were more expensive. Ironically, the financial crisis and the money we 'saved' that day saved the Marlowe's spectacular red seats.

The work of the Trust built on months of preparatory lobbying. One of the targets as a source of funding had been Kent County Council and, in 2007, Colin Carmichael had achieved a pledge from KCC's leader Paul Carter for a "very substantial commitment to the project". Graeme, Colin and I went to see Paul Carter. Graeme again:

"I well remember an early meeting we went to together, to ask for support from Kent County Council. We presented an argument for the importance of a new Marlowe Theatre, both to the economy of East Kent and to the fabric of the community. It was a tough

*meeting; with Paul Carter I remember we were asking for £4 million
– £2 million as a grant and a further £2 million as a loan. We got it
in the end."*

Some time later, Paul, with feigned irritation, revealed to me a
letter, which, before the meeting, he had dictated to send to us. It
informed us that we would be given not 4 million but £2 million
– £1 million as a grant, £1 million as a loan. But he had been
impressed by the strength and ambition of the Marlowe project
and had let the preconceived letter lie unread, in his desk drawer.

This was a generous gesture by the county council. It was
already deeply committed to building the £17.5 million Turner
Contemporary gallery at Margate and was supporting the Theatre
Royal, Margate, as further steps in the regeneration of the seaside
town, and to The Cube in Folkestone. Mike Hill, the cabinet
member for the county's community services, commented:

*'We are determined to support art and cultural events and venues in
Kent, and help them raise their profiles...'*[195]

There was also a determination to bring classical opera back to
Kent, a desire supported by the Festival which remembered with
regret the destruction of Kent Opera 20 years before. We looked
outside Kent to seek a solution – to Glyndebourne, the unique
'Opera House in a mansion' as it was termed when John Christie
founded it in 1933 at his home in the Sussex countryside.[196]
Glyndebourne had assembled a touring company, with an annual
programme and an international reputation. The mission, then,
was to persuade Glyndebourne Touring to embrace in its plans
the as yet unbuilt Marlowe Theatre. Vyvyan Harmsworth was
a member of our Trust. He and his family were supporters of
Glyndebourne. Vere Harmsworth was a major donor and a friend

---

195. Press statement, December 18th 2007
196. Robert Ponsonby, later to become Canterbury Festival's Artistic
Director, but then a trainee at Glyndebourne, was secretary of the
Glyndebourne Arts Trust

of George Christie's; the present Lord Rothermere had been a member of the Glyndebourne Trust's committee. Vyvyan was himself a member. Mark Everett was, by that time, on the Board of South East Arts, including companies such as English Touring Opera in the Marlowe Theatre programme when it was offered and when he could, but the planning was necessarily piecemeal. Together, we made the 'capture' of Glyndebourne a priority. We needed to discover how the new Marlowe could become irresistible to Glyndebourne.

Vyvyan wrote to Gus Christie, mentioning his personal link and the past financial support from his family, and from the Daily Mail Group. Thus it was that he and his wife, Alexandra, and Jo and I, one summer evening, watched a stunning performance of *Peter Grimes* and afterwards chatted with Gus Christie in the bar at Glyndebourne. It was a friendly and open discussion, as much about the challenge of building a new theatre as about the Glyndebourne company visiting it once it was built. But we had one crucial question to which we needed an answer: How big did the new Marlowe orchestra pit need to be to accommodate the Glyndebourne orchestra? Gus smiled: *"We need space for up to 80 musicians and not many theatres have that capacity..."* and the conversation moved on. We reported back to the Trust: if we wanted to attract Glyndebourne, the Marlowe's orchestra pit needed to be flexible enough to accommodate 80 musicians. Mark Everett and designer, Keith Williams, took the challenge in their stride. Sure enough, many months later, when Mark Everett was negotiating with Glyndebourne, one of the first questions he had to field was: *"How big is your orchestra pit? Do you know, we sometimes need space for 80..?"*

We *did* know.

We had another stroke of good fortune as Glyndebourne's general director was David Pickard. David had worked for Kent Opera and there was no need to explain to him the importance of opera to Canterbury. Mark Everett remembers David's visit to the theatre when it was simply a skeleton around a central stage. "David had his memories of the Kent Opera debacle. I also knew that, given the crowded programme of Glyndebourne Touring, one of the other venues on their annual schedule might have to make way if they decided to come to Canterbury. The situation could have been delicate but that subject was never mentioned. We talked about the advantage of the size of the stage, the need to extend the wings and the ability to get into our site with the vehicles involved in a Glyndebourne production. And, of course we talked about the size of the orchestra pit. Paula Gillespie and I had lunch with David and we believed David and his then technical manager would recommend that Glyndebourne come to Canterbury."

Mark was right.[197]

Raising money for the Marlowe presented much the same challenges as with any charitable project. Businessmen and politicians were more likely to support it if they could see a financial return. The Marlowe certainly ticked that box. The Shellard Formula is an assessment of a project's economic impact invented at the University of Sheffield and now generally accepted in charitable circles. According to Shellard, a new Marlowe Theatre would inject into the Kent community around £25 million every year.[198]

The message being proclaimed by the newly formed Marlowe Theatre Development Trust was that this was An Important Project. As such, it needed an injection of style. A royal patron, perhaps. I discussed this with Allan Willett, Kent's Lord Lieutenant and therefore Her Majesty's representative in the county. My company had made a number of documentaries with members of the royal family and, through our contacts and with Allan's support, we opened negotiations. We knew that Prince Edward, the Earl of Wessex, loved theatre. He had worked with Andrew Lloyd Webber and, latterly, had run his own media company. I asked to meet him and he agreed. The preparation for that meeting was meticulous. It

---

197. Glyndebourne Touring would later debut at the Marlowe Theatre Canterbury, in the autumn of 2011 with Dvořák's opera, Rusalka
198. There were those who doubted that figure. Calculations at the end of the first year of the new theatre's life indicated that the Marlowe Theatre had added £30 million to the local economy

began in August and September and on the 12th of that month, we wrote to Prince Edward. Should the meeting with the Prince take place, Brigadier David Ralls, Allan Willett's leading ADC, sent me a briefing note, not least on how to address a member of the royal family, and other such matters.

On October 3rd, I received a reply from Brigadier John Smedley, the Prince's Private Secretary. He had taken my letter, supported by a note from Allan, to the Prince *"who, before further consideration, would welcome a meeting to discuss your plans and how you see him being able to help."* The meeting would take place on November 11th at Buckingham Palace. Early that afternoon, I was escorted through the cordon of security, along endless corridors, in and out of an ancient iron-clad, hand-latched lift and into an airy, well-lit modern office, where the Earl of Wessex stood to greet me. He was welcoming and friendly – but the meeting began disappointingly. He said that he was *"already involved in three other appeals"* and the new Marlowe Theatre *"might be an appeal too far"*. Our meeting lasted nearly an hour. In that time, we discussed the social impact the theatre could (and would) make on the rejuvenation of the region, the stylish shape of the theatre, its footprint and the building timetable; the sources of the £24.7 million we needed; the current and growing success of the existing Marlowe Theatre at the box office; the need to reduce or remove the current £500,000 annual subsidy to the theatre from the city council, which could be achieved partly by increasing the theatre's capacity from 900–950 to 1200; the strength of local support for the project, which had a Friends group of more than 10,000, and the ambition to become a 'producing' theatre, reaching out to a younger generation with a 150-seater Second Space that was an integral part of the Marlowe concept.

This was a negotiation with a busy man, sympathetic to the theatre's aims, but weighing up whether his time would be best used by taking on another project. We had tea and biscuits. He said: *"If I do it, I won't simply be a name on a letterhead. I see its (the theatre's) importance and I would want to do it properly or not at all.*[199] Below is a copy of the letter that I received:

15th January 2008

Dear Peter,

Thank you for your further letter of 12th December 2007 to The Earl of Wessex enclosing an outline of your objectives and strategy in building a new Marlowe Theatre.

Following your briefing on 19th November at Buckingham Palace, His Royal Highness has now given careful thought to your request for him to become Royal Patron of the Marlowe Theatre Campaign and would be delighted to accept for a period of 3 years up to December 2010. I enclose a copy of the general rules of royal patronage for your information...

The Earl of Wessex much looks forward to being able to help your campaign and I look forward to working with you and your board.

Yours sincerely,
John Smedley

Brigadier John Smedley
Private Secretary to TRH The Earl and Countess of Wessex
cc Lord Lieutenant for Kent, Allan Willett

Under the headline 'THEATRE ROYAL', the local press declared:[200] 'EDWARD JOINS NEW MARLOWE PATRONS.' It continued:

'Showbiz royal Prince Edward has agreed to become patron of Canterbury's new Marlowe Theatre.

---

199. Author's note to file, November 19th 2007
200. Adscene, January 25th 2008

'The Prince, who used to run his own TV production company and trained with Andrew Lloyd-Webber's Really Useful Group, announced on Wednesday that he is backing the £24 million project.

'The announcement followed talks between the Prince and film-maker Peter Williams, vice-chairman of the New Marlowe Theatre Development Trust. The Earl will be part of the team until December 2010 when the new theatre is expected to open. The deal was confirmed in November following a meeting with Mr Williams at Buckingham Palace. Mr Williams, 73, from Boughton, said:

"It is fantastic news that he has agreed to be royal patron and we will meet him regularly to discuss the campaign and its progress and to get his advice.

"He is not just going to be a name on a letterhead. He is going to be fully involved in everything we seek to do."

'*Chairman of the new Marlowe campaign board Sir Graeme Odgers said: "His patronage is a huge fillip to the campaign and I am delighted he has found the time in his extremely busy schedule to take on this role."*

'*Leader of Canterbury City Council Cllr John Gilbey said: "Securing the support of Prince Edward for the campaign is a stunning coup. It really raises the profile of the project and completes an amazing line-up of patrons and board members."*

'*Other patrons include Canterbury-born Hollywood heart-throb Orlando Bloom, actress Joanna Lumley, brewery boss Robert Neame, comedian Dave Lee, Sir Robert Worcester, Edwin Boorman, Lady Moira Swire, Lady Northbourne, Lady Vallence and the Lord Lieutenant of Kent Allan Willett. The campaign needs to raise £6 million towards the cost of the new Marlowe. The theatre's three-tier 1,200-seat auditorium will allow bigger shows to be staged and a second smaller space will host experimental and community theatre.*

'*The city council is committed to spend £8.7 million towards the project – the amount needed to bring the existing theatre up to present-day standards. Kent County Council has committed up to £4 million. City councillors are due to vote on whether to proceed with the plans at a special meeting on February 11. Others on the campaign board include motor dealer Paul Barrett. Michael Bukht who founded the Classic FM radio station, architect Andrew Clague and Herne Bay businessman Michael Head.'*

The Earl of Wessex was far more than a 'showbiz royal'. We would meet regularly throughout the campaign. He was our guest of honour when patron, Sir Robert Worcester, threw open his home in Allington Castle in November 2008 for a fund-raising dinner. He would extend his patronage far beyond the three years he had promised and would be there, wittily, to share in the celebration of the new Marlowe Theatre's opening in 2011.

With a strong leadership now in place, matters moved apace. The first big donation of £250,000 had, as we know, been made before the launch of the public phase of the campaign, by Michael Head, a lovely man who had made his money by producing fine and stylish kitchens through his company, Crown Products. SEEDA[201] now gave £2 million to buy an adjoining garage and extend the theatre's footprint. The Bernard Sunley Charitable Foundation pledged £200,000; Fiona Sunley was a consistent supporter of both the theatre and the Festival. In August, the city council unanimously gave to the new theatre planning permission. The council would sell assets worth £11 million to part fund its £13.5 million contributions to the building of the new theatre.

The Marlowe's "£25.5 million revamp" as the BBC put it, was now approved provided £6 million could be raised from private sources over the next three years. *"No pressure then"*, was the view expressed at the next meeting of the Marlowe Theatre Development Trust. Keith Williams, then the UK Architect of the Year for Public and Cultural Buildings, had been asked to design the new building. He was tall, talented and no relation. His vision for the building was far-sighted and completely appropriate. Fly towers for theatres are necessary to contain sets and flats to be moved before and during performances, but they are bulky blocks for any architect to accommodate, particularly in such close proximity to the

201.   SEEDA: South East England Development Agency

cathedral. Keith turned a problem into an opportunity. He fluted the fly tower and, using imaginative lighting, contributed a fresh and exciting spectacle to the city's night skyline. He had pledged to create "a multi-award-winning, world-class contemporary building". And that's exactly what he did.

For personal reasons, Sir Graeme stepped down as chairman and asked me to take his place. At the Board meeting when this was confirmed, I thanked him for his "firm and fair chairmanship" and, importantly, persuaded him to remain on the Board as our President following the sad death of Sir Sandy Bruce-Lockhart. I also took the opportunity of suggesting Ian Odgers and Vyvyan Harmsworth as vice-chairs. We had, at that moment, raised £1.5 million towards our £6 million target. We were able to say as we looked to the public phase of the campaign: "We've already raised a lump of money. This theatre is going to be built – and, now, we need your help to raise *only* £4 million." I stressed the word 'only'.[202]

The public phase of the campaign was launched as the old Marlowe Theatre closed on March 22nd 2009, with a performance titled *The Night of a Thousand Stars*, hosted by Brian Conley and starring Barbara Windsor and Shaun Williamson. Mark Everett spoke from the stage and described the years since its adaptation from its life as a cinema in 1984 as "25 wonderful years, entertaining the people of Canterbury and Kent". For those of us in the audience involved in the rebirth of the Canterbury Festival, the building housed memories of the successful growth of an annual celebration each autumn that was now part of the national arts calendar.

If there were an underlying tension in the campaign, it was in the junction between the city council and the Development Trust, over the campaign's public profile. As we together strove to establish an image for the campaign, Marlowe director, Mark Everett, and I, as chair of the Trust, became a double act. Together we made presentations; Morecambe and Wise but with fewer chuckles. We always made it a joint appeal. 'We' was the keyword.

---

202. Marlowe Theatre Development Trust minutes, 2009

When we used it, no-one in our many audiences thought that Mark was speaking for the city council and I was representing the charitable trust. 'We' meant what it said; together we were trying to build a theatre. One of my niggling regrets is that a single senior councillor and the occasional official criticised the Trust for taking "too much credit" for what became a successful campaign; they did not hear the unity expressed publicly during the hundreds of presentations over the years, jointly made. Together, we sought the high public profile we had all agreed; without it, we would have failed to raise the necessary millions.

It would take two years to build the new Marlowe. To all intents and purposes, it was a new theatre, though the stage originally constructed in 1933 amid the salad days of the movie cinema, survived in the new building, its wings extended. Keith Williams produced a superb theatre. In the weeks before opening, I remember a quiet moment with Mark Everett in the empty theatre, waiting for cast and customers to breathe life into it. We stood in the Upper Circle, stared down on the spectacular red-seated auditorium and observed that the one aspect that could spoil it all was the acoustics. At that very moment, two electricians working on stage, broke their silence as they inspected a complex junction in the wiring. We could hear every word they said to each other. We smiled and moved on…

Altogether, the campaign was fascinating. It embraced the tragic and the comic and a great deal of kindness. Richard Attenborough sadly lost his daughter, Jane Holland, and his 15-year-old granddaughter, Lucy, in the tsunami disaster of 2004. His other daughter, Charlotte, was married to Graham Sinclair, a member of our Trust and, following a series of meetings with our vice-chair, Vyvyan Harmsworth, the Attenboroughs generously supported our campaign and brokered a £250,000 grant from the Foundation of Sport and the Arts. A photograph of Lord and Lady Attenborough (Sheila Sim) hangs in the Marlowe stairwell, passed every day by those who make their way from foyer to circle. Artistes adapted their diaries to play for us. Conspicuously, cellist

Robert Cohen gave up his fee to play a solo fund-raising concert for us at the Gulbenkian Theatre. The theatre was packed. It also happened to be my birthday and Robert, who had appeared many times in the Festival, played a favourite piece by Arvo Pärt, titled *Fratres*. It is one of the best birthday gifts I have ever recieved.

Successive archbishops have supported both the Festival and the Marlowe Theatre and Rowan Williams and his wife, Jane, were familiar friends. Towards the end of their time in Canterbury, Jo and I hosted a private dinner for them in a room in the Abode Hotel. There were perhaps 10 in our party and we had booked seats to go on to the Marlowe to see a Glyndebourne opera. We left the Abode and strolled down the High Street. It was 7.15 and we had plenty of time for a 7.30 curtain-up. As we approached the theatre, it was expectantly lit but strangely quiet. Behind the glass frontage, no-one was moving. We quickened our steps. Had we booked for the wrong evening? Thankfully, no. But the opera was timed to start at 7.15. We were nearly 10 minutes late. Our party occupied much of the front row – row A – in the circle. We entered a packed house and shuffled apologetically into our seats. The curtain rose. It was a great show. Our late arrival had, of course, been noticed. As we left after the show, the accepted truth was that, because the likelihood of a terrorist attack was high, the police had delayed the archbishop's entrance. Shamefacedly, I have to admit it was nothing of the sort. I had simply misread the start time on our tickets!

The new Marlowe Theatre opened on Tuesday October 4th 2011 to the music of the Philharmonia Orchestra. Our royal patron, Prince Edward, Earl of Wessex, who had visited the site quite recently to assess progress, was there to set the seal on a wonderful evening of entertainment, celebration and speeches. Everyone thanked everyone and 1200 people clapped and cheered. Every one of them had, in one way or another, helped to create a theatre that the people of East Kent had hungered for. It was a triumph for the city council for their insight and courage, for Keith Williams for whom it was a tour de force and for the Trust's fund-raising development team who had raised £4.3 million[203] in three years. For consultant, Roger Mitty, it was "*the perfect fund-raising campaign...and I often quote it as such*".

In 2022, the Marlowe Theatre, Canterbury, well led now by director Deborah Shaw, was jointly voted Theatre of the Year. In making the award, *The Stage* praised the Marlowe's mission to be '*an engine house of the performing arts in Kent*', and its role in '*helping the industry to recover from the Covid pandemic...and the work it has undertaken to engage with artists, young people and audiences*'. At the height of the lockdown, the Marlowe made its pantomime available free of charge on-line. It was watched by 92,000 people and was streamed to 91 care homes in Kent and Medway – which seems to me to be a definition of outreach.

Festival...theatre...opera. Three aspects of the arts which have become inextricably entwined in the history of this ancient city – a thriving festival, one of the nation's top theatres and, following the demise of Kent Opera, a strong relationship with Glyndebourne Touring Opera. What has been achieved is the culmination of a campaign that stretches back more than 30 years. The new Marlowe is many things to many people. To benefactors, such as the Sunley Foundation and to Roger De Haan, it is "a truly transformational project for the South East" and "a theatre that would play a vital role in stimulating the regional economy". To patron, Orlando Bloom, it is "a wonderful opportunity to inspire and enthuse the young people of Kent, and to develop their talents". To patrons Timothy West and Prunella Scales, it is "a spectacular new performance space which will attract the very best among the performing arts". To the architectural and travel journalists of the national newspapers, it is "a beauty...sleek and airy...with imaginative use of wood finishes"[204] and "another awe-inspiring space for Canterbury".[205]

---

203. This figure would later be raised to £5 million. Conversation with Clive Relf, the Trust's treasurer, 2021
204. Daily Telegraph, October 8th 2011
205. Sunday Express, October 9th 2011

The Marlowe Theatre is all this, and more. It is a contribution that this generation has made to the history of a most historic city. It sits remarkably comfortably within the ancient city walls. It brings the pleasures of theatre, music, opera, comedy and dance to people of all ages. It is truly a People's Theatre, for this community helped to build it. After all, what is a great city without a theatre, at the heart of a Festival that fought hard and long for its existence?

APPENDICES

Appendix 1: Margaret Babington

Canon Derek Ingram Hill (1912-2003), himself a unique character in Canterbury Cathedral's precincts, wrote this of Margaret Babington (1878-1958):

Margaret Babington was a woman of the greatest hidden potential. I doubt if anyone has hit Canterbury with more of the impact of a bomb than Margaret Babington. Because you see, nobody knew that this quiet clergyman's daughter was to turn out to be the tremendous personality that now you and I know she was. She was a quiet wee woman and she was usually clad in black clothes such as a clergymen's daughter would have used in those days. By the time she had been here for a year, we knew that we had something tremendous in our midst. She had enormous energy; she had tremendous vision; she had a colossal will; she was afraid of nobody and nothing. Incidentally, I think she had private means, which does help, and she stood up to all those people who didn't perhaps agree with her ideas and invariably, but not always, got her way. And Dean Bell, of course, was delighted to back her and support her.

Eleanor Bliss, in her insightful book *The Urgent Miss Babington*[206] set out to "illustrate what an incredible force Margaret Agnes Babington was, both in Tenterden and later in Canterbury. 'Miss Babs' had the knack of getting things done – or 'getting other people to get things done'. I suppose today we would call her a facilitator; I have to say in later life I think she was probably more of a dragon. She learnt her skills in Tenterden, working alongside her father, the Rev John Babington, supporting him in his role as vicar. Then she moved on to Canterbury Cathedral where she

---

206. Canterbury Publishing, 2018

cajoled deans, bishops, the rich and famous, as well as ordinary people like you and me, into taking action alongside her efforts to promote Canterbury Cathedral. She was awarded the OBE 'for services to the Cathedral'.

Margaret was enrolled as an Officer in the Order of St John for services to nursing; she was the first WVS Canterbury co-ordinator at the start of the Second World War. As well as writing a 'best seller' to raise money for the cathedral, she was the driving force behind the early Canterbury Festivals. She toured America and Canada several times, including during the war, giving lectures to raise money for the work of the cathedral. Margaret Babington is recognised as having raised hundreds of thousands of pounds for the cathedral.

By the end of the Second World War, she estimated that she had shown up to 12,000 people around the cathedral, including huge numbers of American and Canadian soldiers who were stationed in the area during the conflict.

Appendix 2: The Canterbury Festival and Kent Opera – A Point of View

A note to file, made by Mark Deller in 2004, recalls his memories of the early years:

The gradual renaissance of the Canterbury Festival as we now know it, began in 1979, when the city council announced that they wished to develop the car park and the site occupied by the 'old' Marlowe Theatre in St Margaret's Street. Somewhat surprisingly, the Council pledged that they would not knock down the theatre until a provision had been made for the building of a new one.[207] It did mean, however, that amongst other things, the repertory company, that had been such a stimulating part of the City's cultural life for 30 years, would cease to exist, and there were no plans to subsidise a resident theatre company in the future. But Kent Opera, the first regional touring opera company, had by this time become an established force in the opera world. Their spiritual home was the Marlowe Theatre in Canterbury, and they had good reason to want to see a new theatre built in the city; more than that, they were keen to ensure that whatever was built would be to specifications that made proper provision for touring opera – adequate stage size, an orchestra pit, ability to fly scenery, etc. The old Marlowe (which itself had been a conversion from the former Central Cinema) has no pit at all, and I well remember from my own experience with the company, that if one exited the stage right, in order then to enter stage left, one had to go out of the theatre and through the car park!

So it was, that in 1979, as a result of Kent Opera's initiative, the Canterbury New Theatre and Festival Trust was established, with

---

207. This followed debates in full council and a meeting between the City Council, Keith Lucas and Peter Williams

Keith Lucas as chairman, to act as a pressure group, not only to see that the city council abided by its commitment to build a new theatre, but also to bring its wealth of experience and expertise to bear on the ultimate design of the building. Various local people, with a keen interest in the arts, were invited to join the Trust; the present Festival Chairman, Peter Williams, and myself among them. The deliberations about a new theatre, whether it should be purpose-built or a conversion of the former Odeon cinema went on for some time – but significantly, two of the things that the Trust pledged in its support of the city council, were a) that it would help to raise funds, and b) that it would assist in the annual programming, by resurrecting (and funding) an annual Canterbury Festival. In both these objectives it was successful; the Trust contributed £20,000 towards the interior décor of the present Marlowe, and the first of the current series of Festivals was held in the autumn of 1984, to coincide with the opening of the theatre.

The Festival programme for that year was devised by a committee, consisting of Norman Platt, the director of Kent Opera, Reg Brown, director of the Gulbenkian Theatre, Michael Marriott (who had recently retired as the Finance director of the Thorndike Theatre in Leatherhead), Brian Arnold, who was 'Mr Music' in Canterbury, Mary Villiers from the National Arts Collection Fund and myself. I was appointed in November 1983 to be the Administrator. I had the task of setting up a Festival Office to co-ordinate the programme and asked to produce a 3-week mixed-arts festival, for a total budget of £50,000. I managed to persuade Michael Waterfield to let me rent a small room at the from of his Waterfields restaurant (of blessed memory) in Best Lane, and he and a number of his friends agreed to organise an 'alternative' Fringe Festival, to complement the mainstream festival programme.

That first festival in 1984 included a week of the National Theatre at the Marlowe, another with the Ballet Rambert and a third with Kent Opera performing Mozart's *Il Seraglio* and a much-praised production of Tippett's *King Priam*, attended by the composer. Also at the new Marlowe, the Philharmonic Orchestra with Sir

Charles Groves as conductor and the young Nigel Kennedy as soloist, gave a concert that included Walton's 1st Symphony and the Elgar Violin Concerto. The Royal Museum, with the support of the NACF, hosted a major loan exhibition of *Treasures from Kent Houses*, and the Canterbury Choral Society performed *Walton's Belshazzer's Feast* in the cathedral. The Festival had some financial support from the city council, South East Arts, KCC, the English Tourist Board and a few sponsors, but it depended largely (as it has done ever since) on the generosity of a large number of enthusiastic local supporters and the revenue from ticket sales.

The success of that first festival encouraged a more ambitious 'Italian' festival in 1985, but despite its undoubted artistic success, there were already signs of tension developing between the artistic ambitions and influence of Kent Opera, and others within the Trust, who took a broader and more pragmatic approach. As well as running the Festival, I was still trying to pursue my principle career as a professional musician and at the end of the '85 Festival. I decided that it was no longer feasible to continue to do both jobs, so I resigned as Administrator. However, by early in 1986, a serious rift had occurred within the Festival Trust, which resulted in the withdrawal of Kent Opera and the subsequent resignation of the chairman (Keith Lucas). The situation threatened, potentially, the whole future of the Festival, so the Trust appointed 'three wise men' to try and resolve the impasse – Reg Brown, city councillor Robin Carver and Peter Williams. Together they steadied the ship; Peter Williams approached Melvyn Bragg to become Artistic Director for 1986, and the TVS Trust gave the Festival a £20,000 grant. Subsequently, Peter Williams took over as chairman of the Festival Trust. I returned to the fold briefly, to help put together the final programme for that year and to oversee the Festival Office move to premises in Ivy Lane, courtesy of the *Kentish Gazette*. Then later that summer I handed over responsibility to a new Administrator, and returned once again to being a musician.

Appendix 3: Tourism in Canterbury

This is the full text of the paper submitted to Colin Carmichael and to the University of Kent's Vice-Chancellor, Robin Sibson, on June 12th 1997. (I enclosed a leaflet on 'Colonial Jamestown: Where a Nation Began'). It was written during the city-wide debate on the siting of a new theatre.

Two basic truths lie at the heart of any debate over Canterbury and tourism. They are:

1) Canterbury's history and, therefore, potential as a centre for tourism could hardly be bettered anywhere in the world, and

2) Canterbury has, so far, failed to fulfil that potential and offers relatively little, particularly to the discerning A/B tourist, other than the Cathedral.

This is not meant to be a comprehensive paper; simply a collection of, I hope, helpful observations.

Opportunities

Canterbury Castle has long been neglected. The exploration of a permanent Son et Lumiere in addition to proper targeting and development would help draw tourists away from the coach park – cathedral – shopping – coach park traipse that appears to be the norm.

Performance venues: We need a comprehensive and co-ordinated review of arts/performance needs in the city. The retention of a theatre in Canterbury is vital. There is already an initiative on the table, through the generosity of the University of Kent, who have offered the Festival and the City a site for a concert hall, on campus. We are pursuing a feasibility study to assess the need for such a building and how best to achieve financial viability (which would then lead to a Lottery Application). I have already spoken to the full Council about this, and thank the city for its contribution to the feasibility study. Given that this possibility is on the table, it enables a more strategic look at this issue/opportunity:

a) The Concert hall should be capable of adaptation for other uses – theatre, an occasional conference centre (which would attract county and regional money), visual arts exhibition space, cinema…

b) Despite the generosity of the University, a city centre site has obvious advantages – though it would be good still to embrace the needs of the University, in that the building might be available as an examination room or for degree-giving, provided there is a flat-floor capability among the variable configurations.

c) The best site for such a building is the most accessible – and if The Tannery site were in play, and a move by the company to Thanet possible from a financial and commercial point of view, the ring road has attractions and advantages over any other.

d) It may be possible to solve the resultant car parking problem by using the other side of the ring road, near the current BT site.

e) Given plans to revitalise the Castle site, and the archaeological and historic potential of the Tannery site and St Mildred's, a grouping of tourism/arts/performance outlets begins to emerge. Add to that:

f) the site is large enough to become a millennium project that would grace the city, attract national attention and demand the highest of architectural and environmental disciplines, and

g) it would get rid of the current Tannery smell

Living History: Expectations of the portrayal of the history of a place or a region are rapidly becoming sophisticated. Canterbury is a long way behind, with the greatest respect to the tiny and cramped *Canterbury Tales* experience (in St Margaret's Street). In the US, the arrival of the first settlers from Britain is marked on a large scale by the recreation of a whole town in 18th century style at Colonial Williamsburg; it sits beside Williamsburg itself, the old buildings having been restored and those that were demolished having been rebuilt. More importantly, a resident's life is lived in 18th century style and at 18th century pace. The workshops and wares are 18th century reproductions made on site in the traditional way; food is baked and sold; nails are made in the forge and used, historic moments are re-enacted; the people are in costume and many craftsmen live there. There are no cars.

On a smaller scale at nearby Jamestown, a working village has been built beside a museum, with replicas of the boats that brought the settlers for the New World; these again are 'crewed' by folk in period gear, in character and answering questions knowledgeably. Glass is blown and marketed in the manner of those times.

In the UK, Shropshire showed the way, with Ironbridge, a village rooted in the Industrial Revolution as a tribute to Telford. Again, people are in costume – but they tend to step out of character in conversation, unlike their US counterparts.

The options for Canterbury, with its historic riches, would seem to be considerable. Pick a century and you could come up with a theme and it needs expert help (with firm local input) to make the decisions. If pedestrianisation within the city walls were to spread, so too would the opportunities – a small, riverside development in the North Lane/Pound Lane area, or a themed area, with St Peter's Street, from the Kings Bridge to the West Gate, at its heart.

There are obvious difficulties – but, to those who understandably object to bearing the pressures of tourism on the city, it is apparent that the visitors are not going to go away. To enhance the amenities may also improve the nature of the tourism itself. Certainly, the educational and artistic attractions of the city would increase by boldly emulating the example of Williamsburg.

Not only are there music performances/and tours, there are also plays and dramatisations. There is also a vigorous educational programme – school tours, guides to literature, illustrated talks and an 'educational resource centre'. The appeal is to the youngsters and to adults.

I also enclose a single sheet guide issued to every visitor to Jamestown, simply for information. Since Disney, Pocahontas, with her Kent connections, has a resonance with the young – but we also have Becket and Wat Tyler (and Rupert Bear!)

P.W.
Chair, Canterbury Theatre and Festival Trust
12 June 1997

Appendix 4: Thoughts on The Perpetual Balancing Act:

Extract from Festival Director Mark Deller's report to the Board and to South East Arts, a strategic report on six Festivals; in May 1998. It is a comprehensive summary, familiar in that it also asks for financial support

The Canterbury Festival's success results in large measure from the quality and range of its programme, and in this respect the Festival has achieved nationwide recognition. In business terms it has been based on a balanced structure of financial partnership consisting of:

a) Corefunding grants (CCC, KCC, SEA)
b) Festival Friends & Fundraising
c) Sponsorship
d) Box Office

Where any one of these falls short, or more fundamentally the balance of support changes to such an extent that it puts a burden on the other constituent parts, the result threatens the whole future of the Festival.

For several years now our corefunding partners have been operating (at best) a standstill policy, with the result that, in the past 4 years, their share of support for the Festival has fallen by almost 50%.

In 1993, revenue grants made up 36% of the Festival's budget; in 1997 that figure had fallen to 19%. During the same period, the Festival's turnover increased by 75%, from £202,000 to £355,000.

Year on Year Figures 1993 – 1998

Year	Expenditure	Box Office	Surplus/Deficit
1993	£198,477	£36,170	£3155
1994	£256,400	£33,530	(£1949)
1995	£239,380	£54,400	£11,101
1996	£279,910	£49,600	£6770
1997	£282,490	£60,670	(£11,651)
1998	£270,650	£67,989	(£5008)
Increase	**Increase**		**Net Surplus**
40%	**88%**		**£2418**

List of significant productions/concerts achieved in the past few years, despite budget restrictions:

1) Concerts

Berlioz	**War Requiem**	Listz	**Faust Symphony**
Berlioz	**Damnation of Faust**	Penderecki	**Passacaglia**
Berlioz	**Grande Messe (1999)**	Janacek	**Glagolitic**
Bliss	**Things to Come**	Rachmaninov	**Vespers**
Burgon	**Merciless Beauty (1998)**	Honegger	**Pacific 231**
Harvey	**Ritual Melodies**	Strauss	**Death & Transfiguration**
Mahler	**Symphony No 1**	Stravinsky	**The Rite of Spring**
Mahler	**Symphony No 5**	Tavener	**The Protecting Veil (1993)**
Mahler	**Symphony No 8 (1996)**	Walton	**Façade**

Nyman   An Eye for a Different (1995)

Officium   Jan Garbarek & The Hilliard Ensemble (1995)

2) Opera

Steadman Harvey **The Plague and the Moonflower** (1990); Stravinsky **A Soldier's Tale** (1993); Britten **The Prodigal Son** (1994); Verdi **Nabucco** (1994); Saint-Saens **Samson & Delila** (1994); George Newson **Mrs Fraser's Frenzy** (1995) (Commission & World Premiere); Matthew King **Jonah** (1994-96) (Commission & World Premiere); Britten **Peter Grimes** (1998); Poulenc **The Breasts of Tiresias** (1999); Ravel **L'Heure Espagnole** (1999)

3) Dance

Richard Allston Adzido African Dance; Ballet Rambert Mark Baldwin; Ballet Nord Mark Bruce; Siobhan Davies Michael Clark; Kokuma Dance Irie Dance; Kathakali Dance Cwmni Dance

4) Jazz

Loose Tubes Steve Williamson; The Jazz Warriors Cubana Bop; Grand Union Jazz Jamaica; Andy Sheppard Fran Kuboye; Tony Coe Orphy Robinson; Lionel Hampton Big Band James Taylor Quartet

5) Festival Club

Perfect Houseplants Hassan Erraji; Acadian Ramblers Eliza Carthy & Nancy Kerr; Seelyhoo Donna and Kebab; Stacey Kent Gary Potter Quartet; N'Faly Kouyate & Dunyakan Richard Fairhurst Trio; Theo Travis The Bushburys; John Etheridge Tarras; Tim Van Eyken Klezmer Swingers; Robert Harbron Ana Maria Velez Group; Mad Pudding

6) Folk/World/Roots

Oysterband Acoustic; Bhundu Boys; Flook; Boys of the Lough; Tarika

7) Drama
National Theatre Dealer's Choice (1996); Teatro Sao Paulo (1998); Compass Theatre; RSC; Actors Touring; Shared Experience; Support for local theatre groups; Playcraft, Lindley Players, Naked Pony

8) Exhibitions
Lucien Pissarro Treasures from the Grand Tour; Cecil Beaton Turner and the Coast of Kent; Henry Moore & the Sea David Hockney; Andre Hallet Eric Hebborn; Sydney Nolan Terrains Vagues; Henri Matisse   Icons of Pop

9) Youth/Community Projects
GameBoy (Rock Musical) (1995); City Lights – Strange Cargo (1997); Candletto – Strange Cargo (1998); Icarus – Strange Cargo (1999); Millenniumania (1999) Whitstable Contemporary Arts, Music for Change, Iris, KIAD

Appendix 5: Vice Presidents of the Canterbury Festival

VPs	Dates
Mr & Mrs Sandy Alexander	1998 - 2003
Brian Arnold	1989 - 1992 & 1995 - 1998
Brig & Mrs M A Atherton	1999 - 2019
Mrs Maurice Atherton	2020 -
Mrs Monty August	1993 - 1999
Prof Stephen Bann	2017 -
Mr & Mrs Mike and Sandy Baxter	2019 - 2020
Mrs James Bird	1989 -2021
Edwin Boorman OBE	1998 - 2011
Mr & Mrs Conrad Blakey	1990 - 1995
Timothy Brett	1989 -
Mr & Mrs Graham & Maggie Brown	2015 -
Prof Alan Bull	1999 - 2006
Mr & Mrs Christopher and Nicki Calcutt	2008 - 2016
Sir James Cayzer	1994 - 2010
Lady Chipperfield	1995 - 2004
Mrs F R Cobb	1991 - 1995
Mr & Mrs Martin & Virginia Conybeare FRCS	2001 -
Mrs Amanda Cottrell	2008 - 2011
Dr Kate Neales and Mr Peter Cox	2013 -
William Dorrell	1990 - 1998

VPs	Dates
Cllr & Mrs Nick and Monica Eden-Green	2017 -
Mrs Jane Edred Wright	2015 - 2020
Mrs Sally Everist	2013 - 2015
Mrs Audrey Eyton	1993 - 2009
Nicholas Fielding	1998 - 2002
Mr & Mrs Alan & Diana Forrest	2017 - 2020
Mr & Mrs Alan & Diana Forrest	2017 - 2020
Mrs Diana Forrest	2021 -
David and Cilla Freud	2017 -
Mr & Mrs Charles & Diane Gaskain	2017 -
Alexander de Gelsey CBE	1989 - 2005
Mrs Romy de Gelsey	2017 - 2018
Mrs Tom Gould (The Cleary Foundation)	1992 - 2010
Mr Alistair Gould (The Cleary Foundation)	2011
Mrs Anna Grant	2013 - 2016 & 2022 -
Graeme Hamilton	1993 - 2000
Mrs Graeme Hamilton	2010 - 2008
Mr & Mrs John and Maggie Harris	2020 -
Peter Harris	1990 - 1993
Mrs Ruth Harrowing	1999 - 2001
Mr & Mrs Philip and Patti Havers	2019 -
Mr & Mrs Peter and Sally Hawkes	2017 -
Tom Head & Kylie Sanderson	2019
Darren Henley OBE	2009 - 2014
Mr & Mrs Peter & Brenda Hermitage QPM	2008 - 2018
Mr & Mrs Neville & Anita Hilary	2008 - 2016

VPs	Dates
David Holman	1993 - 2002
Sir Robert Holton	1994 - 2000
David C Humphreys	2004 - 2015
Andrew Ironside	2013 -
Hon & Mrs Charles and Katie James	2001 - 2016
Mr & Mrs Iain & Susan Jenkins	2006 - 2013
Mr & Mrs George Jessel	2005 - 2010
Hugh Kelsey	1998 - 2001
Mr & Mrs George and Christine Kennedy	2014 -
Mr & Mrs Wolfgang & Dominque Kerck	1998 - 2003 & 2013 - 2016
Mr & Mrs Richard Latham	2006 - 2014
Mr & Mrs Roddy & Caroline Loder-Symonds	1999 - 2020
Mr & Mrs James and Jane Loudon	2010 -
Mrs Keith Lucas	1990 - 1991 & 1998 - 2001
Mr & Mrs David and Mimi Macfarlane	2017 -
Prof Keith Mander	2019 -
The Hon Henry Maude	1990 - 1993
Mr & Mrs Ben Moorhead	2010 - 2015
John Moss	1999 - 2010
Anthony Moubray-Jankowski (de Moubray)	1990 - 1994
Lord Moynihan	2001 - 2002
Mrs Claudette Nihon	1998 - 2002
Mr & Mrs Ian & Juliet Odgers	2013 -
Richard Oldfield	1999 -

VPs	Dates
Mr & Mrs Terry and Valerie Osborne	2013 - 2016
Dr Graham & Dr Jenny Pay	2021 -
Mrs Alicia Pentin	2007 - 2010
Mr & Mrs David and Alicia Pentin	2011 -
Jane Plumptre	2015 -
Mr & Mrs John & Julia Plumptre	2006 -
Dr Mark Rake	2000 - 2007
Dr Mark Rake & Mrs Jill Jordan	2008 - 2013
Keith Rawlings	1998 - 2000
Pierre Remoleux	1989 - 1990
Count and Countess Nicholas Reutner	2013 - 2015
David Riceman	1989 - 1993
Mr & Mrs David Riceman	1994 - 1996
Mrs Pauline Round	1998 - 2002
James Rumbellow	2000 - 2009
Mr Andrea Russo	2008 - 2016
Mr & Mrs Andrew Saunders	2006 - 2009
John Shipton	1989 - 1990
Mr & Mrs Paul and Patricia Smallwood	2009 - 2018
The Countess Sondes	1999 - 2003
Mr & Mrs David & Anne Spencer	2019 -
Rev Nicolas Stacey	1995 - 2014
Mr & Mrs Michael and Sue Stanford-Tuck	2017 - 2018
Dr David Starkey CBE, FSA, FRHistS	2006 -
Peter Stevens	2019 -2021
Mr & Mrs Peter & Beryl Stevens	1990 - 2018

VPs	Dates
Mr Richard Sturt OBE	2010 -
Mrs Fiona Sunley	2015 -
Lady Swire	1989 -
Mrs Camilla Swire	2004 -
Lady Juliet Tadgell	1999 - 2007 & 2013 -
Mrs Daniel Taylor	1998
Mr & Mrs Dominic Taylor	2006 - 2008
Mrs Jo Taylor Williams	1991 -
Stephen Thomson MBE	1993 - 1996
Mrs Loba Van der Bijl	2004 -
Mr & Mrs Charles and Sally Villiers	2006 -
Mrs Henry Villiers	1989 - 1999
Mr & Mrs Fergus Watson	2006 - 2010
Mr Stuart Wheeler	2017 - 2019
Michael Willis-Fleming	1989 - 2007
Sir Robert Worcester KBE	2021 -
Sir Robert and Lady Worcester KBE DL	2008 - 2020
Mr & Mrs Evelyn & Scilla Wright	2006 - 2018
Prof & Mrs Michael and Pamela Wright	2008 - 2014
Alan Wyndham-Green	1989 - 1995

Appendix 6: Festival Friends

Festival Friends – _Official donations to the Canterbury Festival funds 1990-2020_

Year	Chair	Secretary	Donation
2015-2020	Tony Walder	Tina Austin	£25k Plus; £132,000 (including £5,000 to the Spiegeltent)
2012-2014	David Barton	Tina Austin & Laurie Porter	£57,000
2009-2011	Diane Gaskain	Laurie Porter & Sylviane Martell	£48,000
2006-2008	John Harris	Sylviane Martell	£51,000
2000-2005	Alan Bull	Sylviane Martell	£129,000

(In 2004, the Friends moved to become part of the Festival Foundation)

Year	Chair	Secretary	Donation
1997-1999	Anthony de Moubray	Sylviane Martell	£51,000
1995-1996	Peter Harris	Sylviane Martell & Patricia Nightingale	£18,750
1990-1994	Keith Lucas	Deborah Bornoff (Membership Secretary) Des Connolly (Secretary)	£11,500

Appendix 7: Promised Land

Canterbury Festival presents

Promised Land
A Community Opera in Three Acts

By Michael Irwin and Mark Dougherty
From an original idea by Peter Williams

World Premiere: at the Marlowe Theatre
Friday and Saturday, 13th & 14th October, 2006

Commissioned and produced by the Canterbury Festival with funds Provided by Make It Real and the Arts Council of England (South East), Canterbury City Council, Kent County Council,

and East Kent Local Authority Arts Partnership

The production of *Promised Land* received financial support from The Colyer Fergusson Charitable Trust and the performances have been sponsored by Andrew Clague

Synopsis

Prologue

An East Kent beach in summer 1939. Different groups, unidentifiable in summer-wear, mingle contentedly in the sunshine until driven away by a storm that symbolises the start of war.

Act 1

January 1942. Under the Wings for Victory scheme the money has been raised to buy a Spitfire. Everyone in the area has contributed, and a committee is planning the ceremony at which the cheque will be handed over.

Involved in the ceremony is Tom Bateson, a young RAF pilot recovering after a crash. His father, George Bateson, is a prosperous local farmer. Tom is still being cared for by his nurse, Helen Jones, daughter of a miner. She and Tom visit Bateson's farm, where George is eloquent about his love of the land. He clearly disapproves of the growing warmth between Tom and Helen.

Meanwhile the miners, angered by unjust treatment from the pit owners, have gone on strike: Helen's father Trevor Jones is a ringleader. Local people are annoyed by this seeming betrayal of the war effort. The committee is outraged because the adverse publicity seems certain to prevent the presentation ceremony.

There is a mass trial of the miners for breach of wartime strike regulations. Trevor Jones is imprisoned; all the others are fined and ordered to return to work. When they adamantly refuse to do so, there seems no way out of the crisis.

It suddenly emerges that the government has put pressure on the colliery-owners to climb down and meet the miners' demands. Jones is released from prison and the miners return to work. Local opinion is divided, many feeling that the miners have "got away with it", but the Wings for Victory presentation can go ahead. When it does so, the visiting Minister unexpectedly makes a conciliatory speech and thanks the miners for the increase in output that has followed their return to work.

At the close of Act I Tom and Helen are clearly in love. But he has to return to active duty, and the future is uncertain.

Interval

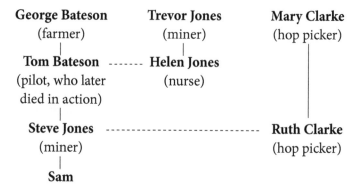

Act 2

The mid 1960s. The act opens in the pithead baths of the colliery. The miners are off on weekend pleasures. Steve Jones is going to take part in a cricket match at Harley Green, and his grandfather Trevor Jones is going along to watch. It emerges that Steve is the son of Helen Janes and Tom Bateson, who died in the War before the two could marry. George Bateson has disowned his illegitimate grandson and has never seen him. Helen has since married and moved to London. Trevor is concerned because Steve has recently expressed an interest in meeting his other grandfather (George Bateson), who in fact lives near Harley Green.

On George Bateson's farm, in a television interview, the farmer reminisces about hop-picking seasons of the past, the festivals of celebration and the whole process of planting, cultivating and picking hops.

At a pub on the village green, cricketers appear after their game. As the men drink, there is some banter, at first friendly, but later hostile and aggressive, between the local farm workers, the miners and the visiting hop-pickers.

Steve and George see and recognise one another, but neither speaks. Steve is drawn to one of the young Londoners, Ruth, daughter of veteran hop-picker Mary Clarke, who is heard to lament the decline of "hopping".

The act closes with a love duet between Steve and Ruth.

Interval

Act 3

It is 1984 – the year of the miners' national strike. Steve and Ruth are now married with a teenage son, Sam. Steve, at first a militant striker, gradually loses hope, while Ruth, originally sceptical, becomes increasingly politicised and active.

Mary Clarke dies, and asks for her ashes to be scattered in the hop gardens where she used to work. George Bateson – now an old man – appears at this ceremony and has a halting conversation with Ruth, in which he asks her about the strike.

After a period of optimism, the miners are gradually forced to end the strike. It emerges that Bateson has died, leaving everything to Steve – but the farm has become so run down that the legacy will be swallowed up by debts, leaving Steve and his family financially ruined after a year on strike.

The act ends at the pithead. The colliery is closed and, in a last ritual the cable is cut, sending the cage crashing down into the mine to smash to pieces thousands of feet below.

Curtain

(Running time including Interval, 3 hours)

Promised Land Cast List

Trevor Jones	**John Upperton**
George Bateson	**Trevor Alexander**
Tom Bateson	**Ian McLarnon**
Helen Jones	**Liza Pulman**
Ruth Clarke	**Liza Pulman**
Steve Jones	**Ian McLarnon**
Colin Thomas	**Richard Morris**
Vicar/Government Minister	**Anthony Hawgood**
Photographer/Magistrate	**Peter Cox**
Sam	**Jacob Austen**

Community Cast

The Children

Camilla Adams
Jennie Evans-Snell
Sam Gooch
Ellie Kerly

Madeleine Knell-Taylor
Elinor Rees
Sophia Shoults
Gaby Smith
Rebekah Smith
Luke Smith
Rebecca Strange

Mike	**Terry Shea**
Lover Boy (Prologue)	**John Rye**

The Miners

Ron	**Sid Moon**
Jack	**John Rye**
Dave	**John Brazier**
Joe	**Daniel Bühler**
Gordy	**David Lewis**
Peter	**David Pentin**
Interviewer	**Sue Canney**

The Hop-pickers

Mary Clarke	**Marilyn Adams**
Frank	**Frank Guthrie**
Mabel	**Glenys Jeff**

Lover Girl (Prologue)	**Carys Nia**	Jeannie	**Carys Nia**
Ice Cream Lady	**Anne Hancox**		
Sadie	**Lyn Powell**		
The Committee			
Lady Mears	**Felicity Foreman**	Stiltwalkers	**Mike Moloney**
General Kelesy	**Frank Guthrie**		**Donal McKendry**
Fenwick MP	**Simon Backhouse**		
William Rook	**James Barber**	The Locals	
Mrs Potter	**Elizabeth Appleyard**	Landlady	**Jill Ackhurst**
Mrs Taylor	**Jane Jones**	Vera	**Eleanor Gracie**
Lilian	**Gill Corble**		
Annie	**Beryl Chalk**		
Sarah	**Barbara Anne Flack**		

Chorus

Jim Akhurst, Brian Andrews, Jacqui Armstrong, Helena Barber, Brenda Bradshaw, Jackie Brittz, Stephanie Brunton, Alexander Bunda (Chani), Louise Chamberlain, Brenda Child, Helen Clark, Hilary Clayden, Inger Coates, Rosie Cullen, Diana Dakin, Philipp Dawson, Tim Derouet, Hilary Derouet, Pilar Diaz, Marshall Eagle, Hilary Edridge, Penelope Fewings, Nicholas Frost, Sarah Gooch, Sue Gregory, Tamara Gummer, Dianna Hagerty, Diane Hamer, Cecilia Hammond, Christopher Harbridge, Joan Hare, Peter Hare, Yvonne Harrop, Kate Hayes-Watkins, Eileen Hiorns, Max How, Lizzy Hughes, Stella Irwin, Graham Jackman, Pearl Johns, Helen Johnson, Martha Jones, Laura Jowers, Elizabeth Knell-Taylor,

Alison Knox, Nicki Leggatt, David Lewis, Denise Miller, Gill Moon, Christel Moor, Phyllis Neaves, Adriana Perera, Jane Pollok, Joan Potter, Liz Rees, Alison Rook, Charlotte Smith, Patricia Smith, Lil Spencer, Isobella Stewart, Gia Stobbs, Sophie Wade.

The Dogs
Skye and Bones.

Props/Stage Management/Costumes

Andrew Taylor	**Janine Greaves**
Jackie Brittz	**Norman Orchison**
Matthew Welch	**Jeanne Taylor**
Naomi Lynch	**Emma Williams**
Lauren Glass	

Assistant Choreographer **Kate Hayes-Watkins**

Orchestra

Musical Director	**Mark Dougherty**
Keyboard 1	**Caroline Humphris**
Keyboard 2	**Bruce Knight**
Guitars	**Johnny Scott**
Bass	**Martin Elliot**
Percussion 1	**Dave Pack**
Percussion 2	**Allan Cox**
Flute	**Tom Hancox**
Clarinet	**Grenville Hancox**
1st Trumpet/Flugel	**Alex Cauldon**
2nd Trumpet/Cornet	**Elaine Williams**
1st Trombone	**Richard Watkin**
2nd Trombone	**Matt Harrison**
Bass Trombone	**Lewis Edney**
Harmonica	**Brendan Power**

Fiddle	**Helen Clarke**
Concertina	**Susan Hudson**
Whistle	**Beryl Chalk**
Repetiteur	**Bruce Knight**
Audition Pianists	**Ben Frost**
	Spencer Payne
	Matthew Shipton

Artistic Team

Liberetto by	**Michael Irwin**
Music composed &	
Conducted by	**Mark Dougherty**
Director	**Syd Ralph**
Designer	**Gary McCann**
Assistant Designer	**Stuart Nunn**
Lighting	**Colin Grenfell**
Choreographer	**Paul Madden**
Associate Costume Designer	
& Wardrobe Supervisor	**Lydia Hardiman**
Production Manager	**Jamie Maisey**
Stage Manager	**Simon Dodson**
Deputy Stage Manager	**Sian Evans**
Assistant Stage Managers	**Kate Tingley and Sue O'Brien**
Sound	**Orbital Sound Ltd and**

Nick Taylor, Porcupine Studios

Vocal Coach	**Peter Cox**
Music Assistant	**Sophie Meikle**
Production Photography	**Katarzyna Zub**
Tadeusz Kluszczynski	

For the Canterbury Festival

Producer	**Rosie Turner**
Project Co-ordinator	**Richard Pollott**
Fundraising	**Amanda McKean**

Marketing	**Louise Griffiths**
Finance	**John Biffin**
Administration	**Sylviane Martell**

For the Marlowe Theatre

Chief Electrician	**Ben Hardstaff**
Deputy Chief Electrician	**John Upward**
Senior Sound and Lighting Technician	**Tim O'Grady**
Stage Manager	**Stephen Stone**
Deputy Stage Manager	**Mark Norrington**

Appendix 8: Board and Trustees

From 1984 till 1986, the following served as members of the Board and Executive Committee of the **Canterbury Theatre and Festival Trust**, under the chairmanship of Keith Lucas:

Brian Arnold, Jack Bornoff, Reginald Brown, Robin Carver, Sir Hugh Casson KCVO PRA CH, Ginette Cobb, Caroline Collingwood, Desmond Connolly, Molly de Courcy, Mark Deller, William Dorrell, Colonel K A Gross OBE, Roland Hurst, Dr David Ingram, Professor Michael Irwin, Keith Lucas, Michael Marriot, Russell MacDonald, Lady Rupert Nevil, John Round, John Shipton, Rosemary Simpson, Donald Sinden, Lady Swire, Mary Villiers, Peter Williams, Michael Willis-Fleming, David Wilson, Cynthia Hawes (*Secretary to the Trust*)

Board Members and Trustees of the **Canterbury Theatre and Festival Trust** since 1986, under the chairmanship of Peter Williams:

Geraldine Allinson, Brian Arnold, Commodore Martin Atherton, Simon Backhouse, Professor Robin Baker, Dr David Barton, Hugo Barton, James Bird (vice-chair), Professor Alastair Borthwick, Colin Carmichael, Michael John Chandler, Sir Geoffrey Chipperfield, Professor Robert Freedman, Diane Gaskain, Dr Christopher Gay, Celia Glynn-Williams, Peter Harris, Darren Henley, Canon Christopher Paul Irvine, Katharine Lewis, Roderick Loder-Symonds, Keith Lucas, Charles James, Richard Jarman, Robert Carsley Jones, Elisabeth Margaret Kerr, Peter Hermitage, Andrew Ironside , Professor Daniel Lloyd, Rear Admiral David Macey, Professor Keith Mander, Dr Keith Mclay, Brigadier John Meardon, Anthony Jankowski de Moubray, Lord Colin Moynihan, Dr Kate Neales, Air Marshal Christopher Nickols, James Nock, Tony Pratt, David Pentin, Dr Mark Rake, Hilary Riva, John Round, Professor Robin Sibson, Stuart Sibson, The Hon Mrs Anne Stacey, Richard Sturt, Hugh Summerfield, Camilla Swire, Patrick

Twigg QC, Loba Van der Bijl, Tony Walder, Professor Roderick Watkins, Peter Williams, Professor Michael Wright, Professor Gillian Youngs

The New Marlowe Theatre Development Trust – Leadership Group and Patrons, 2011
Royal Patron
HRH The Earl of Wessex KG KCVO

Campaign Board:
President and former Chair: Sir Graeme Odgers DL, Chair: Peter Williams, MBE (President, Canterbury Festival), Paul Barrett MBE, Nigel Beevor, Sir Michael Bett CBE, James Bird DL, Michael Bukht OBE, Andrew Clague, Vyvyan Harmsworth LVO (vice-chair), Michael Head, Ian Odgers (vice-chair), Clive Relf (Honorary Treasurer), Graham Sinclair, Charles Villiers

Patrons:
Allan Willett CMG, Her Majesty's Lord Lieutenant of Kent, Orlando Bloom, Edwin Boorman OBE DL, Vyvyan Harmsworth LVO, Jools Holland OBE DL, Dave Lee, MBE, Joanna Lumley, Robert Neame CBE DL, Lady Northbourne, Lady Swire, Timothy West, Prunella Scales, Lady Vallance JP, Tessa Wheeler, Professor Sir Robert Worcester KBE DL (Chancellor, University of Kent)